Digital Innovation Strategy

Based on applied economics and from the perspective of an innovator seeking to develop a new digital business, this textbook is aimed at MBA and advanced undergraduate audiences interested in innovation strategy and competition in digital industries. Step-by-step, the book guides innovators through a dynamic market analysis and business model design, leading to an assessment of the future evolution of the market and the broader innovation ecosystem, and what the innovator can do to position the innovation for continued success. Each chapter defines and provides references for key concepts that can be further explored through suggested readings and study questions. Real-world case studies further facilitate forming a comprehensive view on how to resolve strategic challenges of digital innovation. The topics covered in this text are essential for a broad range of managers, consultants, entrepreneurs, technologists, and analysts to understand in depth.

Aija Leiponen is a Professor of Strategy and Business Economics in the Cornell University SC Johnson College of Business. She is an internationally renowned scholar of innovation and technological change. Straddling the fields of economics and strategic management, her work on digital innovation has been published in leading academic outlets and management reviews and has influenced both digital policy and managerial practice.

Digital Innovation Strategy

Aija Leiponen
Cornell University

CAMBRIDGE
UNIVERSITY PRESS

Shaftesbury Road, Cambridge CB2 8EA, United Kingdom

One Liberty Plaza, 20th Floor, New York, NY 10006, USA

477 Williamstown Road, Port Melbourne, VIC 3207, Australia

314–321, 3rd Floor, Plot 3, Splendor Forum, Jasola District Centre, New Delhi – 110025, India

103 Penang Road, #05-06/07, Visioncrest Commercial, Singapore 238467

Cambridge University Press is part of Cambridge University Press & Assessment, a department of the University of Cambridge.

We share the University's mission to contribute to society through the pursuit of education, learning and research at the highest international levels of excellence.

www.cambridge.org
Information on this title: www.cambridge.org/highereducation/ISBN/9781009208987

DOI: 10.1017/9781009209038

First published 2024

A catalogue record for this publication is available from the British Library

Library of Congress Cataloging-in-Publication Data
Names: Leiponen, Aija, author.
Title: Digital innovation strategy / Aija Leiponen.
Description: Cambridge, United Kingdom ; New York, NY :
Cambridge University Press, 2024. | Includes bibliographical references and index.
Identifiers: LCCN 2023031355 | ISBN 9781009208987 (hardback) | ISBN 9781009209038 (ebook)
Subjects: LCSH: Technological innovations – Economic aspects. |
Information technology – Economic aspects. | Strategic planning. | New products.
Classification: LCC HC79.T4 L4279 2024 | DDC 338/.064–dc23/eng/20230713
LC record available at https://lccn.loc.gov/2023031355

ISBN 978-1-009-20898-7 Hardback
ISBN 978-1-009-20900-7 Paperback

Contents

Part V Gaining Ecosystem Momentum

Figures

Tables

Preface

Overview

This is a textbook aimed at MBA and advanced undergraduate audiences interested in innovation strategy and competition in digital industries. The content is based on applied economics and innovation from the perspective of an innovator seeking to develop a new digital business. The book describes the context and evolution of information and communication technologies, including the internet, and ends with the prospect of an Internet of Things based on 5th generation wireless communication systems. It reviews the strategies related to pricing, networks, standards, and platforms and then embeds the insights in a business model framework to enable bottom-up application of the conceptual frameworks in developing and launching new digital products and services. The final section previews the 5G-enabled Internet of Things to suggest avenues for further exploration of the topics in the evolving communication technology environment. The book is based on the content from a Cornell University course, Digital Business Strategy, taught since 2002.

This book aims to be a rigorous and research-based text on innovation strategy in the digital economy. The book updates and extends beyond currently available materials by providing a comprehensive analysis of digital innovation and competition and by offering a unique perspective into the future of digital industries via case studies of 5G and the Internet of Things. The topics covered are essential for a broad range of managers, consultants, entrepreneurs, and technologists to understand in depth. Digital strategy is emerging as a core course in all leading business schools and will be central in the business curricula for the next decade.

The book updates and extends the basic insights from the economics of information goods and communication networks with recent examples and advances in the strategy literatures on platforms, competition in digital markets, and the roles of intellectual property rights and other institutional and regulatory drivers in the digital economy. Applying basic economic principles, it develops an integrative framework for designing and experimenting with digital business models. Finally, the core conceptual insights are elaborated in the context of the Internet of Things.

The book contains conceptual material illustrated with many timely examples. Each chapter offers examples and each of the seven parts offers a full case reading followed by study questions to discuss and apply the insights. References are included.

The book is intended for professional students and advanced undergraduates in business or applied economics. It is accessible to anyone with knowledge of introductory economics and business fundamentals. It is primarily descriptive but contains some economics material with mostly graphic explanations. Ideally, the reader will have completed a course on introductory microeconomics and introductory business management. However, the examples and business modeling make it also a valuable basic resource for graduate students and strategy professionals in digital industries.

PART I
Introduction

....

> The future is already here, it's just unevenly distributed.
>
> (William Gibson)[1]

Although digital technologies seem to have reached every corner of the economy, there is actually quite a bit of variation with respect to the degree of digitalization. Therefore, digital transformation continues to upset firms, industries, and markets around the globe. The pace of change continues to be rapid and relentless. This book helps you learn from the past and ongoing processes of digital transformation to predict and facilitate future transformation. You will see that the only constant in digitalization is change. The first part of the book introduces the key concepts of digital business innovation, digital disruption, and communication networks, which underpin the deeper analyses of the digitalization of organizations and markets in later parts.

---

[1] *The Economist*, 2001. Retrieved from www.economist.com/business/2001/06/21/broadband-blues in August 2022.

1   What is Special about Digital Business Innovation?

> Once a new technology rolls over you, if you're not part of the steamroller, you're part of the road.
>
> (Stewart Brand)

Innovation is about change: *the introduction of novelty into an economic system.* Managing any type of economic or organizational change is challenging because its effects are usually uncertain and affect participants unevenly. Managing technological change requires a heady cocktail of creativity, flexibility, and perseverance in the face of novelty and turmoil. In this chapter we explore the special features of digital innovation of new businesses, digital business innovation. **Digital business innovation** deals with *improved technology-based business models for information and communication* – core elements of all economic activity. Furthermore, we look at the long-term patterns of technological change and notice how digital technologies arise from the combination of electronics and instruments and lead to new kinds of technologies that accelerate invention activity itself.

One might think that every business is digital business. It is difficult to imagine any economic activity that does not rely on information and communication technologies for their basic functions. Even the most traditional local services such as restaurants and construction companies market and coordinate their activities using websites, computerized booking and scheduling systems, and digital payment systems. At a minimum, a plumber or an electrician has a smartphone to communicate with clients using its call, text, and email functions, even if much of their marketing might still take place using word-of-mouth and the work itself is still based on manual skills and "analog" (as opposed to digital) knowledge. However, digital labor markets such as TaskRabbit and Fiverr are digitizing the job matching process even for these manual trades!

However, not all digital business is equal; some firms are more digital than others. We can distinguish general users of information and communication technologies such as local services and traditional manufacturing and service firms from businesses significantly enhanced by digital technologies[1]. The latter include financial institutions, credit rating services, online retail, and even airlines that all operate in the physical world ("bricks and mortar" as these businesses were called

---

[1] President's Council of Advisors on Science and Technology Report to the President and Congress: Designing a Digital Future (2010). Retrieved from https://obamawhitehouse.archives.gov/sites/default/files/microsites/ostp/pcast-nitrd-report-2010.pdf in August 2022.

during the first internet boom) providing concrete, offline services to people and client organizations. However, their organizational effectiveness and innovation are often significantly reliant on digital technologies that enhance their ability to communicate, coordinate, carry out transactions, collect and analyze information, and make informed decisions. This uneven distribution of digital technologies allows us to examine the most highly digitized business organizations and activities and extrapolate to areas that are probably yet to adopt the most advanced technological solutions. This book intends to help speed up the dissemination of useful digital technologies through business innovation.

In 2015, the most digitized industry was the information and communication technology sector itself – not surprisingly – and agriculture was the least digitized.[2] However, industries such as wholesale trade, utilities, and finance were also quite highly digitized whereas retail trade, hospitality, and health care were surprisingly far from the frontier of digitization, leaving room for new services to enter and offer rapid digital transformation.[3] Just a few years later, digital agriculture started to take off. The extent and rate of digitalization thus varied significantly by firm and industry, often for competitive and strategic reasons.

1.1   Origins of Digitalization

This book will primarily focus on the innovation strategies of dedicated communication and information technology businesses. These organizations are, at their core, built on digital information and communication networks. They offer information products and services or create communication networks for their customers and users. Products and services of such purely digital businesses include digital content and media, communication networks, software, computing services, and so on. These types of service companies have been leading the transformation into a digital society, and by studying how they function, we can shed light on the issues that will affect digitization of businesses that are currently only digitally enhanced or general users of digital technologies.

An interesting boundary object of our study of digital transformation are businesses that provide services offline but at their core define and operate themselves as digital platforms. Boundary objects translate and connect different social and economic worlds. McAfee and Brynjolfsson (2017) called such services Online-to-Offline or O2O services: online information and communication systems support the search, coordination, and matching necessary to provide offline services. They

---

[2] McKinsey Global Institute (2015). Digital America: a tale of the haves and have-mores. Retrieved from www.mckinsey.com/industries/high-tech/our-insights/digital-america-a-tale-of-the-haves-and-have-mores in August 2022.

[3] Gandhi P., Khanna S., and Ramaswamy S. (2016). Which industries are the most digital (and why)? *Harvard Business Review* (April 1). Retrieved from https://hbr.org/2016/04/a-chart-that-shows-which-industries-are-the-most-digital-and-why in August 2022.

include some of the most fascinating service platforms of our time such as eBay, Uber, and Airbnb, but also other types of online markets for physical goods and services – homes, shoes, dog walking, grocery shopping, and even furniture. While the designs and details are diverse, these businesses typically live and die by network effects, and the marketplaces become more valuable with scale. Offline marketplaces also exhibit such scale economies to a degree, but online marketplaces do not have any natural size limit and thus can grow extremely large.

Digital transformation is not limited to service industries, even though information-based service tasks are naturally easier to digitize. Concepts such as the Industrial Internet of Things (IoT) and Industry 4.0 draw attention to the digitization of the manufacturing sector, and even the agricultural sector through the efforts gathering momentum under the umbrella of Digital Agriculture[4]. We can call these industry platforms "Offline-to-Online:" dense data from physical transformation activities are collected and digitally transmitted to an information system that allows their merging, organization, and analysis in support of subsequent decision making.

Although the ideas surrounding the IoT are relatively new and seemingly radical, the development and adoption of digital technologies in manufacturing and agricultural production[5] has been long-standing and gradual. Earlier waves of development took place under the headings of automation, systems engineering, and mechatronics. They all concern the application of computers and instruments to measure and manipulate the physical state of a system. Prior to 1970, progress in automation was primarily driven by inventions in mechanical instrument and control technologies, and after 1970, a dramatic switch to electronic instrumentation took place. At the same time, the degree of automation of such systems considerably increased. Since the year 2000, advanced production systems have rapidly adopted wireless communication. Most recently, the combination of the Industrial Internet of Things (industrial data networks) and 5G wireless telecommunications (ultra-fast and high-bandwidth wireless communications) are enabling full digitization and remote operation of production via system-wide "digital twins."

Figure 1.1 illustrates the economy-wide transition from mechanical technologies to electrical and instrument technologies. It depicts technology flows as measured by cross-industry references (citations) in US patent documents. A patent citation is created when an inventor of a new technology cites an earlier invention as the "prior art" on which the new invention is built. If the citation concerns prior art from other fields of technology, it can be interpreted as cross-sectoral flows of

---

[4] Kite-Powell J. (2020). Welcome to the new world of digital agriculture. Forbes (April 22). Retrieved from www.forbes.com/sites/jenniferhicks/2020/04/22/welcome-to-the-new-world-of-digital-agriculture/?sh=57608b8d10ce in August 2022.

[5] Bryan, S., Fiocco, D., Issler, M., and Perdur, RSM. (2020). Creating value in digital-farming solutions. McKinsey, October 20, 2020. Retrieved from www.mckinsey.com/industries/agriculture/our-insights/creating-value-in-digital-farming-solutions# in August 2022.

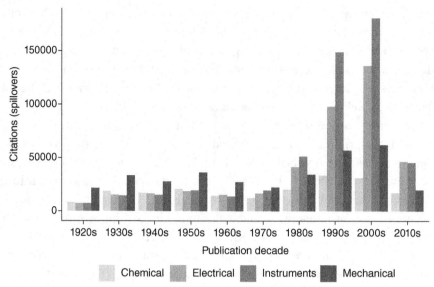

Figure 1.1 Total cross-sector technology flows by field and decade as measured via patent citations
Note: After the 1970s, electrical technologies and instruments became widely adopted in other technology sectors, suggesting large-scale dissemination of these technologies. This illustrates the widespread adoption of electronics, such as computing and communication technologies, and associated instruments, in all sectors of the economy.
Source: Koutroumpis, Pantelis, Leiponen, Aija, and Thomas, Llewellyn D.W. (2020). Digital instruments as invention machines. *Communications of the ACM 64(1): 70–78.*

technology that are spurring additional invention in the recipient industry. Thus, up until the 1970s, mechanical technologies were dominant in influencing invention activities in other fields. After the 1970s, electrical technologies had a much greater impact on invention in the US economy. However, it is interesting that instrument technologies had an even greater impact on other technology fields. If we look more closely within the sectors of electrical and instrument technologies, we will find that it is primarily computers, communication technologies, and control instruments that have had such outsized impact on technological change in other fields of the economy. Together, these three technology fields have driven the rapid and ongoing digitization, automation, and networking of the economy since the 1970s.

1.2   What are the Challenges of Digital Business Innovation?

We define **digital business** as any business that in its core processes is dependent on information and communication technologies to deliver products and services, usually information products or communication services. By **digital**, we mean information and communication that is reduced to (binary) computer code and that can be processed and transferred using computers and communication networks. We particularly focus on the impact of the internet and other communication networks that have enabled extremely high connectivity of social and business relationships. The societal value of information depends very much on the connections through which it is shared.

Innovation involves the creation of novelty, and novelty is difficult to define beforehand and usually uncertain to achieve. Creation of novelty through technological or business invention necessitates a creative step. In an R&D or new business development project the team can define some desirable goals or specifications, such as faster computing performance, but the more ambitious the project, the more likely that the specified goals are not reached. As a result, a radical innovation project such as an order of magnitude increase in microprocessor speed will be very risky. Such attempts to change the future are fundamentally unpredictable and unquantifiable.[6]

Innovation might be faced with both technical and market uncertainty. **Technical uncertainty** concerns whether the technical goals of the project can be reached. For example, the creation of a faster microprocessor requires packing more transistors on a chip that operates on ever-higher frequencies. It is not known at the start whether it is feasible to continue to shrink the manufacturing process beyond single nanometers, or whether there will be scientific discoveries enabling higher frequencies despite their power consumption and heat production.

Market uncertainty concerns whether the commercial goals of the project can be reached. While there has been seemingly relentless appetite for faster computing speeds, during the transition to mobile computing, demand actually shifted significantly toward chips featuring lower power consumption. Battery life is a key performance issue for mobile devices and speed may often be secondary. As a result, Intel's very fast processors lost much market share to ARM's RISC designs that are much more energy-efficient. Market uncertainty can derail even very successful incumbents.

Furthermore, in digital markets for information and communication products, user behavior constitutes another challenging source of uncertainty. **Behavioral uncertainty** can be viewed as a subclass of market uncertainty. When information and communication technologies are used within social groups, it is very difficult to predict what unintended consequences emerge through that process of social construction. **Social construction of technology** entails social interactions among users of technology, and interactions between users and technological artifacts that, jointly, influence how people interpret, adopt, and use the technology in their everyday lives.[7] Unintended consequences can be positive, such as innovative practices that enhance the value of the product, or negative, such as behaviors that reduce the value of the product for everyone. An example of a positive behavioral effect might be the emergence of "memes" as a popular and highly

---

[6] Knight, F. (1921). *Risk, Uncertainty, and Profit*. Boston, MA: Hart, Schaffner and Marx.
[7] See, for example, Bijker, W.E., Hughes, T.P., and Pinch, T., eds. (1987). *The Social Constructions of Technological Systems*. Cambridge, MA: MIT Press.

engaging form of user-generated content. A negative example might be the rise of racist or extremist user groups that may tarnish the reputation of otherwise neutral digital services. Behavioral uncertainty is particularly high in information and communication technology-based services because these technologies display exceptional **generativity** – they are capable of spawning additional innovations.[8] A considerable part of innovation strategy involves the management of all types of uncertainty.

1.3   Why are Information and Communication Technologies so Critical to Economic Performance?

In 2010, the United States President's Council of Advisors on Science and Technology stated that digital technologies are key drivers of economic competitiveness and crucial to achieving policy priorities in energy, transportation, healthcare, education, and national security; they accelerate scientific and technological discovery in nearly all other fields; and are essential to achieving goals of open government. By 2020, the US government's top science and technology priorities included 5G telecommunications, artificial intelligence, advanced manufacturing, autonomous transportation, cybersecurity, privacy, and quantum information science, in addition to priorities related to health, energy, and the environment. A very large part of Science and Technology policy had thus become digital policy. Even after 50 years of rapid innovation, the fast pace of technological change continued in digital industries. There was a constant churn and evolution of information and communication technologies, and early-stage technologies often took more than 10 years to become productive and widely adopted in the economy. The sheer pace of technological improvements continued to be more rapid in digital industries than in many others.

Digital technological advances have translated into unprecedented business innovation opportunities. A comparison of the 10 most valuable companies in the US economy in 2020 and 2000 reveals the tremendous dynamism of the digital economy. In 2000, oil, pharmaceuticals, retail, and banks along with general manufacturing were the dominant industries, although the economy was experiencing the first internet boom with the expansion of the networking infrastructure (Cisco) and the dominance of "Wintel" desktop computing (Microsoft + Intel). Vodafone was busy building the global 3G wireless networks. Oil was still at the top in 2010, but by 2020, the number of digital companies in the top 10 had doubled, with Amazon, Alphabet, Alibaba, Facebook, and Tencent representing a new type of a digital service company that was only invented in the late 1990s and early 2000s (see Table 1.1). These digital services were translating technological advances in information and communication into very large-scale business activity.

---

[8] See Zittrain, J.L. (2006). The generative internet. *Harvard Law Review* 119: 1974–2040.

Table 1.1 The world's most valuable companies by stock market capitalization, 2000–2020

Ranking	2000	2010	2020
1.	General Electric	PetroChina	**Microsoft**
2.	**Cisco**	Exxon Mobil	**Apple**
3.	Exxon Mobil	**Microsoft**	**Amazon**
4.	Pfizer	ICBC	**Alphabet**
5.	**Microsoft**	**Apple**	**Alibaba**
6.	Wal-Mart	BHP Billiton	**Facebook**
7.	Citigroup	Wal-Mart	**Tencent**
8.	Vodafone	Berkshire Hathaway	Berkshire Hathaway
9.	**Intel**	General Electric	Visa
10.	Royal Dutch Shell	**China Mobile**	Johnson & Johnson

Digital companies in bold.

Note: Although digitalization was well under way in the year 2000, non-digital companies dominated the process of value creation until the 2010s. During that decade, digital platform companies grew to an unprecedented global scale and became powerful forces in their markets and broader economies.

Source: Retrieved from https://en.wikipedia.org/wiki/List_of_public_corporations_by_market_capitalization#2020 in August 2022.

Perhaps the most fundamental reason for the dominance of digital businesses in the economy was that information and communication technologies were driving the economy because they facilitated very basic and critical functions of the economy and society, and they were **General Purpose Technologies**: applicable in all parts of the economy.

Fundamentally, all decisions and actions we take depend on the sequence of:

$$\text{Communication} \rightarrow \text{information} \rightarrow \text{decision} \rightarrow \text{action}$$

Communication and obtained information influence everything we do, from looking for a job or a restaurant, to business decisions about market entry and product design, to societal decisions about voting, health policy, or even war and revolution. Thus, when communication technologies make it easier to access relevant information or coordinate with others, we will make more or better decisions that lead to different courses of action. Think about this sequence the next time you make a purchase decision. What were your sources of information and what was the network of communication you relied on to make the decision?

For example, upon buying a new phone you might first explore which phones your peers use by connecting with them in a social network. You might also search and visit comparison websites that write reviews of the latest products. Armed with the recommendations and technical information you would perhaps search for specific products from multiple websites, or use comparison shopping services to locate the best price. Only after that might you visit a specific retail store to purchase it. There is a whole ecosystem of information and communication about products and prices, and a single retailer will have limited control over the information available about their products in this communication network. However, if any of the elements of the information ecosystem are missing or deficient, your ability to optimize your decision may be compromised.

Information and communication technologies might also be called "**Invention Machines**."[9] They accelerate scientific progress by making the process of discovery and technological development more effective. As highlighted by the disproportionate importance of instruments in the process of invention (see Figure 1.1 above), the collection, analysis, and application of data and information are critical for the creation of new knowledge or new technologies. Consider the massive effect of the microscope on the biological sciences. Without such optical instruments, scientists wouldn't have been able to discover cells, proteins, genes, molecules, atoms, or microbes. The microscope revolutionized many areas of science, particularly the medical field, but it also facilitated environmental sciences and engineering. It enabled the development of modern medicine and new materials. The microscope is thus not only a general-purpose technology, applicable in a wide range of industries and technological fields, but also an Invention Machine that accelerated discovery and enabled subsequent inventions. Instruments are technologies that facilitate the collection and manipulation of information that then enters the processes of communication and transfer, decision making, and action. Technologies of information collection, retrieval, and communication are so critical to society and economic activity that their improvements and evolution will shape the very structure and functioning of society.

In today's economy, various computers and communication devices are the primary "instruments" and carry out much of the data collection. When people interact in social media, use mobility apps on their phones, drive around in a connected car, or browse webpages with the intent to buy something, they leave behind a digital trace that the providers of digital services collect, aggregate, analyze, and use for decisions and actions. Additionally, various sensors of physical activity also operate as instruments. Such sensors can detect the state or motion of a physical object. For example, sensors embedded in an engine can measure direction, motion, temperature, or vibration of the engine or its parts. Wirelessly connected sensors can then transmit the data to a remote computer that can analyze and potentially autonomously or with human help make decisions and act to modify the engine operation.

Considering the long-standing and massive economic, societal, technological, and scientific impacts of information and communication devices, we can speculate

---

[9] See Koutroumpis, Pantelis, Leiponen, Aija, and Thomas, Llewellyn D.W. (2020). Digital instruments as invention machines. *Communications of the ACM* 64(1): 70–78. Retrieved from https://dl.acm.org/doi/fullHtml/10.1145/3377476 in August, 2022.

that when data and analytics are networked at scale, very significant technological and economic changes follow, too. We saw such massive and disruptive impacts from the global adoption of the internet, and we can similarly begin to assess how the digital connectivity of physical objects and activities via the Internet of Things will influence scientific and economic progress in the coming decades.

KEY IDEAS

- Information and communication are critical for decision making.
- Digitalization changes how people and organizations find, collect, analyze, and communicate information.
- Rapidly evolving information and communication technologies influence the speed and direction of scientific discovery and technology adoption.
- Instruments, computers, and communication networks create the Internet of Things that promises to bring about a new wave of innovation in the economy.

DEFINITIONS

Behavioral uncertainty concerns user behavior when adopting new technologies and makes it difficult to anticipate how users react to and engage with new digital products and services.

Digital refers to information and communication that is reduced to binary code and that can be processed and transferred using computers and communication networks.

Digitalization refers to the social and economic processes of *adoption* and use of digitized data, artifacts and processes by individuals, organizations, and societies.

Digital business is any business that in its core processes is dependent on information and communication technologies to deliver products and services, usually information products or communication services.

Digital business innovation deals with improved technologies for information and communication that are designed to enable new forms of economic activity.

Digitization is the technological process by which analogue or physical artifacts and processes are *transformed* into digital or digitally-enabled artifacts or processes.[10]

Generativity is the capacity of technologies to spawn (generate) additional innovations.

General Purpose Technologies facilitate and accelerate very basic and critical functions of the economy and the society, and they are applicable in all parts of the economy.

Innovation is about change: the introduction of novelty into an economic system.

Invention Machines are General Purpose Technologies that accelerate scientific progress in many different fields by making the process of discovery and technological development more effective

Market uncertainty makes it difficult to assess whether the commercial goals of the project can be reached.

---

[10] Gradillas, M. and L. D. W. Thomas, "Digi-what? Distinguishing digitization and digitalization," Unpublished Working Paper, 2021.

Social construction of technology is the social process of learning, using, understanding, and creating new social practices when adopting new technologies that are used in cooperation or communication with others.

Technical uncertainty makes it difficult to assess whether the technical goals of the project can be reached.

DISCUSSION QUESTIONS

1. Think of one source of information that has recently become digital and another source of information that is not (yet) digital. Do you think the latter will be digitized in the next five years? What technologies and other resources would be needed to digitize it, and why might it not happen?

2. Modern automobiles have 60–100 digital sensors and instruments, for example, multiple cameras.[11] Choose a particular type of a sensor in a car and explain what information it collects, how that information is analyzed, and what kinds of decisions the generated insights might inform.

3. Pick one of the digital companies in Table 1.1 in the 2020 column and describe how the company used the Communication → Information → Decision → Action sequence to its advantage to dominate its industry. For example, how did the company use advanced communication technologies to collect information that its rivals didn't have, to make better decisions and pursue competitive actions?

4. The Science and Technology priorities of the US government in 2020 included 5G telecommunications and artificial intelligence (AI). How do these technologies enter the Communication sequence? Describe how the company you analyzed in the previous question is likely to apply 5G and AI in coming years.

FURTHER READING

Koutroumpis, Pantelis, Leiponen, Aija, and Thomas, Llewellyn D.W. (2020). Digital instruments as invention machines. *Communications of the ACM* 64(1): 70–78.

McAfee, Andrew and Brynjolfsson, Erik (2017). *Machine, Platform, Crowd: Harnessing Our Digital Future.* New York: W.W. Norton & Co.

Pinch, Trevor J. and Bijker, Wiebe E. (1984). The social construction of facts and artefacts: or how the sociology of science and sociology of technology might benefit each other. *Social Studies of Science* 14(3): 399–441.

Zittrain, Jonathan (2008). *The Future of the Internet – And How To Stop It.* New Haven and London: Yale University Press.

---

[11] See, for example, Tyler, N. (2016). Demand for automotive sensors is booming. New Electronics December 14, 2016. Retrieved from www.newelectronics.co.uk/content/features/demand-for-automotive-sensors-is-booming in August, 2022.

2 Digital Disruption

Innovation is a multifaceted process. It may involve products, processes, or services, or all of the above. It can be radical, incremental, or even revolutionary. The central aspect of innovation is that it introduces novelty into the economic system. It is thus not abstract information, such as a newly patented invention, but something practical and concrete that is developed, implemented, adopted, and applied in real economic activities. Innovations create economic change, whereas inventions may only create scientific or technological change[1] if they are not implemented and adopted in economic activity.

The economic impact of innovations depends on their technological characteristics and the market and organizational contexts in which they are adopted. Technological innovations can be radical or incremental in terms of their magnitude of improvement in the technical performance of the system. Innovations can be competence-enhancing or competence-destroying, depending on the organizational context in terms of whether existing or new capabilities are needed to apply them. Such distinctions help innovators understand who will be well-positioned to commercialize the technological change. Radical innovations are usually more valuable than incremental innovations, but they often require new capabilities and can diminish or "destroy" the value of a firm's existing capabilities, and sometimes it is initially difficult to even understand what investments should be made to develop new capabilities. Radical, and particularly competence-destroying innovations tend to be associated with very severe technical uncertainty. In this chapter we focus on the market impact of innovations in terms of whether they tend to sustain or disrupt existing business models. It turns out that disruptive innovations usually cause rather extreme amounts of market uncertainty.

2.1 Disruptive Innovations Offer a New Performance Trajectory

The concept of disruptive innovation seems to elicit dread and attention among innovators and managers, but it is usually poorly defined and understood. In this chapter we will attempt to be very clear about what disruptive innovation is and is not, and examine its competitive implications. In particular, it is important

---

[1] We use the word *technology* in the sense of knowledge about technical applications of science and engineering.

to understand the limits of the predictive power of theories of disruption. The conditions for disruptive innovation are almost always unobservable, and while a business can prepare for disruption, it is very difficult to predict its timing and magnitude.

Most innovations are gradual and cumulative in nature. They allow innovators to keep improving their product offerings and compete more effectively in their existing markets. These are **sustaining innovations** that offer more and better along the existing performance trajectory. This involves improvement within an established dimension of performance, such as the processing power of microchips. With the constant and somewhat predictable increase in the number of transistors on a chip, these innovations are making computers ever more powerful over an extended period of time. Nevertheless, sustaining innovations can be radical or competence-destroying, such as in the case of a new semiconductor material. The discovery of thin-film amorphous boron nitride[2] promises to extend Moore's law and allow packing even more transistors on a microchip. Its fabrication necessitates very different capabilities than earlier materials, but it continues the same performance trajectory by enhancing the processing power of computer chips. It may be a competence-destroying innovation for chip manufacturers but fulfilling the same needs as earlier technologies for computer users. From users' perspective, this innovation continues the improvement of processing performance and is thus a sustaining innovation.

Disruptive innovations (Christensen, 1997), in contrast, offer entirely new or previously unimportant performance trajectories. In the computing industry, for example, the shift from ever-increasing processing power to mobile devices constituted a disruptive innovation. In fact, when the transition toward mobility took place, customers were offered less powerful devices in exchange for mobility. Whereas the original value proposition of computing devices was focused on ever-higher processing power to run increasingly complex software applications, the new value proposition focused on lightweight devices with extended battery life and built-in wireless connectivity. **Value proposition** is a statement about the aspects of the product that create unusual customer value that articulates why customers should buy this product rather than something else. When such a market shift happens, existing customers who appreciated the original value proposition (processing power) may respond very differently from new and previously unserved or underserved customers who embrace and appreciate the new value proposition (mobility). Old customers may reject the new offering and prefer the old value proposition and the older products. However, if the underserved market segment is large enough, the new value proposition may become dominant in the industry.

While the innovation of mobile computing was incremental in its effects on technical performance (even reducing performance in some ways), it was

---

[2] *The Economist* (2020). A new material helps transistors become vanishingly small. *The Economist*, July 18, 2020. Retrieved from www.economist.com/science-and-technology/2020/07/18/a-new-material-helps-transistors-become-vanishingly-small in August 2022.

nevertheless competence-destroying for existing chip makers such as Intel. It created an opening for new chip makers such as Qualcomm and Samsung, who built their chips based on ARM's (Advanced RISC Machine) designs that were much more energy-efficient than Intel's traditional chip designs. However, changes in consumer behavior were the most surprising aspect of the transition to mobile. Over time, consumers started to use mobile devices as their primary mode of connectivity and even professional users switched to lower-powered laptops and handheld devices. By 2015, there were more mobile-only computer users than desktop-only users, and the majority of internet traffic had shifted to mobile devices, too.[3] A broad behavioral change followed that established mobile computing as the standard and helped the chip market for mobile devices overtake that for high-powered desktop computers and workstations.

The disruptive innovation of mobile computing transformed both computing and internet service industries. Computers had to be miniaturized and wirelessly connected. Internet services had to accommodate small screens and limited or intermittent internet access. Looking at the leading mobile device innovations, most were offered by entrants, not incumbent hardware manufacturers. Initially smartphones were pioneered by handheld device makers Palm and BlackBerry. Nokia tried to enter with its Communicator device but was eclipsed by Apple's iPhone by 2010. Google also tried to enter with its G-phone but it quickly exited and focused on its new mobile operating system, Android. Samsung entered later as a follower that largely based its products on the imitation of successful designs and technologies. No computer manufacturers from the "IBM-compatible" part of the personal computer industry entered mobile computing, and IBM had itself exited already in 2005 by selling its PC unit to the Chinese company Lenovo. Leading PC companies such as Dell and HP stayed primarily in the laptop market that was becoming rapidly commoditized. Ultimately, the mobile disruption thus dramatically shifted the competitive dynamics in much of the computer industry (see Figure 2.1).

2.2   Why is Disruption Challenging for Incumbents?

Given the significant uncertainty about the market response to a disruptive innovation, incumbent firms often, quite sensibly, follow the feedback of their existing customers. If the existing market is substantial, profitable, and growing, there is no point of introducing the disruptive innovation that doesn't serve these highly profitable customers well. This is the "Innovator's Dilemma" identified by Christensen (1997). However, the strategic challenge in this scenario is managing the pace of change: digital innovations tend to get better quickly, and initially scrappy

---

[3] Petrov, C. (2022). Mobile vs. Desktop Usage Statistics. Techjury, August 14, 2022. Retrieved from https://techjury.net/blog/mobile-vs-desktop-usage/#gref in August 2022.

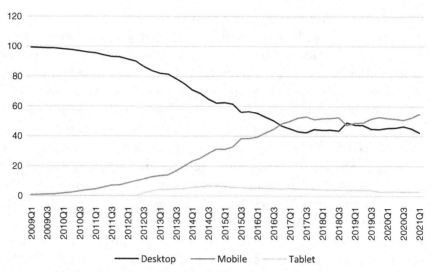

Figure 2.1 Worldwide website traffic by device type
Note: The rise of mobile devices in enabling internet access has been rapid since 2009. Mobile devices overtook desktops as the primary device type for internet access in 2016. Tablet computers have not gained as much market share.
Data source: StatCounter Global Stats. Retrieved from https://gs.statcounter.com/platform-market-share/desktop-mobile-tablet/worldwide/#quarterly-200901-202101 in August 2021.

technologies can become palatable for mainstream corporate customers in just a few years. Consider, for example, the mobile computing disruption. Even if mobile devices initially offered too little processing power for many applications, five or ten years later they actually offered sufficiently high performance for almost all applications. At this point, the incumbent's products may be pushed aside in the market if the disruptive innovations are sufficiently good in both the original and the novel aspects of performance. Then they may be preferable not just to the previously underserved customers, but also to the old and traditional customers who initially preferred the old value proposition.

Open-Source Software (OSS) systems provide an illustration of the disruptive innovation dynamic. When Linux and other OSS operating systems were initially developed, they were not taken as serious contenders to commercial software packages such as Windows. OSS grew inside university labs and off of the efforts of academics and their students. For years, it did not appear to have a major impact in software markets. However, after years of development, many of the students who learned about operating systems by working on OSS in university research labs had graduated and moved on to create and manage computer systems in corporate settings. They realized that OSS could well be adopted in large corporations if they had sufficient IT skills in-house. However, for smaller companies, the lack of skills and resources to adapt OSS programs to the local needs was still a hurdle, even though the price point (free!) was very attractive to them, too. Hence, some of those computer science graduates envisioned a potential market for services that would help smaller companies to adopt OSS packages such as Linux. Indeed, companies like Red Hat that make Linux available to SMEs pioneered an OSS service market. Eventually, Google's Android system adopted the Linux Kernel and IBM acquired Red Hat – open source had gone mainstream. In the web server market, Apache was the original OSS success story and maintained its market dominance in web server operating systems for 20 years. More recently, NGINX (pronounced "engine X"), another OSS system, emerged to challenge Apache. Microsoft's Windows continued to decline in web server software, and it never gained significant market share in mobile computing, although it continued to dominate desktop computing. Thus, after disruptive OSS innovations entered software submarkets, it became difficult for traditional technologies to sustain their positions.

A similar story of the triumph of OSS can be told in mobile computing. Although Google retained some control over Android, the source code was available for modification enabling customization and application by device makers such as Samsung. Despite the fact that the proprietary iOS operating system of Apple was highly profitable, Android became much more widespread globally. Android's disruptive value proposition offered openness and flexibility, which were very appealing to most smartphone manufacturers and consumers in the world. For Google, the roaring success of Android enabled the development of a new **business model** for mobile computing, a whole new constellation and organization of assets and activities that delivered the firm's value proposition, to go along with the operating system. Google would give the operating system for free, require that users have Google accounts and services pre-installed on their devices, and generate profits from advertising enabled by the (ultimately very large) user base and the data collected from consumers. This model differed dramatically from that of Apple that offered well-designed and integrated hardware, software, and content systems but profited primarily from hardware innovation and sales.

In contrast, the previous market leader Nokia and its Symbian operating system alliance failed trying to upgrade their value proposition and business model in response to the threat of disruption from both Apple and Google. As a result, in a shockingly short amount of time (and after a few crucial strategic missteps), Nokia lost its leading market position and sold its device business to Microsoft in 2011. The disruptive innovations of Apple and Google connected smartphones with attractive software and content services. Nokia had no trouble creating the hardware, being a pioneering wireless innovator in handsets and networks, but it could not figure out the complementarity of hardware, software, and services. An incumbent that got stuck in the old value proposition for too long was thus pushed out of the market (see Figure 2.2).

Digital disruption can take place in previously non-digital markets, too. A classic example of its devastating effect in offline services is the fate of travel agencies. Offline travel agencies survived, and thrived, because they could control access to airline booking systems. However, the creation of ITA software for digitally searching airlines' booking systems and the opening up of Global Distribution Systems

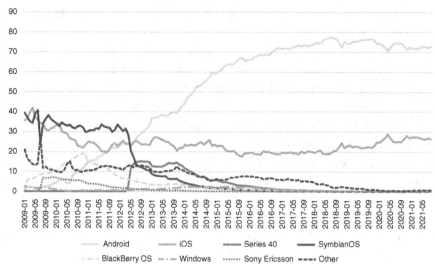

Figure 2.2 Global smartphone operating system market shares
Note: Early leaders in the global smartphone operating systems market included Symbian, Apple, and BlackBerry, but there were several other contenders. By 2012, the Android open-source system promoted by Google became the market leader and has held a dominant position since. Apple iOS maintained a highly profitable niche position, and most other systems have exited the market.
Data source: https://gs.statcounter.com/os-market-share/mobile/worldwide/#monthly-200901-202108 retrieved in August, 2021.

(GDS) such as SABRE, Amadeus, and Travelport enabled online entrants to bypass the traditional travel agencies and directly search for and offer fares. Furthermore, the dominant GDS provider SABRE, originally created as the in-house booking system for American Airlines, went public in 2000 and was no longer dependent on or catering to any single airline. Consequently, Orbitz, Expedia and Travelocity used SABRE and the ITA software directly to create the online travel booking service market.[4] By 2005 or so, a small number offline travel agencies survived only to make unusual or corporate travel arrangements.

Similarly, electronic mapping services used to rely on proprietary maps of which there were only two major providers, NAVTEQ and TeleAtlas. MapQuest and a handful of other online innovators made maps and directions available with funding from advertising, and Google opened up the industry through satellite and "StreetView" imaging that didn't depend on a mapping vendor. In the end, few people were willing to pay for mapping services because they became freely available through these internet services. As a further casualty of the disruption in mapping, London's famous black taxicabs were challenged by the sprouting "minicab" industry, and subsequently by ride-sharing services such as Uber, Ola,

---

[4] Hasbrouck, E. (2010). Google buys ITA software (Part 2: What does ITA software do?). Edward Hasbrouck's Blog. Retrieved from https://hasbrouck.org/blog/archives/001880.html in August 2022.
    Hasbrouck, E. (2010). Google buys ITA software (Part 1: The back story) Retrieved from https://hasbrouck.org/blog/archives/001879.html in August 2022.

and BlaBlaCar. While black cabbies needed to spend months, even years, gaining The Knowledge of London's complex street map, minicab and ride-sharing drivers relied on navigation services such as TomTom that used electronic mapping services. Minicabs could not book fares at the official taxi stands and needed to be pre-booked, which created an additional hassle for customers, but they offered much lower fares. A minicab or Uber driver only needed a clean car and a smartphone to provide their service, as opposed to a special black vehicle and years of training. Again, digital disruption in the industry was prompted by making widely available a critical source of an information good that used to be expensive and controlled by few parties.

The most interesting, and possibly the most challenging, disruptive innovations concern the digitization of hardware or "analog" markets and the associated shift from product markets to service markets (also called "servitization"). Many mobility services fall in this category. On-demand bicycles and cars sell mobility, not vehicles. While the rental car industry has existed for a long time, its value proposition has primarily targeted travelers that have a higher willingness to pay and occasional periods of rental. Car sharing, in contrast, is based on frequent usage and availability in residential neighborhoods where parking is often scarce. Zipcar and other car sharing businesses crafted a market niche that offered a very different value proposition relative to car rental companies and relied on sensors and wireless communication technologies to allow remote monitoring of usage and access. Similar "sharing" (short-term rental) arrangements are of course becoming available in many other industries: residential and commercial real estate, production equipment and tools, engines and other heavy machinery, even jet engines and airplanes.

2.3 Why *Digital* Disruption?

Reflecting the internet's **power to reveal**, digital disruption often involves a new source of information that becomes widely available and undermines the value of an existing source of proprietary information – content or software. In the short-term asset rental markets the new information is often sensor based. For example, location and operation data can be wirelessly lifted from the asset: sensors combined with a wireless connection will tell the asset owner where it is and how it is being used. In many other cases, the new source of information originates from a network of users. It is not necessary any more to subscribe to tightly-held, GPS-based navigation services when Google provides maps and Waze provides crowdsourced information about congestion. In music, peer-to-peer networks of file sharing challenged the legal control of copyrights in content markets. In software markets, networks of programmers contributed to OSS to challenge proprietary software providers. Crowd-based coordination and communication can thus become such a powerful and valuable source of information that industrial powerhouses are challenged – and sometimes toppled.

Continuous improvement in computer processing power, storage, and broadband availability (including wireless connectivity) and associated long-term downward trends in the cost of computing and communication have provided the infrastructure for economy-wide digital disruption. Technological improvements facilitated cost reductions that in competitive markets translated to lower prices and continuous improvement of quality in computing systems. In turn, organizations and individuals made substantial and long-standing investments in information and communication technologies to take advantage of these technological opportunities. Such investments tended to be more pronounced in industries that are information and communication intensive, such as software, financial services, media, education, and professional services. In contrast, industries such as retail and manufacturing were initially slow to make IT investments. Although "e-commerce" attracted a lot of attention from the late 1990s, the share of online retail in all retail reached 10 percent only in 2020. However, with e-commerce expanding, a larger share of revenue is spent on IT now by retailers (cf. Figures 2.3 and 2.4).

To digitally disrupt an existing market, innovators need to locate and exploit a new source of information or a new communication network. Disruptive innovators can make a previously proprietary information resource widely available more cheaply or even free, as in the cases of open-source software or traffic conditions. Then the disruptor must discover a low-cost way to offer the resource. The service offering will usually be embedded in a technological system like a travel booking system or a navigation system. Sometimes the new resource is regulated, and disruption requires changes in the legal or regulatory framework. Such is the case with peer transportation services (e.g., Lyft and Uber have had regulatory conflicts in each jurisdiction they have entered; see Garud et al., 2022) and with peer-to-peer content sharing (e.g., Napster, Grokster, and Aereo were all reviewed and essentially shut down by various US courts). Then, even if a disruptive innovator discovers a dramatically cheaper way to offer a digital service, they may need to convince a larger set of stakeholders to support it. That, in itself, can become prohibitively expensive.

Meanwhile, remember that the concept of disruptive innovation is descriptive but not predictive. It is impossible to know how disruptions play out. It may not be possible to recognize beforehand which novel value proposition offers a distinct trajectory of improvement that is rapidly improving and highly desirable to users while posing a significant competitive challenge to existing companies and industries. Disruptive innovation is thus not a very helpful theory of digital competition. Nevertheless, the pattern of digital disruption has been observed so many times and in so many different industry segments that ignoring the possibility is dangerous in rapidly-evolving industries, as long as digital technologies continue to change relentlessly. To guard against disruption, firms need to be willing to constantly assess their market segments and improve their product offering. For example, as automobile drivers have switched from dedicated devices such as TomTom to smartphone apps like Waze, TomTom has evolved

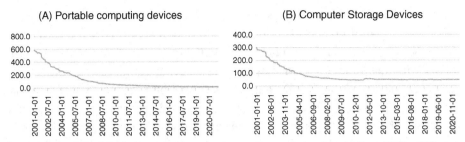

Figure 2.3 Producer Price Index: portable computers and computer equipment (June 2007 = 100) and computer storage devices (December 2004 = 100)
Note: Prices of computing and communication devices have steadily declined over a very long period of time.
Data source: US Bureau of Labor Statistics. Retrieved from https://fred.stlouisfed.org/series/PCU33411133411172 and https://fred.stlouisfed.org/series/PCU3341123341121 in August 2021.

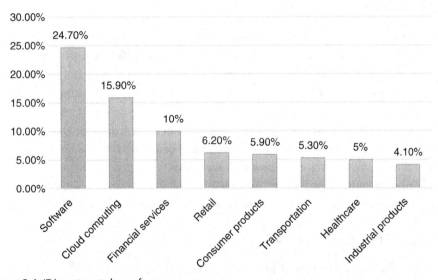

Figure 2.4 IT investment share of revenue
Note: IT investments per revenue are the greatest in software development and cloud computing, but the financial sector, retail trade, and consumer products have also invested significantly in their IT capabilities.
Data source: Flexera survey of CIOs 2020. Retrieved from www.flexera.com/blog/technology-value-optimization/it-spending-by-industry/ in August 2021.

their automotive products toward autonomous driving solutions and electric vehicle charging maps. Smart innovators constantly generate disruption-proof options within their business model.

KEY IDEAS

- Disruptive digital innovations usually offer a new source of information or a new communication network that reduces the value of a proprietary source of information or other type of asset.

- The new digital resource enables new core features and thus a different value proposition that often appeals initially to a different set of users or customers.
- Incumbents often find it difficult to justify switching to the disruptive innovation, because it undermines their existing business model and sources of market power.
- The constant and decades-long improvement and price reductions of information and communication technologies have helped the widespread and rapid adoption of mobile and other computer and information storage devices. This ongoing process of adoption of ever-faster and more efficient ICT devices has supercharged the internet's power to reveal and enabled many if not most digital disruptions.
- As ICTs evolve and disseminate, smart companies scan their markets for potentially disruptive innovations and develop strategies for either adopting or challenging them before they reach the mainstream market.

DEFINITIONS

Business model is the constellation and organization of assets and activities that deliver the firm's value proposition. According to Osterwalder and Pigneur (2010), it includes a revenue model, a cost structure, resources, customer relationships, and partners.

Disruptive innovation undermines the value of an existing, proprietary information resource

The power of digital technologies **to reveal information** stems from their constant improvement and competitive markets that make computing and communication technologies cheaper and more powerful over time.

Sustaining innovation enhances the value of an existing information resource.

Value proposition is a unique offering to create value for customers or users.

DISCUSSION QUESTIONS

1. Think of a disruptive digital innovation (e.g., Airbnb).
   a. What is the new source of information or new network that it offers?
   b. How does its *value proposition* differ from the industry incumbents (e.g., hotel chains)?
   c. On what improvements in *information and communication technologies* does that innovation depend?
   d. How have the *incumbents* reacted to its entry? How do you think they should have responded?
   e. Did its entry have any *regulatory implications*, that is, did it require changes in the legal or regulatory environment?
2. What digital disruptions have depended on the fact that over 70 percent of the (US) population own a smartphone?
3. Why must disruptive innovations offer a value proposition that is different from that of the industry incumbents?
4. Are industry incumbents ever the first to launch disruptive innovations? Elaborate your arguments.

FURTHER READING

Adner, Ron (2002). When are technologies disruptive? A demand-based view of the emergence of competition. *Strategic Management Journal* 23(8): 667–688.

Christensen, Clayton (1997). *The Innovator's Dilemma: When New Technologies Cause Great Firms to Fail*. Cambridge, MA: Harvard Business School Press.

Garud, Raghu, Kumaraswamy, Arun, Roberts, Anna, and Xu, Le (2022). Liminal movement by digital platform-based sharing economy ventures: the case of Uber technologies. *Strategic Management Journal* 43(3): 447–475.

Osterwalder, Alexander and Pigneur, Yves (2010). *Business Model Generation: A Handbook for Visionaries, Game Changers, and Challengers*. Hoboken, NJ: John Wiley & Sons.

3 Disruptive Communication Networks

Communication networks are a key feature of any society, and, in the digital age, much of large-scale communication is digital. The transition to digital began in the 1970s through key inventions in the field of electronics, and the application of computers and telecommunication technologies to build large-scale digital communication systems transformed society. Over time, digital communication and computing technologies were adopted in all sectors of the economy, from agriculture and manufacturing to industrial services to consumer products and entertainment. They are General Purpose Technologies that can facilitate the creation and dissemination of information in everything that we do. Moreover, new generations of communication networks are launched every decade. Therefore, for a digital business innovator, it is important to understand how to shape the emergence and evolution of digital communication networks.

This chapter reviews the origins of the internet and its evolution from a few university labs in the 1970s to a global channel of mass communication and commercialization to the ubiquitous high-speed wireless connectivity by 2020. This overview sets the stage for thinking about future evolution of communication networks and opportunities for innovation therein. While exploring the historical precedents, we will also investigate which design principles have facilitated the growth and impact of the internet. We will argue that the breathtaking dynamism forced the creators of these communication networks to focus on long-term issues rather than concurrent societal problems. They also built the networks to be capable of rapid change and growth, accommodating a very large scale. Constant change and large-scale connectivity also meant that very diverse needs and interests were brought into the online sphere. The network itself thus had to be able to accommodate myriad ideas that generated additional innovations and activities to pursue. The internet was open ended and extremely generative – capable of facilitating follow-on innovation. Thus, the design principles we highlight include:

- design for the future
- design for change
- design for generativity.

3.1 Invention of the Internet

According to the Silicon Valley legend, the idea of the internet was conceived by RAND Corporation scientists tasked with the grand challenge of how the

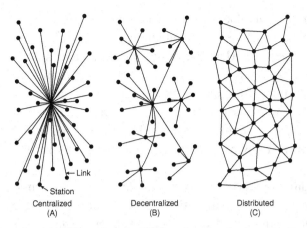

Figure 3.1 Paul Baran's original illustration of a distributed communication network
Note: Baran's Rand memo was the first to propose and analyze the implications of a distributed communication network. Although it met initial resistance, it turned out to be very influential in debates about the internet.
Source: Rand Corporation Memo "On Distributed Communications" (1964). Retrieved from www.rand .org/pubs/research_memoranda/RM3420.html in August, 2021.

nation could communicate after a devastating attack of nuclear war. The 1964 memo by Paul Baran (see Figure 3.1) sketched ideas for a **distributed network** that had no central authority and could therefore operate even if substantial parts of it were destroyed. All nodes of the network would operate as both hubs and spokes, and routing of the messages around the network would only depend on node availability.

According to Baran's path-breaking ideas, a **centralized network** (A) and even a **decentralized network** (B) would be highly vulnerable to strategic attacks if their central node was eliminated. A distributed network (C), in contrast, would be able to communicate effectively if one or even several of the nodes were destroyed. However, the centralized network is more efficient in the sense that each node can reach every other node with just two steps through the central node. The decentralized network is also more efficient than the distributed one as the hub-and-spoke structure shortens the average path length through the network. Thus, the distributed network creates significant redundancy and inefficiency but also reliability as congestion in any hub node will not delay communication among the spokes.

Although the actual global internet is not as distributed as network (C) in the diagram, on each continent there are many central nodes rather than just few. However, occasionally network vulnerabilities do manifest themselves, such as in 2014 and again in 2019 when an underwater cable in the Pacific Ocean broke and international connections between Southeast Asia and the Americas were significantly slowed down.[1] Since 2010, intercontinental connections have increasingly

---

[1] Samui Times (2015). Broken undersea AAG cable slows internet down across Southeast Asia. Samui Times Thailand News, July 1, 2015. Retrieved from www.samuitimes.com/broken-undersea-aag-cable-slows-internet-across-southeast-asia/ in August 2022.

been built by tech giants Google, Facebook, Amazon, and Microsoft, instead of the traditional providers that were telecommunications firms.[2]

Baran also proposed **packet switching**, a technique to split the message into very small "packets." Each packet also had a header that informed network routers of the destination of the packet as well as its order within the original message. The packets would separately find their way over the internet and, once they all reached the destination, they would be assembled back into the original message. However, if any packet was delayed along the way, the whole message would be delayed.

Packet switching is a method to distribute the information content in a message effectively through the communication network. Packet switching facilitates efficient use of the distributed network, because the message will not get stuck in a busy node but each packet will be routed through the least-congested parts of the network. Together with the distributed architecture of the network, packet switching enabled gradual growth of the network with respect to the number of users.

3.2   The Triple Helix of Government, Academia, and Private Enterprise Innovating Networks

To build such expansive communication networks based on these early conceptions, the US government played a central role. The Department of Defense Advanced Research Projects Agency (DARPA) coordinated and funded the efforts to build the ARPANET, the first continental computer network. In addition to US academic and industrial computer scientists, British and French computer scientists' ideas were incorporated in the initial design. The original nodes of the network launched in 1969 included the University of California Los Angeles, University of California Santa Barbara, and University of Utah, as well as the Stanford Research Institute (SRI). By 1974, leading science and engineering universities such as the Massachusetts Institute of Technology, Harvard University, University of Illinois, Carnegie Mellon University, Purdue University, University of California Berkeley, and University College London (UK) had joined the network. Furthermore, major technology companies such as Xerox, and government agencies such as National Aeronautics and Space Administration's (NASA) Ames Research Center in California and DARPA itself in Virginia connected to the growing network (see, e.g., Abbate, 2000, for a scholarly review of the history of internet).

ARPANET was the first network to implement the standardized information protocol TCP/IP (Transmission Control Protocol/Internet Protocol) that allowed the creation of the "network of networks," connecting all computers to the same

---

[2] Satariano, A. (2019). How the internet travels across the oceans. *The New York Times*, March 10, 2019. Retrieved from www.nytimes.com/interactive/2019/03/10/technology/internet-cables-oceans.html in August 2022.

network rather than having many overlapping but not interconnecting networks in place. The early TCP protocol was developed and implemented by scientists from Stanford University in 1974, and for subsequent improvements in routing, scientists from University College London (UCL) and BBN Technologies, a private company, joined the work. The first connection to send messages between US and UK computers using the TCP/IP took place in 1975 between Stanford and UCL. While commercial entities such as IBM, Xerox, and Digital Equipment Corporation continued to develop their own protocols, they also adopted the TCP/IP standard. Eventually this shared and publicly available protocol drove the global adoption of internet technologies.

Although the US government and major research universities cooperated to create the first "inter-net," other academic computer scientists were quick to step in and build complementary technologies and networks. Computer scientists at the University of North Carolina and Duke University created the USENET network to function as a networked discussion board. The core functionality was "newsgroups" that were focused on a particular category of topics or "news." Users were able to post and read news in a wholly unmoderated and anonymous environment. Consequently, it gave birth to such important internet concepts as "flame" and "spam." In the words of computer science professor Gene Spafford from Purdue University, "USENET is like a herd of performing elephants with diarrhea. Massive, difficult to redirect, awe-inspiring, entertaining, and a source of mind-boggling amounts of excrement when you least expect it." Early USENET members included Reed College, the University of Oklahoma, and Bell Labs, and 50 other organizations joined in the first year of operation.[3]

NSFNET was an attempt to extend remote supercomputing resources to scientists in different parts of the country (see Figure 3.2). NSF began funding the development of five computer centers at Cornell University, the University of California San Diego, University of Illinois, Carnegie Mellon University, University of Pittsburgh, and Princeton University. The goal was to allow scientists to connect to these supercomputers from a larger number of research institutions that didn't have in-house supercomputers so that the computing investment and resources could be shared among the institutions. Ultimately, with the broader adoption of the TCP/IP communication standard and growing interest in communicating across the growing networks (e.g., it was possible early on to post articles from ARPANET to USENET but not the other way around), these evolving networks were interconnected to one network of networks, the internet.[4]

European scientists and institutions (particularly University College London and CERN in Switzerland) were instrumental in developing and improving the core ideas and technologies behind these networks. European governments also

---

[3] Emerson, Sandra L. (1983). Usenet/A bulletin board for Unix users. *BYTE Magazine*, October: 219–236. Retrieved from https://archive.org/details/byte-magazine-1983-10/page/n219/mode/2up?view=theater in August 2022.

[4] See, for example www.computerhistory.org/internethistory/1980s. Retrieved in August 2022.

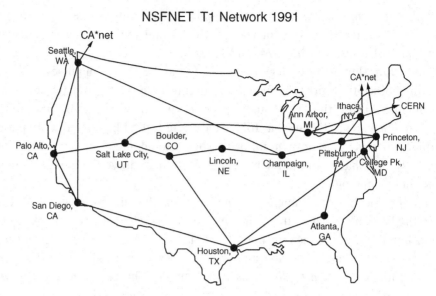

Figure 3.2 NSFNET backbone network in 1991

Note: The National Science Foundation funded a national network of academic supercomputers. By 1991, the network connected major research universities and provided remote computing access to scientists. Soon after, the NSF began privatizing the network to a group of commercial entities.

Source: National Science Foundation via Merit Network Inc. (CC license). Retrieved from https://commons.wikimedia.org/wiki/File:NSFNET-backbone-T1.png in August, 2021.

began to invest in academic communication networks, first within national borders, and soon across borders. In 1988, the NSFNET began to interconnect with European universities in Nordic countries and France. EUnet that evolved from the European Unix Users Group pioneered European internet service provision in the 1980s. By 1989, EUnet had grown to 1,000 nodes in 21 countries. EUnet subsequently became a commercial provider of internet services (EUnet International).[5]

In the late 1980s, NSF also began to consider the privatization of the network. It had accomplished its goal of connecting hundreds of universities and research laboratories, but managing the network had become expensive and cumbersome. Furthermore, several private-sector networks such as MCIMAIL, SprintMail and CompuServe had been launched in the preceding years, and many of these provided email connections to the NSFNET. Nevertheless, the traffic supported by the NSFNET should have, in principle, been aligned with the scientific mission of the NSF, which it was not. These developments prompted a conversation about whether private, commercial organizations could provide the maintenance of the NSFNET in exchange for access fees. The NSF sought input from many

---

[5] See Computer History. Internet History of 1980s. Retrieved from www.computerhistory.org/internethistory/1980s/ in August 2022.

And Internet Society. Teus Hagen. Internet Hall of Fame www.internethalloffame.org//inductees/teus-hagen Retrieved in August 2022.

stakeholders such as the IETF and regional network providers[6]. Whereas the commercial entities IBM and MCI (a telecommunication company) had been overseeing the backbone, other companies did not want to leave the bounty to them. Start-up companies UUNET and PSInet, in particular, were influential in reducing IBM's dominance over the privatized backbone. In a few years, the contested transition was complete and the NSFNET was decommissioned in 1995.[7]

3.3   The Internet as an Evolving Technological and Social System

There were originally many competing ideas for the communication network for computers. While nuclear war was one motivating idea behind Baran's memo, remote access to supercomputing facilities was a real driving force of the initial build-out of ARPANET and NSFNET. USENET, in contrast, was not focused on scientific computing but on exchanging messages, many of which were related to computing but, over time, became overtaken by social messaging. An early "killer app" was the electronic mail, or email, which also became primarily a way to stay in touch socially rather than to engage in scientific exchange. Indeed, email was described as the "federally funded post office." Thus, although the initial ideas for an expansive, distributed computing network have persisted, the internet has become much more than that through the extended and still ongoing process of social construction whereby social interactions shape the ideas and opportunities for technological development. Far from being technologically determined, a communication network is a social system where participants both influence technological development and are influenced by technology themselves. Further, commercialization of the internet allowed for business innovation to enter into the network, tapping into emerging social behaviors and building off of the new technological tools and facilities. The internet is a wonderful manifestation of the **coevolution** of technology, social systems, and the economy, and a demonstration of how the original technological options may enable social and economic evolution of applications and subsequent enhancement of the technologies, provided that interfaces and design options are sufficiently open-ended and generative.

The scientific and military origins of the internet and computing more generally emphasized access to large-scale and high-performance computing. Yet, technological innovations to miniaturize the computer led to the localization of computing through the concept of a "personal computer" (PC). In the early 1960s, computing required rooms filled with electrical appliances such as the early

---

[6] Kahin, B. (2013). Commercialization of the internet. IETF Networking Working Group Request for Comments 1192. https://datatracker.ietf.org/doc/rfc1192/ retrieved in August 2022.

[7] National Science Foundation (2008). The day the world changed. NSF New Release 08–112. Retrieved from www.nsf.gov/news/news_summ.jsp?cntn_id=111824 in August 2022.

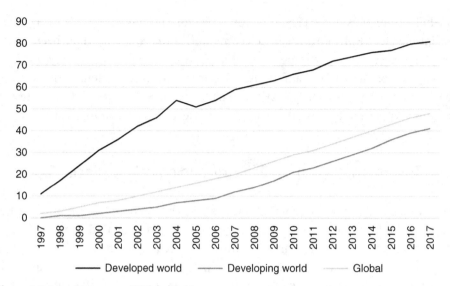

Figure 3.3 Internet users per 100 inhabitants
Note: This figure illustrates the rapid speed of internet adoption in the world starting in the year 1996, and also the significant gap between developed and developing countries.
Data source: International Telecommunications Union. Retrieved from https://github.com/ke4roh/internetHostCount/blob/master/InternetUsersPer100Inhabitants.csv in August, 2022.

Burroughs 205 computer that cost over $1 million and of which only 50 units were built. Just 30 years later, the same amount of computing power (or more) could be found in small grey boxes on millions of home and office desks. However, most of those computers were not connected to the internet. Connectivity to fixed-line IP networks was initially confined to major universities and research institutions, and only over the 1990s did commercial organizations start to adopt internet services. By the late 1990s, home internet connections became feasible through dial-up "modems" (modulator-demodulators) over telephone networks, but they were slow, ranging from 33–56Kbps[8] download speeds and about half that data rate for upload. It made sense to carry out most computing tasks locally.

Although computer processing speeds kept increasing steadily following Moore's Law, the communication bandwidth expanded even more. During the first decade of the 2000s, broadband connections became available to two-thirds of all households in the developed world[9] and many more businesses (see Figure 3.3). This dramatic expansion of connectivity created opportunities for all kinds of business experiments, but also gave a second wind to the idea of remote computing. Once the broadband internet connection is always on and close to 100 percent available, it starts to make more sense to use a "dumb" terminal to access constantly growing

---

[8] WikiPedia. Modem. Retrieved from https://en.wikipedia.org/wiki/Modem in August 2022.
[9] Data from the International Telecommunication Union (ITU, 2015). Retrieved from www.itu.int/ITU-D/ict/statistics/ict/ and http://www.itu.int/en/ITU-D/Statistics/Documents/statistics/2014/ITU_Key_2005-2014_ICT_data.xls in August 2022.

and improving hardware and software resources in the proverbial "cloud." Indeed, from about 2010, the key resource being retrieved from the cloud was data. With **cloud computing**, the idea of the internet had come a full circle.

As internet adoption expanded connectivity, cloud computing became the rebranded term for the original idea of remote computing. The proverbial "cloud" was understood as the nondescript location for the remote computing and storage resource. These ideas were prevalent from the 1960s onward, and in the mid-1980s Sun Computer adopted the slogan "The Network Is The Computer."[10] The first illustration of the "cloud" has been traced back to the Compaq computer company's strategic plan from 1996.[11]

Compaq was among the early entrants into the emerging cloud computing market segment. It envisioned its current customers would purchase computing resources via NSPs, that is, Network Service Providers such as Internet Service Providers (ISPs) and telecommunications companies such as Regional Bell Operating Companies (RBOCs, also called "Baby Bells") which were the regional telecom service providers following the antitrust-related break-up of AT&T, at

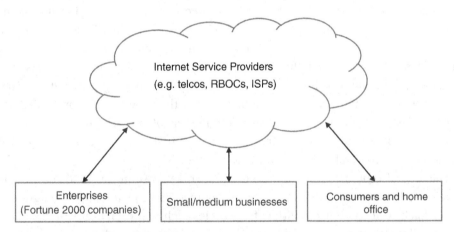

Figure 3.4 1996 Compaq Internet Solutions Division strategy memo
Note: In this memo, Compaq stated that "Internet cloud will have substantial impact on Compaq customers." This strategic plan is among the first to describe how local computing would become cloud computing as internet services became more prevalent and powerful. It was notable because in 1996, internet connectivity was low (see Figure 3.3) and broadband access was rare.
Original source: Compaq, 1996. Adapted based on https://s3.amazonaws.com/files.technologyreview .com/p/pub/legacy/compaq_cst_1996_0.pdf in August, 2021.

---

[10] Perry, T. S. (2019). Does the repurposing of Sun Microsystems' slogan honor history, or step on it? IEEE Spectrum, July 30, 2019. Retrieved from https://spectrum.ieee.org/does-repurposing-of-sun-microsystems-slogan-honor-history in August 2022.

[11] Regalado, A. (2011). Who coined "cloud computing"? MIT Technology Review, October 31, 2011. Retrieved from www.technologyreview.com/s/425970/who-coined-cloud-computing/ in August 2022.
     Compaq Computer Corporation (1996). Internet Solutions Division strategy for cloud computing. CST presentation, November 14, 1996. Retrieved from https://s3.amazonaws.com/ files.technologyreview.com/p/pub/legacy/compaq_cst_1996_0.pdf in August 2022.

the time nicknamed "Ma Bell." Compaq's Internet Services Division realized that a large share of computing resources might move to the cloud, in which case the company would try to sell hardware and software solutions to those NSPs, which it assumed would become cloud computing service providers (see Figure 3.4).

3.4   Innovating a Mobile Internet: The Emergence of 5G

The next step in the evolution of the global network was the emergence of mobile broadband. The idea had been proposed years earlier, and during the 1990s, mobile voice communication, text messages, and mobile hotspotting were becoming immensely popular. Smartphones were adopted, starting in 2000 with the launch of the first BlackBerry that became an instant hit, and mobile internet telecommunication services overtook the personal computer-based internet communications within a decade. In 2010, with the launch of 4G wireless, the internet had become truly mobile.

While in hindsight wireless telecommunications seem to have evolved gradually, each new generation was a noticeable step in terms of enabling new communication activities and applications. AT&T launched the first Mobile Telephone Service in 1946. It evolved from radio telephony, which was originally invented in the early 1900s. Early radio telephones were clunky and heavy devices that included a larger transceiver device connected with a dialing pad and handset. They were often mounted in vehicles because of the weight, therefore called car phones. Early radiophones, sometimes described as 0G phones for "zero generation," were extremely important for seafarers and first responders but rarely used by ordinary individuals because of their cost and size.

The idea of cellular telecommunication networks arose in the 1970s to provide wireless telecommunication coverage for more users and for larger geographic areas. Each "cell" provided multiple frequencies such that each user would be able to find a free frequency from one of the nearby base stations. Motorola's prototype phone that made the first cellular call in 1973 weighed 2.4 lbs (1.1 kg). These wireless telephones were analog devices, meaning they did not convert the radio signal into digital bits. The first commercial cellular network, 1G or first-generation wireless, was launched in Japan by Nippon Telegraph and Telephone (NTT) in 1979.

Multiple generations of mobile telecommunication systems have since been launched, with a new and substantially better system every 10 years or so. The first mobile telephony system was 1G; 2G was the first digital communication system; 3G launched the mobile internet; 4G offered mobile broadband that enabled video streaming and made mobile devices into entertainment centers; and 5G facilitated the creation of large-scale data networks (i.e., the **Internet of Things** and other smart networks.[12]) The generations were defined in terms

---

[12] Mitra R.N. and Agrawal, D.P. (2015). 5G mobile technology: A survey. *ICT Express* 1(3): 132–137.

of their speed of transmission. To be called **5G wireless** the network's download speed experienced by the user had to be greater than 100 Mbps (megabits per second). Different versions of 4G achieved up to 100 Mbps download speed (but the typical 4G/LTE network download speeds varied by around 30 Mbps), and 3G reached 8Mbps, although the early 3G speeds were much lower.[13] 5G targeted speeds of 100–300 Mbps, so up to an order of magnitude faster mobile download speeds compared with 4G.

The spectrum of radio wave frequencies is a limited natural resource. Because radio waves propagate irrespective of regional or organizational borders, the use of a portion of the spectrum in one geographic area may affect the ability to use the same portion in other areas and cause harmful interference, as was discovered when the *Titanic* sank. Spectrum therefore needs to be managed at national and international levels. ITU Radio Regulations is an international treaty ratified and applied by all ITU Member States. It has been in force since 1906 and is updated every four years by the ITU World Radiocommunication Conferences. Every satellite, aircraft or ship, television or radio station, mobile device, and defense, air traffic or maritime radar uses a specific frequency band as prescribed by the Radio Regulations. The global allocation of frequency bands by ITU allows all radio-communication services to co-exist without interference. It gives stakeholders, including those involved in 5G development, the certainty that these bands will be available for use and protected in all countries in the foreseeable future. In other words, it provides certainty for long-term investments, which is the basis for the sustainable development of the ecosystem.

Each new generation of wireless communication entailed billions of dollars of investment, first, into the development of the improved technologies and, then, their implementation in telecom networks. For example, the air interface for 5G called New Radio provided a level of spectral efficiency in terms of bits per second per Hertz that will be at least double compared to that of 4G. In other words, each transmitted radio wave would transfer significantly more data. Telecom service providers needed to make massive investments to expand spectrum resources so that more data can be transferred. They also needed to improve the antennae in the base stations in order to accommodate many more devices per square mile, and upgrade software and computational capacity in the network controllers in order to enhance reliability and to reduce latency. The roll-out of consumer 5G networks to upgrade 4G LTE networks in urban and suburban areas up to a speed of 100 Mbps from an existing 20–30 Mbps entailed an estimated cost of 72–85 euros ($85–100) per user.[14] This was a very feasible capital expenditure for telecom

---

[13] See, for example, Ken's Tech Tips (2018). Download speeds: What do 2G, 3G, 4G, and 5G actually mean? Ken's Tech Tips, November 23, 2018. Retrieved from https://kenstechtips.com/index.php/download-speeds-2g-3g-and-4g-actual-meaning Retrieved in August 2022.

[14] Oughton E.J., Frias, Z., van der Gaast, S., and van den Berg, R. (2019). Assessing the capacity, coverage and cost of 5G infrastructure strategies: analysis of the Netherlands. *Telematics and Informatics* 37: 50–69.

operators. In contrast, in rural areas, similar speeds could cost up to 700 euros per user, making the investment difficult to justify given monthly subscription prices. Overall, the cost of the last third of the population in terms of population density within zip code areas was estimated to be twice the amount of the first two-thirds. Because of this extremely high cost of development and investment, communication networks tended to persist for several years, and sometimes decades in order for telecom operators to be able to generate a return on investment.

Each generation of wireless telecommunication systems took about 10 years to develop and lasted for about 10 years in use, although different regions adopted new systems at different times and rates. Since 3G, global technology firms and telecom service providers have engaged in extensive coordination to build global standards that allow all devices from different firms to work with all networks by different operators in the world. For 3G this didn't quite work out – there were initially multiple standards – but for 4G practically all major markets were a part of the same wireless network. This was also the goal for 5G and a huge global effort was made to achieve convergence through standard-development activities coordinated by the International Telecommunications Union and the international standardization alliance 3GPP. The development of the 5G standard started officially in 2012, and the first version of the global standard named IMT-2020 was completed in early 2021 at the ITU. Thus the development took at least eight years, and the network will continue to evolve and improve, with updates and new features to be developed for several years.

However, 5G is not just a faster network, it will have additional features that pave the way for the Internet of Things, or IoT. The IoT is a new type of a communication network that is not just about communication among people but also among autonomous devices. 5G will connect people, objects, data, applications, transport systems, and cities in "smart" networked communication environments.[15] In 2020, 50 billion devices were estimated to be connected to the global IP network.[16] Humans could interact with various kinds of automated systems, or even have machines communicate directly with one another to achieve production, transportation, decisions, or trade. The 5G system was designed to support applications such as smart homes and buildings, smart cities, 3D video, work and play in the cloud, remote medical surgery, virtual and augmented reality, and massive machine-to-machine communications for industry automation and self-driving vehicles. This required extremely fast and responsive communication networks enabling data-intensive activities that depend on a quick response time from system participants such as vehicle-to-vehicle communication of autonomous cars. The 5G network intended to deliver much more speed and data-transfer capacity relative to 4G to support such massive machine-to-machine communications with

---

[15] See ITU (2020). ITU's approach to 5G. ITU News, October 15, 2018. Retrieved from https://news.itu.int/5g-fifth-generation-mobile-technologies/ in August 2022.

[16] Mitra and Agrawal, n. 16.

highly reliable services for time-critical applications. With such ambitious goals, 5G networks faced considerable operational challenges such as meeting high levels of stability, security, and reliability.

Higher speed and lower latency are features of 5G that enable new kinds of applications. Furthermore, the growth of 5G coincides with a few other, closely related and complementary digital innovations such as cloud and distributed computing; big data and analytics; machine learning; and the Internet of Things. With the help of these communication and computing technologies, it became possible to create high-fidelity and real-time digital representations of the physical world. Whether it be augmented-reality entertainment, big data-enabled machine learning and decision making, autonomous transportation, or remote diagnostics of production machinery or even home appliances, all recent ground-breaking digital innovation ideas depended on wireless communication systems to deliver the envisioned applications.

3.5   Innovating Communication Services: The Web

Both the fixed and mobile versions of the internet crucially depended on the invention of the World Wide Web (WWW) as a software system to connect and structure content and devices. As the World Wide Web evolved from a tedious, text-based information repository to a massive, indexed, and searchable set of constantly evolving and connected information, our engagement with the information and its providers expanded and deepened.

Whereas early technologies such as Gopher, Telnet, and FTP allowed users to connect to remote computers and retrieve files, the user needed to know exactly what files they required and where to look for them. Only after the World Wide Web connected the files themselves could search engines such as Archie, Excite, and Lycos begin to catalog the webpages in a systematic way to provide easier access to information the user needed. Initially searching across WWW documents was not very systematic. For instance, Yahoo started as a list of the founders Jerry Yang and David Filo's favorite web pages, or "Jerry and David's Guide to the World Wide Web" in 1994.[17]

Google was not the first search engine but arguably had the best technology. The Page Rank algorithm probably provided an order of magnitude improvement in the match between user needs and webpage suggestions. Google's algorithm continues to be a trade secret, but we know that it continuously crawls and indexes webpages, and then creates a ranking of the pages based on the number and quality of links to a specific page.

The WWW, file transfer protocols, and search were early and essential enabling technologies to make increasingly connected information efficiently accessible to

---

[17] See Pickert, K. (2008). Yahoo! CEO Jerry Yang. *Time*, November 19, 2008. http://content.time .com/time/business/article/0,8599,1860424,00.html. Retrieved in August 2022.

a growing number of users. However, most users were still connecting to simple webpages using slow modems over telephone networks. An expansion of broadband networks was a necessary condition for the next stage of internet-based content, the so-called Web 2.0, or the Age of Mass Collaboration.

Once networks based on the open standard Internet Protocol had substantial capacity and were widely available, the new way of connecting with strangers online could begin. The open-source software movement was the harbinger of social and distributed creativity on the web. This mode of distributed software development started in the late 1980s and 1990s, often through USENET newsgroups which at the time were the easiest way to catch the attention of a large number of people with shared interests. Linus Torvalds posted the first, rather modest, message about Linux in a newsgroup called "comp.os.minix" in 1991:

> Hello everybody out there using minix –
>
> I'm doing a (free) operating system (just a hobby, won't be big and professional like gnu) for 386(486) AT clones. This has been brewing since april, and is starting to get ready. I'd like any feedback on things people like/dislike in minix, as my OS resembles it somewhat (same physical layout of the file-system (due to practical reasons) among other things).
>
> I've currently ported bash(1.08) and gcc(1.40), and things seem to work. This implies that I'll get something practical within a few months, and I'd like to know what features most people would want. Any suggestions are welcome, but I won't promise I'll implement them :-)
>
> Linus (torvalds@kruuna.helsinki.fi)
>
> PS. Yes – it's free of any minix code, and it has a multi-threaded fs. It is NOT portable (uses 386 task switching etc), and it probably never will support anything other than AT-harddisks, as that's all I have :-(. (Linus Torvalds)

The Apache OSS project for server operating systems was also launched in the early 1990s, and the Mozilla project in 1998 when the source code of the early Netscape browser was released into the public domain. On the heels of the open-source movement came the peer-to-peer file-sharing services of Napster, Gnutella, and Kazaa. Furthermore, Wikipedia was launched in 2001, and early social networks such as Friendster in 2002. With expanding broadband availability and enhanced search capabilities, connecting to such collaborative projects became easy and compelling.

The collaborative web made it clear that anyone can easily be both a consumer and producer of information goods online. By the late 1990s, the ethos of the web had shifted to that of "Remix" – a culture where it is acceptable to adopt, absorb, edit, recycle, recombine, and recirculate anything and everything digital, spawning the Napster generation of prosumers (producer-consumers).[18] This led

---

[18] Lessig, L. (2008). *Remix: Making Art and Commerce Thrive in the Hybrid Economy*. New York: Penguin Books.

to massive legal debacles and tensions between generations of information consumers. Who owns or has rights to shared or remixed content, and what are the boundaries of fair use?

From the perspective of network traffic, the launch of collaborative and creative video sharing on YouTube in 2005 was a watershed moment. In contrast to text, music, or software files shared in earlier services, YouTube was about video content that involved an order of magnitude increase in file sizes. One hour of high-quality audio creates a file size of over 100 megabits, whereas one hour of high-definition video takes a file size of three gigabits. When converted to text pages, 3 gigabits corresponds to 200 thousand pages![19]

While YouTube was an instant hit among users, it led to legal, strategic, and, eventually, political complications. Legally, video file sharing created similar intellectual property conflicts as music file sharing through Napster. However, with the Napster precedent (it was shut down because of detrimental court decisions in 2001 and later relaunched with a completely different business model), YouTube was more attentive to Digital Millennium Copyright Act (DMCA) complaints about infringing content and dealt more effectively with such challenges. Strategically, however, YouTube was an unwieldy business proposition. Video files take up an enormous amount of costly storage, and the path to monetization of the service was not obvious. In 2017, the profitability of YouTube's advertising model remained uncertain, but it certainly benefited from Google's dominance in online advertising.[20] Also, the cost of storage was trending down, and YouTube had created subscription plans to compete in the commercial video streaming market with Netflix, Amazon, and newer entrants such as Disney+. In 2019, Google's parent company Alphabet revealed that YouTube generated $15 billion in revenue, and while profits were not disclosed, analysts estimated that the unit was finally profitable.[21]

With YouTube pioneering video sharing and Netflix launching video streaming and ultimately replacing its original business model of DVD rentals, video content soon took up the majority of traffic on the internet. In 2018, YouTube and Netflix together sent over half of all bits traveling around the US internet. This started to attract both network owners' and policy makers' attention, leading to a divisive policy debate concerning net neutrality. How to mitigate network congestion while keeping the internet open, innovative, and competitive? As of 2022, this debate raged on.

---

[19] KLDiscovery company website. Retrieved from www.sdsdiscovery.com/resources/data-conversions/ and Hildenbrand, J. (2020). How much mobile data does streaming media use? Android Central, August 10, 2020. Retrieved from www.androidcentral.com/how-much-data-does-streaming-media-use in August 2022.

[20] Yu, B. (2017). Medium Sep 6, 2017. Retrieved from https://medium.com/@intenex/where-are-you-getting-hard-data-that-youtube-isnt-profitable-a00aed0672ac in August 2022.

[21] Statt, N. (2020). YouTube is a $15 billion-a-year business, Google reveals for the first time. The Verge, February 3, 2020. Retrieved from www.theverge.com/2020/2/3/21121207/youtube-google-alphabet-earnings-revenue-first-time-reveal-q4-2019 in August 2022.

At the same time, collaborative technologies and online communities grew in political influence around the world. Wider availability of information about government agencies and their policies made political decision making more transparent. Even drafts of new legislation that were difficult to access in the "analog" era became immediately available online for much broader assessment and discussion. A whole new class of political commentators sprang from the "blogosphere"; individuals who became mass distributors of opinions and commentary on all matters social, cultural, and political. The notion of a "blog" derived from "web log" that was essentially a log of activity or thought by an individual. Companies such as WordPress made it easy for anyone to become an online publisher and a "blogger." People even started to create their own "TV" shows under the heading of v-logs, or video logs. Anyone could become a "somebody" on the web, or as the famous New Yorker cartoon put it, "on the web, no-one knows if you're a dog."

Networks of political observers also set up services that enabled political or corporate whistle-blowing. The most famous of these was of course WikiLeaks, founded in 2006 by Julian Assange. The original goal of WikiLeaks was to "publish material of ethical, political, and historical significance while keeping the identity of our sources anonymous, thus providing a universal way for the revealing of suppressed and censored injustices."[22] Against this noble goal, some of the choices made by WikiLeaks of revealing identities of intelligence officers or confidential communications of national security employees were highly controversial. So were their decisions to publish Edward Snowden's materials obtained illegally from the US National Security Agency as an external contractor. Despite the criticism and the continued exile of Mr. Snowden, these publications revealed the extent of domestic surveillance by the US government through programs such as the Prism that had been poorly vetted by the legislature and thus were borderline illegal themselves. The ramifications of the Snowden case triggered major changes in the legal approval process for domestic surveillance in the United States.

Outside of the United States, the Arab Spring movements in several African and Middle Eastern countries were organized using social networking services. Many of these digital revolutions succeeded in overturning existing authoritarian governments and thus had a major impact on global politics. The Arab Spring also initiated the unrest in Syria, but there it was met with exceptional willingness on the part of the existing regime to kill its own citizens. Arguably, this was the starting point of the devastating war in Syria that led to millions being killed or displaced, and a massive influx of migrants and refugees in Europe, fomenting the rise of nationalist right-wing politicians in many European countries. All unintended consequences of Twitter and Facebook!

The degree to which the rise of white nationalism and right-wing populism in the US and Europe can be traced to online communication, social networks, and the backlash against the tsunami of migrants is for political scientists to analyze.

---

[22] Dumas M.B. (2012). *Diving Into the Bitstream: Information Technology Meets Society in a Digital World*. New York: Routledge.

To a casual observer it seemed that the traditional institutions of Western democracies were struggling to adjust and accommodate the much more volatile social forces brewing in online communities. When everyone was capable of putting out authoritative-sounding commentary, large swaths of the population seemed to have lost sense of what information was reliable and trustworthy and what was sheer propaganda. Clickbait eroded the credibility of traditional media, and millions believed conspiracy theories such as those propagated by QAnon.[23] As noted by Marshall McLuhan in 1960, "World War III will be a guerrilla information war." Few statements can turn out to so accurately predict events 50 years into the future. The political events described above have demonstrated, yet again, to those wishing to get access to power that controlling social and communication networks is critical for instigating and influencing major political events. Slowing down communication networks can enhance election success of the ruling party's preferred candidates,[24] political opinions can effectively be planted and spread in social groups through Facebook communities (cf. Cambridge Analytica), and it had become a lucrative business to provide data, analytics, and access for powermongers of various sorts. Regulating and monitoring such activities was proving to be extremely difficult.

3.6 Summary: A Framework for Innovating the Digital Society

This chapter has reviewed the history of innovating the internet, from ARPANET to the World Wide Web and 5G wireless. It is clear that this 50-year stream of innovation has fundamentally changed the world. Not always for the better, but always irreversibly: whenever information has been revealed, it can never be un-revealed. The only thing that seems certain is that economic and societal upheaval will continue. It is also notable that these transformational innovations were created through the constant interaction and cross-fertilization between governmental agencies, universities, and other research institutions including scientific funding agencies, business organizations, and individual citizens, inventors, and consumers. Government policies and nonprofit scientific discovery were particularly crucial in the early stages of computing and the internet. Communication policies continue to shape the markets and the innovation system to this day. The 5G network was less a product of government investment, but it was created through a global system of coordination among governments, technology companies, and scientific institutions. System-level technological revolutions tend to require broad collective action, and when entry into and exit from these processes of innovation are open and easy, significant innovations are more likely to emerge.

---

[23] See Roose, K. (2021). What is QAnon, the viral, pro-Trump conspiracy theory? *The New York Times*, September 3, 2021. Retrieved from www.nytimes.com/article/what-is-qanon.html in August 2022.

[24] Ackerman, Klaus (2017). Limiting the market for information as a tool of governance: evidence from Russia. Paper presented at the NBER Summer Institute. Retrieved from http://conference.nber.org/confer/2017/SI2017/PRIT/Ackermann.pdf in August, 2022.

Let's revisit and explore the design principles for digital innovation that this recent history of digital innovation underlines. First, design for the future: rapid evolution means today's innovations are outdated tomorrow. From the original ideas of the internet through the evolution of the interactive Web 2.0 to the mobile internet of today, it is clear that at the time of innovation and investment, innovators usually have a very limited understanding of the needs and applications emerging just a few years later. Creators of ARPANET did not envision the popularity of USENET newsgroups. The concept of email quickly changed from scientific exchange to social discussion. Open-Source Software emerged as academic computer scientists' pastime and ended up toppling large software companies. At the same time, designing new communication networks often takes several years. Therefore, 5G innovators would be wise to anticipate that their current service concepts will quickly be outdated and seek to incorporate emerging needs and interests from underserved and new user groups in their designs. While future user needs will be difficult to predict, the trends in the cost and capacity of the underlying data networks are much more predictable and can be built into new product designs. A digital innovator needs a technological roadmap that facilitates prediction of the trajectory of innovations and improvements.

Second, design for change: future-proofing your innovation means flexibility and adaptation. With quick anticipated obsolescence, new products and systems should be designed as open-ended such that user feedback and innovations can easily and quickly be incorporated into product upgrades. While we reviewed the history of successful innovation here, there is an even deeper history of failed innovations. One of the epic fails was WAP, an attempt by telecom operators in the early days of the mobile internet to create "walled garden" types of wireless services instead of providing unobstructed access to the open internet. While the WAP protocol itself was not closed, operators used it to create closed "portals" that primarily pointed to their own curated content and required that any content accessed beyond that was provided in Wireless Markup Language, WML, instead of the usual HTML of the open internet. Few websites chose to present their content in WML and hence the services available via WAP portals were very limited. The closed nature of the WAP and WML-based service models precluded user feedback and limited access to innovative ideas, and as a consequence, this system failed to evolve with user needs.

Third, design for generativity: diverse communities each create their own interpretations of the innovation and use it in unpredictable, and often creative, ways. Diversity of user groups turns out to be an advantage for innovators. While it is initially more costly to accommodate a wide variety of user needs, a rich set of user groups actually provides the innovator with access to simultaneous experimentation and user innovation. Thus, a smart innovator seeks to expose their innovation to many different types of users and groups to accelerate and enrich their feedback. If they initially focus on a homogenous set of users, the innovation may fail to scale to the general population. Furthermore, the network needs to have open and standardized access points that allow diverse user groups to append the network with their own innovations. The rapid adoption of the Android mobile operating system depended on the massive proliferation of mobile applications that required only about $100 and fairly basic skills in software development to launch. The technical and economic bar to express creative ideas in this system was extremely low.

KEY IDEAS

- The original ideas behind new communication services tend to become quickly outdated and replaced by new concepts that emerge as large numbers of people and diverse social groups use the service.
- Designing, building, and establishing a new communication network typically takes several years.
- Each generation of the internet, from ARPANET to 5G, has launched transformative societal change.
- During the decade of the 2020s, fundamental innovations continue in both physical and software-based communication networks.
- Successful innovators in this extremely dynamic environment focus on long-term technological and economic changes, emphasize design flexibility and openness, and engage diverse users in many different contexts.

DEFINITIONS

5G wireless telecommunication networks must have download data rates above 100 megabits per second; ability to handle the volume of at least 1 terabits per second per square kilometer; traffic capacity of 10 megabits per second per square meter in hotspots; latency below 1 millisecond in data exchange; and mobility up to 500 km per hour in high-speed trains and 1000 km per hour in airplanes.

Centralized networks have one central node that controls the flow of information around the network.

Cloud computing involves accessing remote computing resources such as data and applications via the internet.

Coevolution in biology refers to reciprocal adaptation of interacting species. In the economy, coevolutionary processes refer to the series of events where one event or action causes others which in turn cause other actions and reactions. While there are causal sequences, it is difficult to identify the original event that set the dynamic process in motion.

Decentralized networks have many nodes that have some amount of control of the network traffic.

Distributed networks have all nodes capable of controlling traffic, and all nodes dependent on others for resources.

Internet of Things (IoT) is the communication network of devices such as tiny embedded sensors, autonomous machinery, or home appliances.

Packet switching was the radical innovation related to the distribution of information around the internet. Packet switching divided information into small standardized packets the transfer of which could be individually optimized and subsequently reassembled to form the original information content.

DISCUSSION QUESTIONS

1. Identify one successful communication network (e.g., email) and one communication network that ultimately failed (e.g., first social networks like Friendster, MySpace, or the later entrant Google+). Using the design framework, investigate and compare how the successful network differed from the unsuccessful one with respect to future-orientation, openness, and diversity of user groups.
2. How would you take into account that 5G enables significantly faster wireless uploads and downloads of data and content when designing a new communication network or service?
3. If 5G was launched in 2020, when would you start planning for 6G?
4. When do you think governments should participate in the innovation of new communication networks?

FURTHER READING

Abbate, Janet (2000). *Inventing the Internet*. Cambridge, MA: The MIT Press.

Greenstein, Shane (2015). *How the Internet Became Commercial: Innovation, Privatization, and the Birth of a New Network*. Princeton, NJ: Princeton University Press.

Tufekci, Zeynep (2017). *Twitter and Teargas: The Power and Fragility of Networked Protest*. New Haven, CT: Yale University Press.

CASE 1: BARNES & NOBLE AND THE E-BOOK REVOLUTION

The book market was among the first to be digitally disrupted. Jeff Bezos founded Amazon in 1994 on the assumption that books are easy, although not cheap, to sell and ship over the internet. In the mid-1990s, lots of new types of "dot-com" businesses were founded to sell regular items over the internet. Garden.com, Stamps.com, and Pets.com were early experiments in figuring out online business models for physical products. They all failed though. During that "new economy" boom, founders had ample funding and made many mistakes that now seem elementary: selling for prices well below variable cost, spending too much on advertising and office perks, and attempting to scale without solving the operational challenges of shipping heavy items (pet food?) to individual buyers. Amazon struggled with many of the same challenges, and it took the company nine years to make its first annual profit in 2003[25].

Barnes & Noble was a traditional bookseller, originally founded in 1886 as Arthur Hinds & Company in New York City; it then changed name to Hinds & Noble and ultimately to Barnes & Noble in 1917 thanks to the evolution of the business

---

[25] Perez, J.C. (2004). Amazon records first profitable year in its history. InfoWorld. January 28, 2004. Retrieved from www.infoworld.com/article/2668062/amazon-records-first-profitable-year-in-its-history.html in August 2022.

partnerships of the founders. By 1990, Barnes & Noble had become the largest national chain of bookstores in the United States, and the company was listed in the New York Stock Exchange in 1993. Barnes & Noble prided itself as having "revolutionized bookselling by making our stores public spaces and community institutions (...) where every kind of customer, young and old, may browse, find a book, relax over a cup of coffee, talk with authors, and join discussion groups."

Barnes & Noble was a long-standing and well-managed company that entered early into e-commerce and e-books. Nevertheless it struggled to maintain its dominant status in the book market.

Case 1.1 Entry into E-Commerce

In 1997, Barnes & Noble launched its first website and, with it, an online bookstore. barnesandnoble.com was organized as an individual subsidiary, with its own leadership and independent decision making. In 1998, a 50 percent ownership share of barnesandnoble.com was sold to Bertelsmann, a major German media and publishing house that controlled the Big Six book publisher Random House. Nevertheless, Barns & Noble considered the online bookstore a key part of its growth strategy:

> The Bertelsmann investment in barnesandnoble.com, together with the expected completion of an initial public offering (IPO) for this company, has placed us in an extremely enviable position, especially given the increasingly competitive nature of the bookselling industry. Very simply, we now have two well-capitalized vehicles that can be used to explore new opportunities, in retail and in e-commerce. (Annual Report 1998, p. 17)

Indeed, in just two years, the online store had become a top internet destination, and the fourth most-visited e-commerce site. It had the largest in-stock inventory of any online bookseller, with 750 000 titles. In 1998 the online sales grew almost 400 percent and the company improved many of the website features such as software sales, one-click ordering, a new search engine and overall design, and also enhanced the inventories of discount books, rare books, and out-of-print books. Under development were music, movie, and business-to-business content offerings. The company's slogan articulated the ethos: "If we don't have your book, nobody does." In early 1999, barnesandnoble.com prepared for a listing in the NASDAQ market under the ticker "BNBN." Barnes & Noble had successfully entered the world of online commerce.

After recovering from the financial crash of 2000, the online sales of Barnes & Noble were growing again and the segment was projected to make a profit in 2004. While its ranking as an internet destination was slipping with increased entry and competition in online retail, co-marketing arrangements with America Online, Google, and Microsoft Network and affiliate agreements with 189,000 other websites were going to enhance its appeal and renown. In 2004 the mothership re-acquired a controlling ownership stake in barnesandnoble.com. The online store had been publicly listed in 1999 but the original owners had retained 40 percent of the ownership shares each. Now Barnes & Noble acquired the shares of Bertelsmann to have a 75 percent controlling stake after some stock arrangements with employees. Later in the year, barnesandnoble.com was delisted and fully merged with an existing, wholly-owned subsidiary of Barnes & Noble. E-commerce had now become a central element in the long-term strategy of the corporation.

Having become a major competitor in online book selling, Barnes & Noble made a big splash in 2009 when it first introduced the e-bookstore and the Nook, "the most full-featured e-book reader in the market" for $259 and started selling e-books via barnesandnoble.com, now called BN.com. The e-bookstore made over 1 million titles available for the Nook device but also for tablets, smartphones, and PCs. The original Nook featured e-ink's electronic paper screen, 3G and WiFi connectivity, and was built on the Android open-source operating system. The company also made the e-reader software application available for Windows computers and Android devices. However, in the 2010 Annual Report the company announced decreasing sales due to the economic downturn, increased competition, and the expanding digital market for e-books, e-book readers, and digital distribution of content at the expense of paper books. Nevertheless, the company believed its footprint of more than 1,300 stores to be a major competitive asset. It planned to integrate the retail space with the digital offerings by using retail stores to promote and sell digital devices and content.

Nook was a feature-full device but it was launched almost two years after Amazon's Kindle. Kindle initially sold for $399 and also featured an e-ink display. It offered a wireless connection via Sprint's Whispernet network and immediate access to 90,000 titles.[26] Subsequent WiFi-connected versions were cheaper and did not require a telecom service contract, and eventually the device included a touch screen with a software-based keypad. Nevertheless, Nook competed favorably against Kindle in terms of device design and title availability.

However, the reading market was changing. There were widespread concerns that people, and particularly the younger age groups, were reading less. Book sales were stable since 2008 (see Figure C1.1), despite rapid growth in the e-reading market.

The market also saw a few new trends emerge. First, digital audiobooks had been introduced in the late 1990s (audiobooks themselves had been published since the 1930s on vinyl records), but were becoming more popular in the late 2000s. Audible was founded in 1995 to commercialize a portable media player but it soon pivoted toward audiobooks. In 2003 it became the exclusive audiobook provider for Apple's iTunes store, and in 2008 Amazon announced

---

[26] Hall, C. (2020). Amazon Kindle: A brief history from the original Kindle onward. Pocket Lint, October 20, 2020. Retrieved from www.pocket-lint.com/gadgets/news/amazon/137303-amazon-kindle-history-kindle-to-the-kindle-oasis in August 2022.

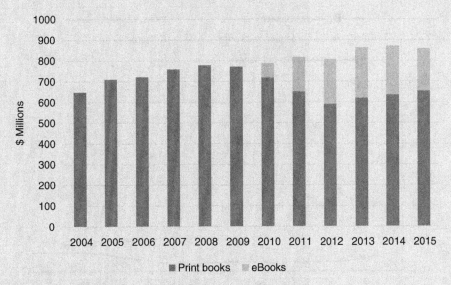

Figure C1.1 US book unit sales 2004–2015
Note: Total sales of books in the US grew slowly, but the volume and share of print books decreased.
E-books grew rapidly from 2010 to 2013 but declined after 2013.
Data source: Nielsen Bookscan and PubTrack Digital. Retrieved from www.nielsen.com/us/en/insights/
report/2016/2015-us-book-industry-year-end-review/# in August 2021.

it was acquiring Audible. It became the dominant creator and distributor of audiobooks in the US by 2013.[27] In 2018, the Audiobook Publishers Association reported nearly $1 billion of sales and a 25 percent growth rate.[28] Barnes & Noble jumped on the audio bandwagon in 2014 by releasing the Nook audiobook app on app stores.[29]

Second, the publishing industry was experiencing new forms of competition. While the total industry revenue had been flat since 2008,[30] the "Big Six" publishers (Random House, Penguin, HarperCollins, Simon & Schuster, Hachette, and Macmillan) were increasingly challenged by independent publishers and even self-publishing by authors. In fact, digital selling platforms such as Amazon and Barnes & Noble enabled and encouraged self-publishing.[31,32] Particularly

[27] Alter, A. (2013). The new explosion in audio books. *Wall Street Journal*, August 1, 2013. Retrieved from www.wsj.com/articles/the-new-explosion-in-audio-books-1375980039?tesla=y in August 2022.

[28] Audio Publishers Association (2019). U.S. publishers report nearly $1 billion in sales as strong industry growth continues. APA News Release, July 17, 2019.

[29] Kozlowski, M. (2014). Barnes and Noble puts a priority on audiobooks. GoodEReader, November 19, 2014. Retrieved from https://goodereader.com/blog/audiobooks/barnes-and-noble-puts-a-priority-on-audiobooks in August 2022.

[30] Statista (2022). Net revenue of the book publishing industry in the United States from 2008 to 2020. Retrieved from www.statista.com/statistics/271931/revenue-of-the-us-book-publishing-industry/ in August 2022.

[31] Barns & Noble Press. Self-publish your book with Barnes & Noble Press. Retrieved from https://press.barnesandnoble.com/ in August 2022.

[32] Semuels, A. (2018). The authors who love Amazon. *The Atlantic*, July 20, 2018. Retrieved from www.theatlantic.com/technology/archive/2018/07/amazon-kindle-unlimited-self-publishing/565664/ in August 2022.

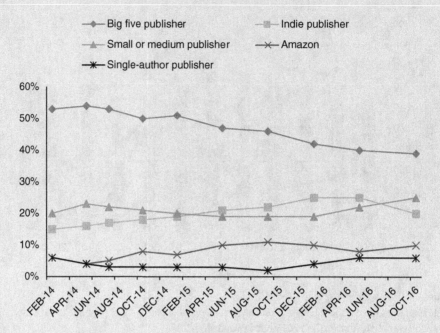

Figure C1.2 Market share of e-book publisher types by gross sales
Note: The market share of the "Big Five" publishers (at the time of the case, the Big Five included Penguin Random House, Hachette, Simon & Schuster, Harper Collins, and Macmillan) was declining in e-book sales, whereas Amazon and independent publishers were growing. Small and medium-sized publishers and single-author publishers were relatively stable between 2014 and 2016.
Source: American Association of Publishers, reprinted at https://publishingperspectives.com/2015/11/innovation-is-the-only-way-to-increase-ebook-sales/ Retrieved in August 2021.

in e-books, the revenue share of major publishers was declining and those of independent publishers, Amazon, and single-author publishers were increasing (see Figure C1.2). The growth of indie publishing was even more conspicuous in terms of unit sales, showing that the average prices of e-books published by independents was significantly lower.

In self-publishing, entry had been particularly rapid: 300,000 books were published in the US in 2009, and over a million books in 2017. More than two-thirds of the books of 2017 were self-published. Three-quarters of self-publishing authors in 2018 used Amazon's platforms Kindle Direct, Create Space, and KDX.[33] With so much entry into book authoring and price pressure in bookselling, median incomes of authors had declined by 21 percent between 2013 and 2017, and by over 30 percent for authors using traditional commercial publishers. Only self-publishing incomes had increased, but those still did not rise to the level of commercial publishing incomes.[34]

[33] The Authors Guild (2019). Six takeaways from the Authors Guild 2018 author income survey. The Authors Guild, January 5, 2019. Retrieved from www.authorsguild.org/industry-advocacy/six-takeaways-from-the-authors-guild-2018-authors-income-survey/ in August 2022.
[34] The Authors Guild (2019). U.S. published book author income survey. Retrieved from https://authorsguild.org/news/six-takeaways-from-the-authors-guild-2018-authors-income-survey/ in August 2022.

Case 1.2 The Book Ecosystem

The book industry ecosystem included a variety of parties that were differently affected by the transition to digital markets and e-books. While authors and editors were still critical suppliers of e-books, the content did not need to be printed on paper or shipped around in physical products. Downstream, bookstores were still essential, too, and the reading devices represented a new part of the ecosystem (see Figure C1.3). Firms entering the e-book market deployed various strategies to provide an e-reader.

One of the earliest entrants into the e-reader device segment was Rocketbook in 1997. The start-up behind it had even pitched the device prototype to Amazon's founder Jeff Bezos, but Bezos didn't think it would succeed because it would need to be plugged into a personal computer for downloads. However, Barnes & Noble invested in a 50 percent stake in the company and participated in the trial marketing. It turned out Bezos was right and only 20,000 units were sold before the company was acquired by Gemstar in 2000[35] and soon the operations were shut down.

Early e-books were offered for reading on computers or PDA devices, or personal digital assistants that were about the size of a smartphone and typically held a calendar and a note-taking application. However, reading was not a pleasant experience because the light-emitting, low-resolution computer screens were straining for the eyes. The reading experience was truly revolutionized by Sony with its electronic paper technology jointly developed with Philips and e-ink. Sony's PRS-500 e-reader was first commercialized in Japan in 2004 and then in the US in 2006 for a price of $399. At the same time, Sony opened its

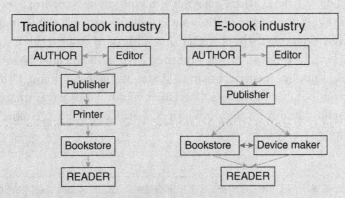

Figure C1.3 Traditional and e-book industry ecosystems
Note: Whereas the print book industry operated as a traditional value chain, the e-book industry had eliminated the printing function and the reading device represented a novel element in the ecosystem.

---

[35] Kozlowski, M. (2018). The tale of Rockebook – the very first e-reader. GoodEReader, December 2, 2018. Retrieved from https://goodereader.com/blog/electronic-readers/the-tale-of-rocketbook-the-very-first-e-reader in August 2022.

online Sony eBook Library.[36] Nevertheless, skepticism associated with e-readers was articulated by the WSJ blogger Christopher Lawton: "This tech blog has always been skeptical of digital e-book readers. Maybe because we think the feeling of a stiff hardback or welted paperback book is timeless. Or maybe it was because major e-book vendors such as Sony and Amazon.com never released how many units of the devices they actually sold."[37] Despite the naysayers, in the first two years Sony sold 300,000 units, exceeding all expectations including its own.

Another major book industry contender was Borders. It chose to offer its e-books via the independent Kobo e-reader,[38] in addition to Sony's e-reader and other tablets, smartphones, and computers. Kobo's device launched to good reviews in 2010. As a stand-alone device, it allowed accessing content from the Kobo International E-Book Store and other bookstores.

Finally, tablet computers also doubled as reading devices. Early tablet computers in the 2000s by Microsoft, Nokia, and others were valuable market experiments but didn't capture the mass market. However, 2010 was a big year for the tablet market with Apple launching the iPad, and Dell and Samsung also releasing similar devices. In early 2011, Motorola, BlackBerry, and major computer manufacturers also announced new tablet computers. Now this device category could also work with e-reading content providers, although none of them featured electronic paper and thus offered an inferior reading experience but a multipurpose device.

Case 1.3 E-Book Pricing Debacles

The transition to digital formats put pressure on the relationships among the book ecosystem partners. With Amazon's growing dominance in paper book sales and the evolution of the digital music industry since Napster, major book publishers were concerned about losing their ability to control the distribution channel. Shifting to e-books meant that they needed to consider how to mitigate digital piracy. Amazon's market share, on the other hand, implied that to reach a large number of readers, publishers had to work with Amazon despite its habit of selling books for very low prices. Furthermore, the economics of book publishing changed.

---

[36] Pilato, F. (2004). Sony LIBRIe – the first ever E-ink e-book reader. MobileMag, March 25, 2004. Retrieved from https://mobilemag.com/2004/03/25/sony-librie-the-first-ever-e-ink-e-book-reader/ in August 2022.

[37] Worthen, B. (2008). Turns out Sony e-book readers sell after all. Wall Street Journal, December 3, 2008. Retrieved from https://blogs.wsj.com/biztech/2008/12/03/turns-out-sony-e-book-readers-sell-after-all/ in August 2022.

[38] Biggs, J. (2010). Borders launches the Kobo eReader and eBook store. TechCrunch, May 7, 2010. Retrieved from https://techcrunch.com/2010/05/07/borders-launches-the-kobo-ereader-and-ebook-store/ in August 2022.

The typical profit and loss statement of a publisher included costs of goods sold exceeding 50 percent of revenue potential. Manufacturing tasks such as covers, printing, freight, and fulfillment typically amounted to 30–40 percent of revenue. Traditionally, authors would get royalties based on a percentage of sales, often at 10 percent of retail price. Thus the cost reductions for e-books meant that prices could also decrease without sacrificing profit margins, but, without adjusting the royalty agreement, authors' incomes would also decrease.

Indeed, the pricing of e-books became a heated aspect of competition. Amazon was committed to very low prices, even at the expense of profitability. It allowed publishers to set their wholesale prices, but it offered most e-books for $9.99 in the US. In the early e-book market it paid about $12 wholesale price per title,[39] losing $2 on every sale. However, it succeeded in building the market and driving growth, and by the Christmas season of 2009 it was selling more e-books than paper books.[40]

Apple entered with a different strategy, called the agency model. The established App Store model was to take 30 percent of commission of all "in-app" sales. As a result, publishers could offer their e-books via Apple's bookstore and price individually, and Apple would simply take a 30 percent cut on the sales price. Apple suggested retail prices around $13–15, implying a substantially higher price compared to Amazon. This gave publishers an illusion of pricing power, but actually generated lower revenues. For example, if they priced the same title at $15 in Apple's iBookstore that Amazon was selling for $9.99, they would certainly sell fewer copies than if they had priced the book at $10. However, out of the $15 price, Apple would charge $5 as commission and the publisher would gain only $10 per copy. In other words, they would sell fewer copies and collect less revenue with Apple's revenue-sharing scheme (see Table C1.1).

Nevertheless, five of the major publishers that included Hachette, HarperCollins, Macmillan, Penguin, and Simon & Schuster worked out an arrangement with Apple that involved coordination of their prices under the agency mechanism. Random House was aligned with the five publishers in interest but it wisely stayed out of the negotiations. Coordination of prices among competitors is illegal in the US, particularly if it results in price increases. Indeed, the publishers and Apple were found in violation of antitrust laws. Judge Denise L. Cote of United States District Court in Manhattan wrote in her decision:[41]

---

[39] Maher, R. (2009). Kindle fantasies are running wild – but, for now, Amazon is losing its shirt. Business Insider, November 20, 2009. Retrieved from www.businessinsider.com.au/e-readers-should-drive-profits-for-both-distributors-and-book-publishers-2009-11 in August 2022.

[40] Blodget, H. (2009). Kindle milestone: Amazon sold more Kindle books than physical books on Xmas. Business Insider, December 26, 2009. Retrieved from www.businessinsider.com/henry-blodget-kindle-milestone-amazon-sold-more-ebooks-than-physical-books-on-xmas-2009-12 in August 2022.

[41] Cote, D. (2013). Apple e-book opinion and order. Retrieved from www.documentcloud.org/documents/725381-apple-e-book-opinion-amp-emails.html in August 2022.

Table C1.1 Typical profit and loss of paper book and e-book publishing

	Print	Digital
Copies printed	100,000	100
Copies sold (90%)	90,000	90,000
Book price (wholesale)	$12.50	$5.00
Total revenue	1,125,000	450,000
Reserve for returns & lost books (30%)	337,500	90,000
Net revenue	787,500	360,000
Cost of goods sold		
Cover art	4,000	4,000
Proofreading/copyedit	10,000	10,000
Interior design	3,000	0
Permissions	1,000	1,000
Manufacturing (100,000 copies)	200,000	5,000
Freight (2% of net)	15,750	500
Author's royalty (10% of retail price)	187,500	75,000
Total COGS	421,250	95,500
Gross profit	366,250	264,500
Selling expenses		
Fulfillment fees	78,750	36,000
Marketing	56,250	56,250
Galley mailing	3,000	3,000
Total selling expenses	138,000	95,250
Overhead (15% of net revenue)	118,125	118,125
Net profit	110,125	51,125
Net profit margin	*9.79%*	*11.36%*

Note: In digital production of e-books, revenues, costs, and profits were significantly lower, but profit margins were higher, relative to print books.
Source: Maher & Blodget (2009) Business Insider, retrieved from www.businessinsider.com/henry-blodget-kindle-milestone-amazon-sold-more-ebooks-than-physical-books-on-xmas-2009-12 in August 2021.

Apple seized the moment and brilliantly played its hand. Taking advantage of the Publisher Defendants' fear of and frustration over Amazon's pricing, as well as the tight window of opportunity created by the impending launch of the iPad on January 27 ("the Launch"), Apple garnered the signatures it needed to introduce the iBookstore at the Launch. It provided the Publisher Defendants with the vision, the format, the timetable, and the coordination they needed to raise e-book prices. Apple decided to offer the Publisher Defendants the opportunity to move from a wholesale model – where a publisher receives its designated wholesale price for each e-book and the retailer sets the retail price – to an agency model where the publisher sets the retail price and the retailer sells the e-book as its agent. (pp. 11–12)

This collusion arrangement also imposed severe financial penalties on the publishers if they didn't jointly force Amazon to switch from the wholesale model to the agency model and cede retail price setting to the publishers. In other words, publishers agreed to not do business with Amazon unless it changed its business model.

Whereas the publishers settled their cases, Apple appealed the decision. The Supreme Court of the United States declined to hear the case so the Appeals Court's decision would stand: a massive fine of $450 million for Apple's anticompetitive behavior.[42]

Despite this setback for the publishers and Apple, by 2012, Apple and also Barnes & Noble had gained footholds in the marketplace. While Amazon initially controlled 90 percent of the e-book market, in 2012 Barnes & Noble had about 25 percent and Apple 11 percent of the market, pushing Amazon down to about 60 percent. However, the struggles were not over. How could Barnes & Noble create a sustainable competitive advantage, and a profitable business (see Table A1.1), against the e-commerce giant Amazon on one side and the electronics giant Apple on the other side?

DISCUSSION QUESTIONS

1. Are e-books a disruptive innovation? Describe the value proposition of e-books and compare against that of paper books and the definition of disruptive innovation.
2. Barnes & Noble was an established firm in the book ecosystem, yet it was among the first to start selling online and offer e-books. What strategies facilitated its early entry into digital markets?
3. Sony's e-reader was the first to offer a display with e-ink. What factors do you find in the case that may have prevented it from dominating the e-reading market?
4. Who are the potential user groups of e-reading and how could Barnes & Noble design its products and services to address their diverse and evolving needs?
5. In 2012 Barnes & Noble was "between a rock and a hard place," competing with Amazon and Apple for e-reading market share. Describe strategies that might help it enhance its market power in the e-book ecosystem by differentiating from its main competitors.

---

[42] Liptak, A. and Goel, V. (2016). Supreme Court declines to hear Apple's appeal in e-book pricing case. *The New York Times*, March 7, 2016. Retrieved from www.nytimes.com/2016/03/08/technology/apple-supreme-court-ebook-prices.html in August 2022.

CASE DATA APPENDIX

Table A1.1 Barnes & Noble financial statement 2008–2013

Millions of dollars	2013	2012	2011	2010	2008
Sales					
Retail	4568	4853	4927	4947	5122
College	1763	1744	1778	844	--
NOOK	780	933	695	105	--
Total sales	6839	7129	6999	5808	5122
Cost of sales	5156	5211	5197	4122	3532
Gross profit	1683	1918	1801	1687	1590
Selling and administrative	1675	1739	1629	1395	1264
Operating profit (loss)	(220)	(55)	(57)	83	152

Notes: NB: Year 2009 was later reinstated and is missing from here.

The sales revenues of Barnes & Noble steadily declined over the case period, whereas its costs increased. As a result, the company experienced growing losses.

Source: Annual report 2013: www.annualreports.com/HostedData/AnnualReportArchive/b/NYSE_BKS_2013.pdf retrieved in August 2021.

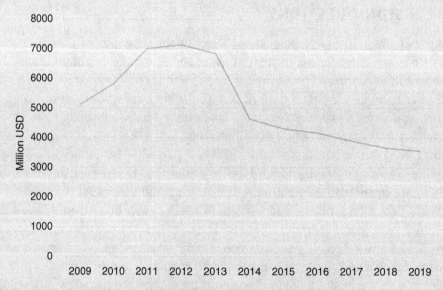

Figure A1.1 Barnes & Noble revenue 2009–2019
Note: The revenue of Barnes & Noble declined rapidly in 2014 and the downward trend persisted thereafter.
Source: www.netcials.com/financial-revenue-history-usa/890491-BARNES-&-NOBLE-INC/#firstlist retrieved in August 2021.

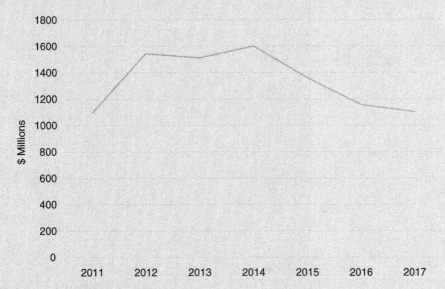

Figure A1.2 US publishers' e-book sales revenue
Note: US publishers' e-book sales grew briskly between 2010 and 2012, but have since stalled and declined.
Source: Association of American Publishers (AAP) StatShot Monthly. Retrieved from https://medium.com/
newco/how-to-stop-the-killing-of-ebooks-81b81f7106d6 in August, 2021.

PART II
Information Products and Sources

....

We saw in Part I that there seems to be a lot of "disruption" in the digital economy. The evolving information and communication technologies constantly introduce new sources of information in the economy that enable entrepreneurs to challenge established companies that have built their business models on protected sources of information. Innovators can then take advantage of these new resources to launch disruptive innovations that undermine the market positions of incumbents. Part II begins with a discussion of how the production process and the resulting cost structure of information goods differs from those of physical goods, leading to significant, qualitative differences in competitive dynamics. These economic characteristics of information influence how information goods are traded and priced. We also explore how information is consumed to understand both the demand and supply sides of the information market. Frictions and inefficiencies tend to distort information markets because people are systematically biased in their valuation of information goods. We will highlight a few key behavioral distortions and how innovators can account for those in their go-to-market strategies.

4   Production of Information Goods

The increasing penetration of information and communication technologies in the economy enabled the emergence of digital business practices in a wide range of industries. The digitization of information products, service processes, product information, and pricing altered the functioning of the markets. Once products and processes are digital, communication technologies facilitate the instantaneous exchange of information. This immediate availability of product and service information and pricing enhances competition: digital networks can accelerate and even automate product and price comparison, making consumers more powerful in the marketplace. This chapter focuses on the economics of digital information products and implications for strategy.

4.1   Economics of Information Production

Many types of products and services contain information, but it is not always digitized and used separately from the physical good. For example, cars contain information about the shape, components, and operation of the physical object. With the advance of information and communication technologies it has become possible to detach the information component, if it is valuable, and utilize it separately to draw insights about the product's performance. In the case of cars, the fleet owner might collect valuable information about its location, functioning of the components, and speed and acceleration. Insurance companies would like to know how safely the insured driver behaves in traffic and offer service packages targeted to more or less safe drivers.[1] Information about the product shape and materials was already generated and codified during the design and manufacturing phases, when the vehicle was designed using software programs and manufactured based on the largely autonomous operation of industrial robots following computerized instructions. Thus, a physical product potentially generates a lot of information that can be collected and analyzed.

There are also large categories of goods that primarily consist of information. Such content goods comprise movies, news, books, music, and many other

---

[1] Toplensky, R. (2020). Driver data is a help and a hazard for auto insurers. Wall Street Journal, November 30, 2020 www.wsj.com/articles/driver-data-is-a-help-and-a-hazard-for-auto-insurers-11606729983. Retrieved in August 2022.

information products and services. When information is offered in digital form, it is no longer dependent on a specific physical format. News or novels do not need to be printed on paper, and movies do not need to be printed on discs or copied on magnetic tape and coiled up inside a plastic case. They can be easily distributed over the internet without any physical packaging. However, they do require digital formatting which is a digital good in itself and can be used as a strategy to control distribution.

Information can be very costly to produce. Writing a novel or a textbook may take a year of an author's time, and a movie can cost hundreds of millions of dollars to create. When an author or a creator makes such investments, she does not know how many consumers may ultimately be interested in buying the content. These are sunk investments, meaning that they cannot be recovered if the project fails. However, the cost of dissemination will be minimal compared to the cost of creation. Furthermore, it will be difficult to control the dissemination of the good. Once information is reduced to bits, users may be able to easily share it with others, and competitors can easily imitate it, reducing the profit opportunities for the creator.

In economic terms, the large cost of creation is a **fixed cost**, and the small cost of distribution is a **variable cost**. The sum of all fixed and variable costs is the **total cost**. In practice, the variable cost is also the **marginal cost**, because producing one more unit only requires distributing another digital copy of the good, and this cost of distribution is typically very small and relatively constant. Information goods usually have very high fixed costs but very low and more or less constant marginal costs. This creates two strategic issues: **increasing returns to scale**, and the need to pursue a **differentiation strategy**.

Let's examine a very simple information production function and its cost implications.

If we assume that a digital music album costs $100,000 to create and $0.01 to distribute, the fixed cost is $100,000 and the constant variable cost is $0.01. This would lead to the following cost function:

$$\text{Total cost} = \text{Fixed cost} + \text{Variable cost*Quantity}$$

$$\text{Marginal cost} = \partial(\text{Fixed cost} + \text{Variable cost*Quantity}) / \partial\text{Quantity} = \text{Variable cost}$$

$$\text{Average cost} = \text{Total cost/Quantity} = \text{Fixed cost/Quantity} + \text{Variable cost}$$

For a quantity of 500,000 units, the total cost would be $100,000 + $0.01 * 500,000 = $105,000. As we see from the reasonably realistic example, variable costs are relatively meaningless for many information producers.

If marginal cost is constant, this cost function leads to an ever-decreasing **average cost**. The fixed cost is simply divided by more and more units sold. Figure 4.1 illustrates both total cost (TC) and average cost (AC) functions. Average cost will approach but not reach the marginal cost. This means that the larger the firm (the more units it can sell), the more profitable it will become. In other words, there are strong **increasing returns to scale**. Once the firm **breaks even** (sells enough

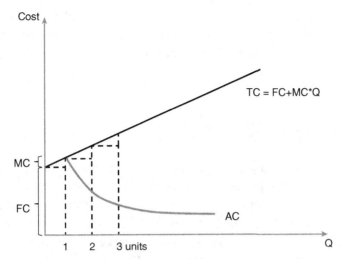

Figure 4.1 Cost structure of information goods when marginal cost is constant
Note: When the marginal cost of producing an additional unit is constant, total costs grow linearly with production quantity. Average costs decrease and approach the marginal cost.

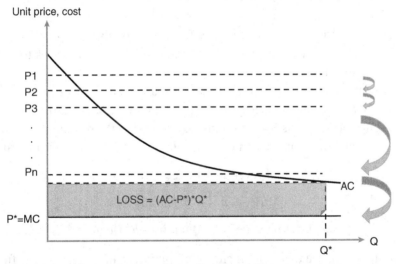

Figure 4.2 The impact of price pressure on firm profitability in information markets
Note: In competitive markets, price will approach marginal cost meaning the firm will become unprofitable if it is easy for rivals to enter.

to cover the fixed cost), every additional unit sold is almost pure profit! However, selling enough to cover fixed cost can be tricky and require significant business model innovation and durable product differentiation.

In competitive markets, low marginal cost means that prices are very low, too. If the price is above marginal cost and entry is very easy, competitors will enter and prices will decline until it equals marginal cost. Once the price falls below marginal cost, it does not make sense to ship the next product so entry will stop. Figure 4.2 illustrates this dynamic and shows how competition puts pressure on pricing until price equals marginal cost. Unfortunately, in information markets, when price is constant and equals marginal cost that is also constant, the firm will always be losing money: for any amount of quantity sold, marginal cost will be below average cost. Hence, if price falls below average cost, the firm will be unprofitable.

4.2   Differentiation Strategy

Considering that price competition will not be sustainable for information producers (because it will drive prices too low), digital firms need to look for strategies to differentiate and compete under a "monopolistic" framework. Monopolistic competition takes place in a market that has many small firms with differentiated products. In this setting, firms have some **market power** but not enough to significantly influence their rivals' strategies. However, firms have some market power such that if they reduce prices, they will gain some customers, and if they increase prices, their sales will fall. The demand curve is thus downward sloping rather than flat as is the case under the ideal of perfect competition. In perfectly competitive markets, firms are price takers – either they offer the commodity at market price or else (all) buyers will buy from their rivals. In monopolistic markets firms offer slightly different products and can adjust their prices to attract a targeted amount of demand.

Let's assume the monopolistic information market has a linear demand function: Price = $a - b$*Quantity, where a and b are parameters. Then, the firm's revenue function simply equals Price * Quantity. Combining the demand function with the total revenue function, we can express total revenue in terms of quantity:

$$\text{Total revenue} = \text{Price} * \text{Quantity}$$

$$\text{Price} = a - b * \text{Quantity}$$

$$\Rightarrow \text{Total revenue} = a * \text{Quantity} - b * \text{Quantity}^2$$

As usual, to determine the optimal choice of quantity (and price) for the firm, we need to explore when marginal revenue equals marginal cost for this firm. With the linear demand function and the simple cost function we specified earlier, the firm should increase production quantity until (or set price where) marginal revenue (that is decreasing with quantity) equals marginal cost (that is a very low constant or zero, and equal to variable cost). The logic is that any quantity below that point (Q^*) will generate less profit than Q^*, and any quantity above Q^* will also generate less profit. The firm's profit function is simply the difference between total revenue and total cost, and the firm attempts to maximize profit by selecting quantity:

$$\text{Profit} = \text{Total revenue} - \text{Total cost}$$

$$= a * \text{Quantity} - b * \text{Quantity}^2 - \text{Fixed cost} - \text{Variable cost} * \text{Quantity}$$

Marginal profit = ∂Profit / ∂Quantity = $a - 2b$ * Quantity - Variable cost = 0

If Variable cost = c = Marginal cost

$\Leftrightarrow$ Quantity = $(a - c) / 2b$

Price = $a - b$ * Quantity

$\Leftrightarrow$ Price = $a - b$ * $(a - c) / 2b = (a + c) / 2$

It is worth noting that optimal quantity and pricing do not directly depend on fixed cost. Also, the slope of the marginal revenue curve, $2b$, is exactly double the slope of the demand curve.

Figure 4.3 presents the optimization problem graphically for the case where marginal cost c equals zero. This is a realistic case for many online businesses that distribute information automatically from a website, and the actual variable cost is a fraction of a cent (essentially the cost of electricity to complete the transaction). If marginal cost equals zero, optimal quantity Q^* is found at the intersection of marginal revenue (MR) and the X-axis. That level of quantity allows the firm to charge the price P^*, making a profit that equals $P^**Q^* - AC*Q^*$. In other words, fixed cost is very important for profits because it largely determines the average cost.

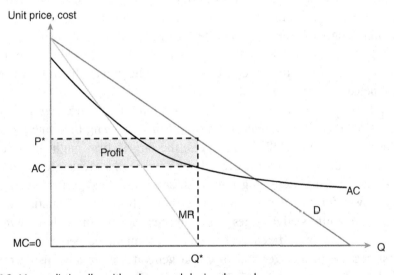

Figure 4.3 Monopolistic seller with a downward sloping demand curve
Note: An innovator of a differentiated digital good might face a demand curve that allows the company to set its price in order to maximize profits.
D = Demand = $a - b$*Quantity
MR = Marginal revenue = $a - 2b$*Quantity
AC = Average cost = Fixed cost/Quantity + Variable cost
P^* = optimal price = $a/2$
Q^* = optimal quantity = $a/2b$
MC = Marginal cost = 0

Thus, the good news is that information producers can make a profit if they manage to sufficiently differentiate themselves from competitors. The challenge is that differentiation is difficult to maintain under incomplete **excludability** – when information is primarily protected by copyright, rivals can often "recreate" the content without using exactly the same sequence of symbols (letters or numbers) and the new version is no longer protected by copyright. This makes long-lasting differentiation quite difficult for the information industry. For instance, copycat news outlets can simply rephrase the news and present it as their own content. For this reason, news outlets have been struggling to maintain profitability in the digital economy. They must find other ways to differentiate themselves.

4.3 Cost Leadership

The only alternative to differentiation is trying to maintain profitability by being the lowest cost producer. If firms are in a highly competitive market offering very similar commodity products, they are essentially price takers and must all offer the market price. If competition is tough, then price will equal marginal cost. An example of a commodity information market is movie listings. In Ithaca, New York, at least three online services provide movie listings of the three theaters in town. The information is easily available but there is value to having showtimes aggregated in one (or multiple) places rather than moviegoers having to search individually from each theater's website. In the movie listing business, creating a system to collect and display the listings is a fixed cost, while marginal cost is practically zero. Therefore, the price of this publicly available information has been competed down to zero, too.

However, it is conceivable that information producers differ with respect to their cost structures. For example, even if all firms are using the same production technology and equally skilled employees, the largest firm might have a lower average cost and make a profit, even though its smaller rivals are unprofitable, simply because of the increasing returns to scale described earlier: average cost is always lower for a larger but otherwise similar firm. In information markets, larger size also confers advantages in the adjacent advertising market. Even with zero price and the same fixed cost, larger firms might be better able to cover their cost because of a larger audience that generates more advertising revenue. Nevertheless, revenue opportunities from online advertising are very limited, and commodity information providers need to attract very large audiences to generate substantial revenue (see Figure 4.4).

To compete under the constant pressure of commoditization, digital firms can thus follow either differentiation or cost leadership strategies. Because incomplete excludability erodes the value of information over time, firms following a differentiation strategy need to constantly reinvent their content. In contrast, cost leadership without differentiation is rarely observed in digital information

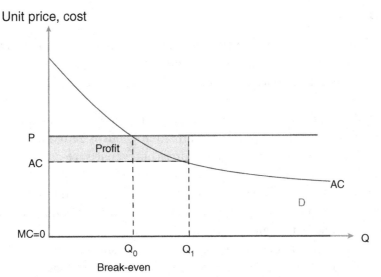

Figure 4.4 Competitive seller with a flat demand curve
Note: When the firm is a price taker with a decreasing average cost, the only way to stay profitable is to maintain a sufficiently large scale.

markets. A neat example is weather forecasting. Weather information is publicly and widely available in the US through the National Weather Service, a government agency. Just redistributing the public weather information is an option for information producers, who may try to create more intuitive visualizations and packaging of the public information. There might be minor differentiation through this packaging effort but the information content would essentially be the same. They could then fund the service through advertising revenue. However, both AccuWeather and The Weather Company have gone significantly beyond simple repackaging to build their own weather models. AccuWeather is an interesting privately-held company from College Station, Pennsylvania. Joel Myers, the company founder, was a meteorology scientist who did his graduate studies at Penn State University in the same town. He developed models that could more accurately predict microgeographic weather patterns. For example, he could provide particularly pertinent forecasts for car dealers and ski hill operators.[2]

While AccuWeather and other weather services provide local forecasts free online, they also sell customized forecasts to their enterprise clients, presumably making most of its $100 million revenue in this manner. Dr. Myers described how difficult it was in the early days of the company to sell such customized information: it took him 25,000 cold calls over 10 years to attract 100 paying customers!

---

[2] Yakowics, W. (2016). This entrepreneur made 25,00 cold calls to build a $100 million weather business. Inc. Magazine. Retrieved from www.inc.com/magazine/201607/will-yakowicz/joel-myers-accuweather-forecast.html in August 2022.

KEY IDEAS

- Information goods are associated with high fixed costs of creation and very low variable costs of dissemination. Therefore, the marginal cost of an additional unit sold is often very close to zero.
- Low costs of distribution are good for consumers, but they make it difficult for information producers to charge a price and make a profit. In many commodity information markets, the price of information goods is zero and the service is funded through advertising or other sources of revenue such as markets for data or referrals.
- Information producers need to accumulate market power through differentiation to be able to charge for access. Therefore, most information goods depend on constant innovation and creativity.
- Because many digital businesses experience increasing returns to scale, a large size is beneficial because the average cost per unit sold keeps shrinking. As a result, even very low prices can create a profitable business when the size of the network is extremely large.

DEFINITIONS

Average cost is total cost divided by the number of units produced.

Break even happens when total revenues exceed total costs.

Differentiation strategy involves designing products and services that are in some ways different, ideally better, than those of competitors.

Excludability allows an innovator to exclude unauthorized users of their product. If excludability is incomplete, there will be users who can access and benefit from the product without paying for it.

Fixed cost is the cost that has to be spent before producing a single unit of the product or service. It often includes facilities, machinery, and administrative activities.

Increasing returns to scale are observed when average cost is decreasing as the firm's production quantity grows. Also called scale economies. Returns to scale can also be decreasing or constant, depending on the trend of the average cost curve when the firm's production grows.

Marginal cost is the cost of producing an additional, "marginal" unit of the product.

A firm has market power when it is able to "set prices," meaning it can increase its price without losing all customers.

Total cost equals fixed and variable costs for the quantity produced.

Variable cost is the cost of producing a unit of the product.

DISCUSSION QUESTIONS

1. Microsoft acquired Skype for $8.5 billion in 2011. Computer-to-computer ("Skype-to-Skype") calls are free but it charges 0.20 cents ($0.002) per minute for calls to landlines or mobile phones. Each minute costs Microsoft 0.01 cents ($0.0001) in server usage.

a. Skype has estimated that its demand function is P = 3–5E-10 * Quantity (minutes of consumption). What quantity does it sell for the price of $0.002?

b. What is the average cost for Microsoft at that quantity (minutes consumed)?

c. How many minutes does Microsoft need Skype to sell to cover the fixed cost of acquisition and the variable cost of server usage?

d. Does Microsoft maximize Skype's profit with the price it has set?

2. It costs hiphop artist Jebz £25,000 to digitally record an album of 10 songs and £1 to handle the sales fulfillment of one unit of the album via their website. Half of their 100,000 fans are not willing to pay anything for the album, and half are willing to pay £5.

1. Work out Jebz's total cost, total revenue, and profit.

2. How much is their average cost?

3. A music label called Lemon offers to promote the album to new audiences, promising 30,000 new fans who are willing to pay £3 for the album. However, Lemon will take a 30 percent commission of all sales. Should Jebz make the deal?

4. What is their average cost if they do make the promotion deal?

FURTHER READING

Bhargava, Hemant K. and Choudhary, Vidyanand (2015). Information goods and vertical differentiation. *Journal of Management Information Systems* 18(2): 89–106.

Jones, Roy and Mendelson, Haim (2011). Information goods vs. industrial goods: cost structure and competition. *Management Science* 57(1): 164–176.

Varian, Hal R. (2003). Buying, sharing and renting information goods. *Journal of Industrial Economics* 48(4): 473–488.

5 | Pricing of Information

Because information is an **experience good**, we usually know if we like or value the information only after we have consumed it. However, after we have already consumed it, there is little reason to buy it. This is Arrow's paradox that makes information particularly tricky to value and price. Additionally, all sorts of cognitive biases influence whether people view information as useful, truthful, or valuable, and the value of information also depends on the context of use. Not only do idiosyncratic preferences influence whether someone enjoys books by Austen or Auster, but the value of many information services depends on how essential they are in the situation, and how much additional value creation they enable. For example, someone may not be willing to pay at all for streaming music on a regular day, but on a day when they host a dance party they might be willing to pay quite a bit for a few hours of access. Those are the magic words: **willingness to pay** (WTP).

Of course, the value of physical products may also vary over time and across situations: ice cream is more valuable on a hot day and mittens are more valuable on a cold day. However, digital information products are different from physical products in that their marginal cost does not provide a "natural" lower bound below which the product is unlikely to be sold. While ice cream is rarely handed out for free by commercial entrepreneurs, music or books may be free.

Because there are so many factors that influence the valuation of information, digital information producers should expect wide variation in potential consumers' willingness to pay. Some people, sometimes, are willing to pay a lot, most people are willing to pay nothing, and others may be willing to pay a tiny bit. The challenge for the digital innovator is to discover who is who.

Digital pricing strategies thus revolve around distinguishing who is willing to pay, how much, and for what features. The good news is that, in information markets, the opportunities to discover willingness to pay and to offer differentiated packages of the same information are abundant. Therefore, most (successful) digital businesses attempt to do at least some **price discrimination**, that is, offer a different price for the same good to different buyers. According to the US Federal Trade Commission, "price discriminations are generally lawful, particularly if they reflect the different costs of dealing with different buyers or are the result of a seller's attempts to meet a competitor's offering."[1]

---

[1] See FTC's guide to the antitrust laws. Retrieved from www.ftc.gov/tips-advice/competition-guidance/guide-antitrust-laws/price-discrimination-robinson-patman in August 2022.

  Also note that the FTC defines the Robinson-Patman Act that provides the antitrust guidance to apply for commodities, not services, and purchases but not leases. In service markets – much of the digital economy – such limits on price discrimination do not seem to apply.

Price discrimination can be accomplished by making individual offers to each customer (first-degree price discrimination), by offering different bundles of features and by charging different prices for them (second-degree price discrimination), or by segmenting the market and offering different prices to buyers in different segments based on their inferred willingness to pay (third-degree price discrimination).

Individual offers potentially yield the greatest revenue, but the associated transaction costs may exceed the benefits. It takes time and effort to negotiate every single price. Some of that can perhaps be automated, but only up to a point. Offering differentiated bundles is much easier, as it allows buyers to self-select into different options and prices. The information producer does not need to collect and analyze any data about buyers. However, designing the bundles can involve a lot of (costly) trial and error. Market segmentation is also fairly simple but it involves transaction costs, too. For example, discounts for students or retirees require that the seller check the credentials of the buyers to receive the lower prices. Again, some of these strategies can be automated but any price constraint always involves some cost to set up and monitor.

5.1 Personalized Pricing

Fully individualized, often dynamic, price schemes can be challenging to design but are quite feasible to execute in digital markets. **Dynamic pricing** refers to a rate that evolves over time based on the demand and supply conditions or other market parameters. Airlines have traditionally utilized some degree of dynamic pricing with their "yield management" techniques, for example, when passengers buy their tickets last minute, signaling that the travel is likely to be urgent and the passenger's willingness to pay is high[2]. However, the e-commerce environment allows companies to not only consider the state of the market but also the characteristics of the potential buyer.[3] In addition to general and market information such as product availability, timing, and the nature of the product, firms can use cookies, IP addresses, technical specifications of the computer, the buyer's purchase history, and voluntary registration information to predict the buyer's willingness to pay and to offer a price they are likely to accept.[4] While consumers may not like the fact that their own information may be used "against" them (if a higher willingness to pay is predicted), it can also be difficult to detect.[5]

---

[2] Elmaghraby, Wedad and Keskinocak, Pinar (2003). Dynamic pricing in the presence of inventory considerations: research overview, current practices, and future directions. *Management Science* 49(10): 1287–1309.

[3] Kannan, P.K. and Kopalle, Praveen K. (2001). Dynamic pricing on the internet: importance and implications for consumer behavior. *International Journal of Electronic Commerce* 5(3): 63–83.

[4] See, for example, *The Economist* (2012). Caveat Emptor.com. *The Economist*, June 30, 2012, www.economist.com/leaders/2012/06/30/caveat-emptorcom. Retrieved in August 2022.

[5] Richards, Timothy J., Liaukonyte, Jura, and Streletskaya, Nadia A. (2016). Personalized pricing and price fairness. *International Journal of Industrial Organization* 44 (January): 138–153.

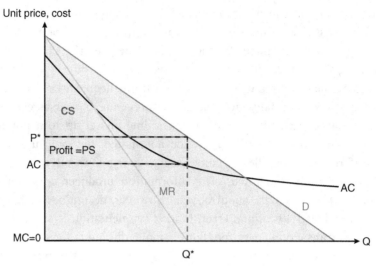

Figure 5.1 Personalized prices

Note: When a company is able to perfectly personalize its price offers and when the marginal cost is very low, it can theoretically capture all the consumer surplus available in the market. However, price personalization may not be a low-cost service, but as long as its cost does not depend on the quantity supplied, such as if the negotiation cost is constant, then the same analysis applies, but the firm will set quantity Q* at MR = MC.

Figure 5.1 illustrates the advantages of **personalized pricing** when marginal cost is zero. Under monopolistic competition, the firm would select quantity Q^* which maximizes profits by setting marginal revenue equal to marginal cost. The corresponding price is P^*. This would lead to a profit the size of the rectangle PS (producer surplus). Even with this monopoly price, consumers as a group would gain surplus the size of the triangle CS (consumer surplus). However, if the firm has complete control of the pricing process, and can negotiate individualized prices as well as figure out willingness to pay with reasonable accuracy, its profit will consist of both consumer and producer surplus.

In fact, with zero marginal cost and a high degree of control of the market, it is in the interest of the firm to keep selling to all buyers with positive willingness to pay (i.e., WTP>MC), and capture the whole large triangle. However, in reality, such negotiation costs would likely make marginal costs actually significantly greater than zero. In digital information markets, we see such personalized selling practices in markets for large information platform access. For example, Bloomberg and Thomson Reuters sell most information packages based on negotiated prices. Similarly, many enterprise software package prices are negotiated. The negotiation process allows the seller to keep the "market price" secret and through personal engagement gain information that helps estimate the potential buyer's willingness to pay. Indeed, the marginal cost of a sale is not zero but perhaps hundreds of US dollars if it requires that a skilled salesperson engages in a lengthy conversation with the potential customer to define their needs and financial status. As we will see in cases and examples later in the book, selling is not a cheap or easy activity.

5.2   Group Pricing

Next we examine third-degree price discrimination, also called **group pricing** or **segmentation**. Figure 5.2 illustrates a situation with two market segments, high vs. low willingness to pay. The low willingness to pay segment also has a higher price elasticity – a small decrease in price generates a larger change in quantity demanded.

D_1 represents consumers who have a high willingness to pay and are not very price sensitive. Consumers described by D_2, in contrast, have a lower overall willingness to pay and higher price sensitivity – these types of individuals respond very strongly in terms of quantity demanded when price is increased or decreased.

Assuming that the marginal cost of the information good is close or equal to zero, we can again draw marginal revenue curves (MR_1 and MR_2) and find the quantities demanded when the prices are optimized, respectively, for the two separate segments. We notice that the optimal price is always higher for the less sensitive segment ($P_1 > P_2$). In the real world we can observe discounts for students and retirees, and prices for the same textbooks being lower in less wealthy markets.

However, such group pricing requires a substantial amount of control, too. Students have to provide information about their schooling status, and consumers from more-developed markets shouldn't easily be able to visit less-developed markets and bring the good back to their home market for sale at a higher price. In other words, the company has to be able to prevent arbitrage – buying low and selling high. Sometimes this pricing strategy works very well (as with the widely prevalent student and senior discounts, even though they do increase transaction costs), but there are not always good mechanisms available to detect lower WTP consumers.

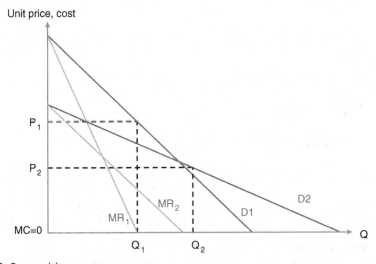

Figure 5.2 Group pricing

Note: In segmented markets, two or more consumer groups differ by their response to price changes. The more price elastic user group should be offered a lower price, even if the marginal cost of servicing users in the two groups is the same.

5.3   Versioning

When segmentation is not easily available, firms may use second-degree price discrimination strategies by **versioning** (Shapiro and Varian, 1998), or providing bundles of features that buyers themselves select. Many digital goods are a part of a technological system, consisting of a variety of features, and it is often easy to build different combinations of features more or less for the same cost. The versioning strategy, as well as bundling and **nonlinear pricing** more broadly, involves some flavor of a "two-part tariff."

In its basic form, a **two-part tariff** means that one first needs to pay to enter the network, and then buy some quantity of goods provided. For example, subscription shopping such as Dollar Shave Club or Stitch Fix entails a low subscription fee and payment per bundle bought. Products may be shipped monthly, based on the consumer's general preferences, in bundles of five items or so. If the individual likes the items, they pay and keep them, otherwise they return them.

The advantage of subscription shopping, and nonlinear pricing more generally, is that by charging different prices for different bundles, consumers can buy more or less based on their willingness to pay, whereas the seller can usually obtain a part of the consumer surplus and gain higher profits. Figure 5.3 demonstrates the logic of this strategy.

We have again two distinct types of consumers, D_1 with high WTP and low sensitivity and D_2 with low WTP and high sensitivity. Ideally, the company would like to charge two distinct prices, p^* and p_1, but it cannot distinguish which shoppers

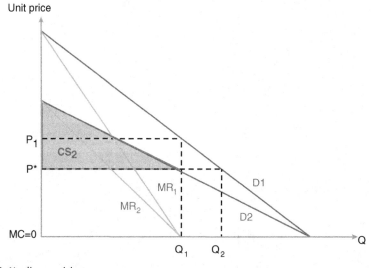

Figure 5.3 Nonlinear pricing
Note: When the firm has customers with different levels of willingness to pay but no good mechanism to identify the customer types, it can offer a two-part tariff such as a membership fee and a unit price. This allows it to capture the amount of the consumer surplus of the low WTP types from all buyers.

are which type. However, it can design a "subscription" fee and a marginal price, as in the subscription shopping case. The firm should charge p^* per unit, and CS_2 as the subscription fee. Now both types of consumers will buy some goods. D_1 will buy quantity Q_1, and pay $CS_2 + p^* * Q_1$. D_2 will buy quantity Q_2 and pay $CS_2 + p^* * Q_2$. Compared to a single linear price, which would optimally be p^*, the seller will now profit $2 * CS_2$ more. Without nonlinear pricing, in some market conditions the preferences might be so divergent between the two types that for the seller it is optimal to only serve the high WTP-type consumer. Nonlinear pricing allows the company to serve both types of consumers. Thus, even if the firm may gain much of the consumer surplus, particularly for the low types of consumers, consumers may still gain from being able to consume at all.

Nonlinear pricing strategies are particularly helpful when consumer preferences are very dispersed, such as when some consumers like service A a lot but service B only a little, and others like service B a lot and service A only a little. These services could, for example, be topic sections of a news service. Some consumers want to follow international news and others primarily follow sports. By selling each topic area separately it can be difficult to find linear prices that enable the firm to reach profitability. The firm may need to sell according to the low willingness to pay and price each service low to sell to both types of consumers, or price high and only sell to one type of a consumer. However, bundling the services A and B for a medium price may allow the company to profit much more significantly. The news distributor could offer both international and sports news in a bundle that is priced higher than a single topic section, and sell to the whole market. Subscription shopping schemes discussed above deploy both pricing strategies – nonlinear pricing and bundling. Bundling is also often observed with software products (Windows operating system + web browser), communication services (the "triple play" of internet, TV, and fixed-line telephone service) and other information products (such as TV or cable channels).

In information markets, creating various versions of the same underlying product can be very easy and inexpensive. Sometimes it involves creating one single product and switching off some features for the lower-end packages, as in the case of the Windows operating systems. Versioning does not necessarily require a two-part tariff. It can use the quality and features of the product in other ways to distinguish high and low WTP consumers. Many information products are offered in three or more versions. In 2021, the DirecTVNow Over-The-Top (over the internet) TV streaming service offered six different packages including "Plus" (40 channels), "Max" (50 channels), "Entertainment" (65 channels), "Choice" (85 channels), "XTRA" (105 channels), and "Ultimate" (125 channels). Additionally, the service offers Spanish-language channel package "Optimo Mas" (90 channels, but for a price lower than that for "Entertainment" with 65 channels). All channels involve a very high fixed cost of creating or acquiring the content, but offering one or more channels to a household does not influence the variable cost of streaming. Such bundling and versioning strategies are thus purely about price discrimination. The Spanish-language package, furthermore, highlights the company's prediction that Spanish- speaking households on average have a lower willingness to pay for content. They thus use language to segment the content market.

5.4   Versioning and Freemium

Following Hal Varian's exposition of the versioning strategy,[6] we will assume that there are two types of consumers, each with a high or low willingness to pay (WTP) for quality. Consumer 1 is interested in a little bit of quality, up to q_1, whereas consumer 2 is interested in a lot of quality up to q_2 (see Figure 5.4). If the seller was able to perfectly price discriminate and the marginal cost of quality was zero, the seller would ideally sell the service with quality q_1 to consumer 1 for a price of the triangle A (this consumer's entire consumer surplus). They would also sell to consumer 2 with quality q_2 for the price of the large triangle A+B+C, their whole consumer surplus.

However, if the firm is not able to perfectly discriminate the two types of buyers, they can still offer one or two levels of quality. Depending on the distribution of the types in the market, the firm could offer quality q_1 for price A and have

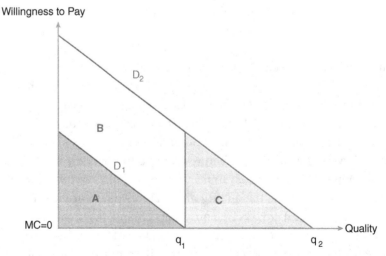

Figure 5.4 Pricing versions of information products
Note: When a firm has two types of customers with different levels of WTP for quality (additional features), the pricing of one version influences the pricing of the other. To have consumers properly separate into the two versions, the price of the higher quality product can't capture the whole consumer surplus of the higher WTP-type buyer.

[6] Varian, H.R. (1997). Versioning Information Goods. UC Berkeley, Unpublished Manuscript, January 1997. Retrieved from www-inst.cs.berkeley.edu/~eecsba1/sp97/reports/eecsba1b/Final/version.pdf in August, 2022.

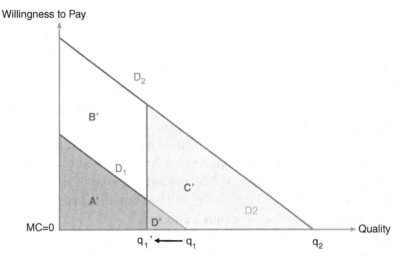

Figure 5.5 Profit-maximizing version pricing
Note: Depending how many of each type of customer the firm has, it can maximize profits by adjusting the lower-quality level which allows it to capture more consumer surplus in the high-end market.

both types buy the lower-end product, or it could offer the higher-end product of quality q_2 for price A+B+C but only have high WTP-types buy the product. The firm could also offer both quality levels, but pricing would need to induce the consumers to self-select into the product that corresponds to their WTP. This pricing strategy can be tricky to discover.

If the firm simply offers q_1 for A and q_2 for A+B+C, the high-end consumers are likely to notice they will actually gain a consumer surplus of B if they buy the lower-quality product q_1. Therefore, if the firm offers q_1 to both consumers, then it has to offer the high-quality product q_2 to consumer 2 for the price of A+C only. To be willing to buy the high-end product (or be indifferent between the two), consumer 2 needs to gain the same amount of consumer surplus from both products, equal to B. However, the seller can do even better. They can lower the low-end quality offered to q_1' and take over some of the consumer surplus available to consumers of type 2. If there are equal numbers of consumers 1 and 2, the firm will optimally select q_1' such that revenues from consumer 1 lost (D') equal revenues gained from consumer 2. In other words, q_1' enhances the firm's profits by allowing it to capture some more of the consumer surplus of high-end customers. To decide whether to offer multiple versions, the firm should consider whether the market share of the lower-quality version, offered alone, is greater than the market share of the higher-quality version, offered alone.[7] If the lower-quality market share is larger, then adding a lower-quality version makes sense. The feasibility of versioning also depends on variable costs. When costs decrease, adding lower-quality versions becomes more feasible (see Figure 5.5).

---

[7] Bhargava, Hemant K. and Choudhary, Vidyanand (2008). When is versioning optimal for information goods? *Management Science* 54(5): 1029–1035.

Freemium is an important versioning strategy in digital markets. It helps to overcome the experience good problem related to information goods and to sponsor network effects and achieve critical mass in network markets. Freemium involves a low-end product or service that is free and higher-end products that are for fee. For example, many gaming apps are free to play in App Store or Play Store, but to achieve a higher level of performance or access more interesting activities, there are in-app purchases available to boost the gaming experience. Similarly, the free version of Skype allows internet users to call each other for free, but calls to reach people on their landlines or mobile phones are for fee. Providing a free version is a feasible strategy when the marginal cost of another copy is practically zero. It allows the firm to "proliferate" the market and build an installed base, and in that way offer low-cost marketing to acquire customers.[8]

However, designing a freemium product strategy can be challenging. The seller needs to decide which features to offer free vs. for fee, and how to price the for-fee products. This is why experimentation with prices and product design are essential to get it "right." A key goal of the freemium strategy is to support the "**conversion**" of free users to paying users, without whom the innovation will not succeed.[9] Thus, without at least some of the free users becoming paying users, there is usually no point in offering the free version. Building in features that automatically push users over the payment threshold is ideal. For example, Dropbox launched with a significant amount of free storage, but, over time, as people use the service, they tend to accumulate a lot of large files such as photos. In a year or two, many of them choose to start paying a low monthly fee to be able to continue accumulating content.

Freemium forces the firm to lower all prices in the market. The logic is the same as in the analysis of versioning where the two types need to be willing to self-select into their preferred products. In Figure 5.6, q_0 reflects the quality offered with the free version. Then the lower-quality, for-fee version can only be priced at A', and the higher-quality version at A'+C. Additionally the firm may shift q_1 left as described earlier, depending on how many consumers are in each group. Finding q_0, q_1, and q_2 as well as the best possible prices for each is not a simple task. It usually requires systematic and extensive experimentation, or "A/B testing."

KEY IDEAS

- A digital innovator should attempt to distinguish the willingness to pay of each potential buyer. Each buyer type can be offered a different price through mechanisms of price discrimination.

---

[8] Boudreau, Kevin J., Jeppesen, Lars Bo, and Miric, Milan (2021). Competing on freemium: digital competition with network effects. *Strategic Management Journal* 43: 1374–1401.

[9] Wagner, Thomas M., Benlian, Alexander, and Hess, Thomas (2014). Converting freemium customers from free to premium – the role of the perceived premium fit in the case of music as a service. *Electronic Markets* 24: 259–268.

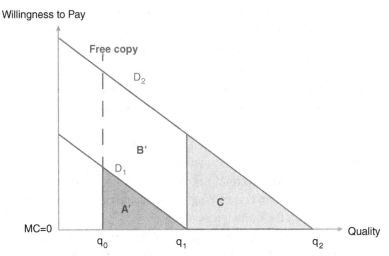

Figure 5.6 Version pricing when the lowest version is free

Note: If there is a free version of the product available in the market due to piracy or freemium strategies, then the prices of both higher-quality versions need to be decreased.

- Personalized pricing requires negotiating a customized price point with each buyer. This is typically feasible only for large purchases because the negotiation takes time and is costly.
- Segmentation necessitates ways to recognize buyers with high vs. low willingness to pay. Each market segment is then offered a different price. Segments can be defined, for example, based on geography, demographics, or profession.
- Versioning involves creating slightly different product or feature bundles that buyers select. If the marginal cost of producing each bundle is constant and low, as in software and other information goods, versioning can be achieved by offering the same product and by switching off some of the features for low-end bundles.
- Freemium is a versioning strategy where the lowest-end product is offered for free. It helps to attract new users to a network product, but it reduces the price that can be charged to the high-end buyers.
- Nonlinear pricing schemes such as bundling and subscription shopping have many quality and price parameters that can be challenging to estimate and necessitate experimental testing to discover.

DEFINITIONS

Dynamic pricing evolves based on the state of the market, such as buyer characteristics and the number of buyers or capacity. As a result, each buyer may receive an individual price offer.

Experience good is a product that must be consumed to determine its quality. Quality can't be observed by just inspecting the product.

Freemium pricing is a form of versioning where the lowest-quality version is free and higher-quality versions are for fee.

Nonlinear pricing might take the form of bundling or quantity discounts, or involve subscription or membership fees. Then price of the bundle does not grow linearly with the number of products in the bundle. It often includes a **two-part tariff** where the first part is an "entry fee" and the second part is a unit price.

Personalized pricing is first-degree price discrimination whereby the seller makes individual offers to each buyer in the hope of capturing much of the total consumer surplus.

Price discrimination means offering different prices to different buyers. The product offered may be the same or have slightly different versions of the same.

Segmentation, or group pricing, is third-degree price discrimination where the seller attempts to segment the market according to observable characteristics of the buyers that are correlated with their willingness to pay.

Versioning is second-degree price discrimination and requires that the seller designs multiple packages or bundles of the product that have sufficiently different features and that separate buyers with a high WTP from those with a low WTP.

Willingness to pay is the basis for all types of "value pricing." Then the seller seeks to discover how much each potential buyer is willing to pay for a product.

DISCUSSION QUESTIONS

NatLangPro offers a data analysis package that helps analysts complete Natural Language Processing tasks very easily. It sells the package to individual analysts, small boutique consulting firms, and large corporate customers.

1. In which market could it maximize profits by engaging in personalized pricing?
2. NatLangPro estimated that its overall demand function (measured in millions of units sold) is $P = 300-2Q$ in the Indian market and $P = 200-3Q$ in the Italian market. The annual fixed cost of operation (marketing and R&D) is $100M but the product is distributed directly from the website for a $0 variable cost. What is the optimal price for each of the markets and what pricing strategy do you recommend the company deploy?
3. After more careful market research, NatLangPro found that within each geographic market, individuals, SMEs (small and medium-sized enterprises) and corporations are interested in different features. Individuals tend to want just a GUI (Graphic User Interface) and basic analytics and are at the most willing to pay $50. SMEs want GUI, basic analytics, and the visualization package for a maximum price of $500. Corporations usually want the GUI, advanced analytics, visualization, and a 24h/7 online chat service and are willing to pay $2000. Half of the Indian market consists of SMEs, 40 percent of individuals, and 10 percent of corporations. Half of the Italian market consists of individuals, 30 percent of SMEs, and 20 percent of corporations.
   a. Why should the company not offer three feature levels: basic (GUI, basic analytics) for $50, medium (GUI, basic analytics, visualization) for $500, and advanced (GUI, advanced analytics, visualization, and chat) for $2000?
   b. Describe how the optimal offers for each country would differ.

The hiphop artist Jebz is contemplating how to price their new album of 10 songs. We previously learned that 50,000 of her fans are willing to pay £5 for the album, and 50,000 are not willing to pay anything at all. However, in a small-scale promotion Jebz's marketing team noticed that 40 percent of the fans who were initially not willing to pay anything changed their minds to paying £3 for the album after they were able to download the hit song "Ya Hipsta" for free. Of these low-WTP fans, 10,000 are college students.

1. What pricing strategies would you consider for the album?
2. Would a freemium strategy make sense? How much would the high-WTP fans pay?
3. How much consumer surplus would the high-WTP fans gain under the freemium strategy? How would you change their offer to entice them to spend their whole WTP?
4. Would a segmentation strategy generate more revenue than the freemium strategy?

FURTHER READING

Bhargava, Hemant K. and Choudhary, Vidyanand (2008). When is versioning optimal for information goods? *Management Science* 54(5): 1029–1035.

Boudreau, Kevin J., Jeppesen, Lars Bo, and Miric, Milan (2021). Competing on freemium: digital competition with network effects. *Strategic Management Journal* 43: 1374–1401.

Choudhary, Vidyanand, Ghose, Anindya, Mukhopadhyay, Tridas, and Rajanm, Uday (2005). Personalized pricing and quality differentiation. *Management Science* 51(7): 1120–1130.

Gu, Xian, Kannan, P.K., and Ma, Liye (2018). Selling the Premium in Freemium. *Journal of Marketing* 82(6): 10–27.

Kannan, P.K. and Kopalle, Praveen K. (2001). Dynamic pricing on the internet: importance and implications for consumer behavior. *International Journal of Electronic Commerce* 5(3): 63–83.

Richards, Timothy J., Liaukonyte, Jura, and Streletskaya, Nadia A. (2016). Personalized pricing and price fairness. *International Journal of Industrial Organization* 44 (January): 138–153.

Shapiro, Carl and Varian, Hal R. (1998). Versioning: the smart way to sell information. *Harvard Business Review* November–December: 106–114.

6 Consumption of Information

6.1   Cognitive Biases and Digital Markets

"Human minds, brilliant but buggy," said the famous psychologist Daniel Kahneman.[1] Indeed, human cognition has evolved over millennia to respond swiftly to various kinds of dangers – spiders, snakes, heights, and predators in the forest. We respond to such physical threats intuitively and decisively. These cognitive features probably kept the human population alive and thriving through difficult conditions.

Our brilliant minds are decidedly more "buggy" when it comes to information processing in modern, especially digital, environments. Behavioral economics has highlighted many **cognitive biases** (see Table 6.1) that afflict our economic decision making. We may choose people like ourselves for important jobs, even though individuals with very different characteristics might be ideal, or we may focus on irrelevant characteristics such as ethnicity or accent in such situations. Such "homophily" was helpful in primitive situations where kinship guaranteed loyalty and protected "our" group from invaders, but it is not likely to make our business organizations more effective in the global economy. We may also focus on recent, available information because our brains interpret that as more relevant for the current situation, whereas, optimally, we might benefit from a deeper dive into collecting more representative or comprehensive data and analyzing it appropriately. Even the way information is presented influences whether we believe it. Overall, our brains would much rather jump to conclusions that seem "right," that is, confirm our expectations.

Kahneman explains that we can think of such intuitive judgment and decision making through his concept of "System 1." System 1 decisions depend on where the presented information originates, whether it is framed positively or negatively, whether it confirms our previous beliefs, and whether it is complex or straightforward. In short, we tend to be biased toward easy, intuitive, prejudiced, simple, positive, shallow, and familiar explanations. Everything else is hard work.

In fact, most humans, most of the time, like to avoid deep thinking. Thinking through complex problems is tedious and uncomfortable, and it is taxing to concentrate for long periods of time. However, this is what the "System 2" cognitive processes require. System 2 is a slower thinking process that does not cut corners

---

[1] Kahneman, Daniel (2011). *Thinking Fast and Slow*. New York: Farrar, Straus and Giroux.

Table 6.1 Some common cognitive biases

Effect	Description
Anchoring	Tendency to get "stuck" on the initial piece of information.
Availability	Tendency to focus on available information, including the most recent or most memorable information.
Confirmation	Tendency to prefer information that confirms preconception.
Endowment	Tendency to value something that we own more than we would be willing to pay for it if we didn't own it. That is, the willingness to pay < willingness to accept for an object.
Framing	Tendency to draw different conclusions from information depending on how it is presented.
Loss aversion	Disutility from a loss is perceived as greater than the utility of gaining the same amount.
Rare events	Tendency to exaggerate the expected utility from low-probability events.
Representativeness	Tendency to form assumptions about an individual based on the group that the individual represents.
Psychological ownership	Tendency to value objects one has created higher than things one has not expended effort for. Related to the "IKEA effect," which is the tendency to value objects greater having constructed or compiled them.

Note: Behavioral scientists have characterized several common patterns of behavior that influence our decision making and often make us depart from objectively rational choices.

but tries to ensure that the facts add up to a logical, replicable, and verifiable solution. This process takes more time and effort and is thus costlier to individuals and organizations, but, for decisions that truly matter such as hiring new talent, a thorough assessment is worth it.

Thorough assessment usually requires ample data. In a study of decision-making biases in hiring, Hoffman, Kahn, and Li[2] explored whether automated recommendations based on data make better or worse decisions than experienced managers. While managers might be subject to the cognitive biases described above, they might also have a better tacit understanding of the job requirements than those generated via analyses of information that can be codified into a computerized recommendation system. So, do managers or computers make better hiring decisions?

In sad news for managers, the study suggests that the adoption of an automated job testing procedure improved hiring outcomes in terms of tenure and productivity. Those HR managers who frequently overruled the recommendation of the automated test result systematically and significantly degraded their hiring outcomes. In other words, managers were better off relying on the test result alone,

---

[2] Hoffman, M., Kahn, L., and Li, D. (2018). Discretion in hiring. *Quarterly Journal of Economics* 133(2): 765–800.

and whenever they overruled the test based on their interview or other information about the applicant, they tended to hire less suitable employees. Along the same lines, Rivera[3] provides evidence that shared leisure activities between the job candidates and the interviewers such as golf or jogging influence hiring decisions. Although it is nice to connect with colleagues about hobbies, sharing a leisure interest is unlikely to improve productivity. These studies highlight the potential for automating business decisions that are repeated and associated with significant amounts of data.

6.2   Valuation of Information

In addition to evaluating emerging information using quick heuristics that lead to biased decisions, we tend not to be very good at commercially valuing information. In contrast to many physical objects, the value of information depends greatly on the context in which it would be used. Furthermore, due to its nature as an experience good, information can be difficult to evaluate before access. This was the classical challenge of Arrow's Paradox (cf. Chapter 5). Because of such evaluation problems related to information, consumers tend to undervalue information before they experience it, leading to depressed values of willingness to pay.

On the seller side, information goods might be overvalued for multiple reasons. One reason is psychological ownership arising from originally creating the information.[4] As we saw in Chapter 5, information goods can be very labor-intensive and costly to create. Writing a book, creating and recording an album's worth of songs, or compiling a large database of, say, weather observations can take hundreds of hours of labor. Feeling "ownership" of the created material is natural and common, and can lead to valuations that significantly exceed those of potential buyers. Interestingly, the intellectual property law doctrine called "sweat of the brow" states that content or data that involves painstaking effort to create, even if it is not particularly novel or original, such as a telephone directory, can be protected under copyright. A creator of such a good can legally exclude others from copying such a compilation, even though the regular copyright applies only to original creations. The law thus, in a sense, recognizes psychological ownership of information goods and awards limited legal rights to exclude other users and protect the material. However, copyrights do not resolve the potential market failure arising from divergent valuations between sellers and buyers.

---

[3] Rivera, Lauren (2012). Hiring as cultural matching: the case of elite professional service firms *American Sociological Review* 77: 999–1022.

[4] Morewedge, Carey K., Monga, Ashwani, Palmatier, Robert W., Shu, Suzanne B., and Small, Deborah A (2021). Evolution of consumption: A psychological ownership framework. *Journal of Marketing* 85(1): 196–218.

Information can also create a situation described as **Curse of Knowledge**.[5] Curse of knowledge makes it difficult to ignore information that one possesses, even when it is advantageous to do so. For example, when a seller is estimating the willingness to pay of a potential buyer, the seller may have much more detailed information about the product than the buyer, creating a situation of **asymmetric information**. This is particularly pertinent when the product is complex or sophisticated, or has other aspects of unobservable quality such as a technological invention. Upon reading a patent, the buyer may have a rather limited view of how the invention works and what it might be used for, whereas the seller as the inventor of the technology may have explored many potential use cases and be able to estimate its value. It might be difficult to credibly communicate all those use case details to the buyer, and, hence, the seller's and buyer's valuations of the invention might diverge.

Furthermore, the seller's knowledge might be "cursed" in that they do not comprehend the buyer's information set regarding the invention. If the seller perceives the invention as much more valuable than the buyer does, and does not understand the buyer's basis of valuation, a market failure may result whereby the buyer does not accept the seller's offer. It is difficult to "un-know" things that one already knows.

The Curse of Knowledge can also lead to a hindsight bias. At the time of making decisions a person may have less detailed information about the situation than later on. After the fact, when evaluating the course of action, it is difficult to set aside the information that was obtained after the incident. As a result, hindsight bias may arise and influence subsequent decisions such as damage awards in legal trials.

Asymmetric information and the Curse of Knowledge can systematically bias the valuation of digital information goods. Usually the biases make sellers value the good too high and buyers value the good too low. Divergence of valuations can create a market failure whereby very little trading takes place even though there might be social value to be gained from exchanging information goods.

6.3 Judgment and News Consumption Online

Data and analysis can often overcome the limitations of human judgment. Nevertheless, human judgment may be particularly deficient in digital environments like websites and social media. These environments are highly conducive to System 1-type intuitive action, as opposed to thorough deliberation à la system 2. Online environments are designed for quick flipping, scrolling, clicking, and browsing instead of deep concentrated immersion in a complex topic. In social networks such as Facebook, we tend to spend time looking for short-form

---

[5] Camerer, Colin, Loewenstein, George, and Weber, Martin (1989). The Curse of Knowledge in economic settings: an experimental analysis. *Journal of Political Economy* 97(5): 1232–1254.

entertainment and fun when we are bored, not seeking reliable information about a specific topic. Furthermore, the business logic of such applications is based on making us stay on the service for a long period in order to present as many ads as possible. Hence, they bombard us with outrageous material such as clickbait that appeals to curiosity, disgust, intrigue, and suspicion. While such topics keep us "engaged," the website or app can serve us advertisements. According to Pew Research, more than 70 percent of US adults go online several times daily, and a quarter of US adults are online almost constantly, a behavior resembling an addiction.[6]

When we consume information online quickly and half-heartedly, we tend to be gullible and prone to poor judgment. It is very easy to manipulate images and make up stories to create credible content, especially about topics that are associated with political tensions and about which people have very strong feelings, such as immigration and political movements such as Black Lives Matter.[7] With the arrival of deepfake technology, video manipulation is becoming feasible, too.[8]

Internet "trolls" can exploit this human gullibility and either earn advertising revenue or exploit heightening societal tensions, such as in the case of Russian internet operations that posed as Black Lives Matter activists on Facebook. As explained by the US Representative and Member of the House Intelligence Committee Adam Schiff, Russian trolls understood that Facebook "algorithms tend to accentuate content that is fear- or anger-based, that helps it pick up an audience, go viral, and be amplified." When we are emotional about an issue, we are even more gullible and less likely to carefully scrutinize the sources and factual basis of a news item. Hence situations like "pizzagate" can arise, whereby a man believed social media conspiracy theories about Hillary Clinton running a pedophile ring out of a pizza restaurant in Washington, DC. He raided the place with a rifle to "liberate" the children. Luckily no children were in the restaurant and no one got hurt.[9]

While such examples of information consumption biases are extreme, the fact that most citizens in industrialized countries consume news from social media

---

[6] Perrin, A. and Aktske, S. (2021). About 3 in 10 US adults say they are 'almost constantly' online. Pew Research Center March 26, 2021. Retrieved from www.pewresearch.org/fact-tank/2018/03/14/about-a-quarter-of-americans-report-going-online-almost-constantly/ in August 2022.

[7] Silverman, C. (2017). Black Lives Matter is bringing food to victims of Harvey but people are sharing a false story about BLM blocking erelief effors. Buzz Feed News, September 1, 2017. Retrieved from www.buzzfeednews.com/article/craigsilverman/conservative-fb-pages-spreading-false-claim-about-blm in August 2022.

[8] Roose, K. (2018). Here come the fake videos, too. *The New York Times*, March 4, 2018. Retrieved from www.nytimes.com/2018/03/04/technology/fake-videos-deepfakes.html in January 2022.

[9] See Glaser, A. (2018). Russian trolls were obsessed with Black Lives Matter. Slate, May 11, 2018. https://slate.com/technology/2018/05/russian-trolls-are-obsessed-with-black-lives-matter.html and Wells, G. and Seetharaman, D. (2017). New Facebook data shows Russians targeted users by race, religion, politics. Wall Street Journal, November 1, 2017. www.wsj.com/articles/russian-ads-targeted-facebook-users-by-profile-1509563354?mod=djemalertTECH and Douglas, W. and Washburn, M. (December 6, 2016). Religious zeal drives N.C. man in "Pizzagate." *The Courier-Tribune*, The Charlotte Observer. Retrieved in August 2022.

does give rise to problematic commercial and political issues. According to the Pew Research Center, six in ten Americans get news from social media, most often from Reddit, Twitter, or Facebook. By 2018, news sourcing from social media exceeded that from print newspapers.[10] Most Americans also recognized that the fake news phenomenon had left people confused. Nevertheless, people trusted themselves to be able to recognize fake news.[11] Perhaps another form of cognitive bias was at play there. As a result, a national poll in 2020 showed that a significant share of US citizens believed Qanon's conspiracy theories.[12]

Fake news is defined as news articles that are intentionally and verifiably false and could mislead readers. Lower entry barriers to mass media and the suitability of social media for dissemination of questionable material facilitate and magnify this problematic phenomenon. The prevalence of smartphones and expanding broadband availability also contribute to its spread.

Analysts have pinpointed both commercial and political motivations for fake news: fake news businesses may either attempt to profit from advertising or manipulate political opinions. Gentzkow et al.[13] presented the first economic model of fake news. In their framework, consumers enjoy both actual knowledge and news reports that are consistent with their prior expectations. In other words, we like news that confirms our worldview. Consumers tend to choose news outlets that maximize their utility by providing valuable knowledge and enjoyable – and agreeable – content.

In this scenario, if truth is difficult to reveal, rational consumers will judge news to be of higher quality if it is closer to their expectations. They may thus prefer news that confirms their views, because of the psychological utility they obtain. When such preferences affect consumers' decision making, even mainstream media will have a "slant." Practically speaking, all media is biased to some degree, by choosing or emphasizing reports that their readers are more likely to prefer, because profit-motivated outlets will attempt to maximize the number of readers and either sell them subscriptions or serve them advertising. While this does not usually imply that the mainstream media lie about the facts, they may

---

[10] See Pew Research Center (2018). Social media outpaces print newspapers in the U.S. as a news source. Pes Research, December 10, 2018. Retrieved from www.pewresearch.org/fact-tank/2018/12/10/social-media-outpaces-print-newspapers-in-the-u-s-as-a-news-source/ in August 2022.

[11] See Pew Research Center (2016). News use across social media platforms 2016. Pew Research, May 26, 2016. Retrieved from www.journalism.org/2016/05/26/news-use-across-social-media-platforms-2016/ in August 2022.

[12] See Ipsos (2020). More than 1 in 3 Americans believe a "deep state" is working to undermine Trump. NPR Ipsos poll, December 30, 2020 www.ipsos.com/en-us/news-polls/npr-misinformation-123020 and Pew Research Center (2016). News use across social media platforms 2016. Pew Research May 26, 2016. Retrieved from www.journalism.org/2016/05/26/news-use-across-social-media-platforms-2016/ in January 2022.

[13] Gentzkow, Matthew, Shapiro, Jesse M., and Stone, Daniel F. (2016). Media Bias in the Marketplace: Theory. Ch. 14 in *Handbook of Media Economics, vol. 1B* (Amsterdam: Elsevier), edited by Anderson, Simon, Waldofgel, Joel, and Stromberg, David.

select, embellish, or style their reporting based on the preferences of their audience. Traditionally, major media outlets have attempted to provide truthful reporting because they cared about their long-standing reputation.

Fake news operators, in contrast, take advantage of both the nature of information consumption in the digital environment and the diversity of consumers' preferences. They make no effort to report accurately, hence they substantially lower the fixed cost of production – they just make up the content. They also do not attempt to build a reputation for quality, which for real news outlets takes a long time and requires great investments. They simply manufacture outrageous content in hopes of a large volume of clicks that enables advertising revenues to flow in from ad auction systems. Such business models can be highly profitable, as recent examples suggest.[14]

However, fake news comes with significant social costs. By exacerbating the mistaken beliefs of consumers (citizens), these businesses make it easier for other fake news outlets to enter and increase skepticism regarding legitimate news producers. The boundary between fake and real news becomes increasingly blurred, and consumers' confusion can be politically exploited. As a consequence, foreign powers have increased their attempts to stir outrage and increase division to influence political outcomes in their adversary countries.[15] Ultimately, the growth of the market share of fake news vs. real news can alter the selection of election candidates and thus undermine democratic institutions. More generally, patterns of online consumption of information have contributed to the increasing fragmentation and reduced perception of the reliability of information sources, contributing to the decline of trust in mass media and heightened political polarization.

6.4   Machine Decisions

Artificial intelligence (AI) is an evolving set of computational techniques that allow computers to make decisions. **Machine learning** means that computers analyze large amounts of data to generate models and predictions without being explicitly instructed. Access to big data can thus improve the precision of predictions or decisions. A training dataset is used, first, to teach the computer about a specific set of issues, such as recognizing images. The computer is fed a large number of images, together with information about what they represent. With a large enough number of images, a computer can "learn" then to recognize and predict other images. Thus, when the computer is presented with a new set of

---

[14] See Subramaniam, S. (2017). Inside the Macedonian fake-news complex. Wired, February 15, 2017. Retrieved from www.wired.com/2017/02/veles-macedonia-fake-news/ in August 2022.

[15] Whiskeyman, A. and Berger, M. (2021). Axis of disinformation: Propaganda from Iran, Russia, and China on COVID-19. Fikra Forum Policy Analysis, February 25, 2021. Retrieved from www.washingtoninstitute.org/policy-analysis/axis-disinformation-propaganda-iran-russia-and-china-covid-19 in August 2022.

images, it will be able to predict what the images represent by interpreting the pattern of information on the image file.

While it is conceivable that enough data and processing power could be harnessed to predict "everything," applications of artificial intelligence remain narrow. For example, computers can learn to predict whether X-ray images present an image of a tumor or a normal organ. Similarly, computers can be used to generate transcripts of voice recordings or detect fraudulent transactions out of transaction data. Such applications can be very valuable, but limited to very specific sets of questions. General artificial intelligence is a long way into the future.

While computers are less likely to make intuitive, "System 1" decisions, they are not devoid of bias. Machine predictions depend on the type of training data that are used. The concern with **algorithmic bias** is that the data may in themselves contain biased outcomes. For example, the goal might be to predict successful start-up ventures based on the data about venture teams and other business features. However, the data might mainly contain ventures with white male founding teams and not be representative of more diverse sets of entrepreneurs. The computer might then predict that successful start-up ventures have white male founding teams, even though the white-maleness is not truly a characteristic that matters for innovation. There are also many examples of computers interpreting facial features of Black and Asian individuals more poorly than those of white individuals, because they are underrepresented in the data.[16] Moreover, if different demographic groups have different physiological responses to medical conditions or treatments, being underrepresented in the data can lead to dangerous predictions about diagnoses or treatment paths. This is already well known from the insufficient clinical testing of drugs on women leading to their higher mortality.[17] In another study, Black patients were assigned systematically lower medical risk scores than white patients by an algorithm used to make referrals to more advanced medical care.[18] Researchers found that the bias was created by including as a factor the patient's previous year's total healthcare costs, and that Black patients had used significantly less healthcare for similar medical conditions. The scholars concluded that, as a result, systemic racism that caused Blacks to consume significantly less healthcare for the same conditions was effectively baked into the recommendation system. We can see that existing societal biases can be perpetuated and even amplified when decisions are automated.

---

[16] Simonite, T. (2019). The best algorithms struggle to recognize black faces equally. Wired, July 22, 2019. Retrieved from www.wired.com/story/best-algorithms-struggle-recognize-black-faces-equally/ in August 2022.

   Singer, N. and Metz, C. (2019). Many facial-recognition systems are biased, says U.S. study. *The New York Times*, December 19, 2019. Retrieved from www.nytimes.com/2019/12/19/technology/facial-recognition-bias.html in August 2022.

[17] Davio, K. (2018). Women are still underrepresented in clinical trials for cardiovascular disease drugs. AJMC, May 2, 2018. Retrieved from www.ajmc.com/view/women-are-still-underrepresented-in-clinical-trials-for-cardiovascular-disease-drugs in August 2022.

[18] Ledford, H. (2019). Millions of Black people affected by racial bias in health-care algorithms. Nature, October 24, 2019. Retrieved from www.nature.com/articles/d41586-019-03228-6 in August 2022.

Considering machines are catching up with or surpassing humans in many specific applications in the next 10–15 years, where might we expect humans to continue to have an advantage over machines? Most experts believe it will be more difficult to automate decisions involving creativity or emotion. Computers are good at answering questions but not at asking important and meaningful questions. Therefore, humans will have an edge as entrepreneurs, innovators, scientists, and creators. They can excel in activities requiring the ability to persuade, motivate, inspire, and lead other people. They will also be preferred in tasks that entail emotional connection and caring. Overall, the early evidence of the impact of AI on labor demand is negative: AI adoption is associated with the automation of some tasks formerly performed by labor (Acemoglu et al. 2022). Is your job AI proof?

KEY IDEAS

- Digital environments accentuate our inclination to rush to conclusions and accept intuitive explanations. However, decisions based on quick and superficial analyses are often biased or incorrect.
- Computers can avoid superficial explanations and using intuition, but the quality of their analyses depends on the quality of the underlying data.
- People often exhibit cognitive biases, and computers often exhibit algorithmic biases. These two types of biases have different sources and implications.
- Fake news relies on cognitive biases of online consumers of information.
- Techniques of machine learning are progressing rapidly, but their applications remain specific. General artificial intelligence is not expected for a long time.

DEFINITIONS

Algorithmic bias arises from non-representative data used for statistical analyses and leads to erroneous, biased inference.

Artificial Intelligence is a set of computer methods that allow computers to analyze (learn from) data, generate predictions of outcomes, and recommend or make decisions.

Asymmetric information afflicts many economic transactions and relationships. A seller might have more information about a product than a buyer does, and they might either strategically withhold the information, or they might not be able to credibly share the information even if they wanted to.

Cognitive biases induce people to make decisions that are irrational, or against their best interest. They are particularly prominent when we make quick decisions based on intuition or perception, rather than based on a thorough analysis.

Curse of Knowledge is a cognitive bias whereby people might not be able to understand how their gained knowledge influences their decisions or perceptions of a situation.

Fake news is verifiably false information presented as news with the intention to mislead.

Machine learning is a subfield of artificial intelligence where computers use training datasets to learn models or recognize patterns that the computers can subsequently use to predict outcomes in other datasets.

DISCUSSION QUESTIONS

1. In your experience (or based on some online browsing), how do clickbait creators take advantage of cognitive biases such as confirmation, framing, or rare events? Can you think of other instances where commercial entities attempt to influence decision making by exploiting cognitive biases?

2. Both asymmetric information between sellers and buyers and the Curse of Knowledge can create a divergence of valuations of the market participants, leading to few sellers finding willing buyers. Why are information markets particularly prone to these types of problems? As a seller in such a market, how would you address each source of inefficiency?

3. The traditional news company NewsForYou has an annual fixed cost of $1 million whereas a fake news operator MakinItUp's annual fixed cost is just $100,000. Both news companies generate revenue from advertising at the rate of $3 CPM (per 1,000 ad impressions, i.e., each time the advertisement is shown to a reader). Their variable costs are zero. Their front pages impress five different ads to each page visitor. On average, users visit the site 10 times per year. How many users does each news creator need to break even?

4. How can a traditional news organization compete against a fake news organization? Think about the revenues and costs in Question 3. Which ones can the NewsForYou more easily improve and how?

FURTHER READING

Acemoglu, Daron, Autor, David, Hazell, Jonathon, and Restrepo, Pascual (2022). Artificial intelligence and jobs: evidence from online vacancies. *Journal of Labor Economics* 40(S1): S293–S340.

Allcott, Hunt and Gentzkow, Matthew (2017). Social media and fake news in the 2016 election. *Journal of Economic Perspectives* 31(2): 211–236.

Camerer, Colin, Loewenstein, George, and Weber, Martin (1989). The Curse of Knowledge in economic settings: an experimental analysis. *Journal of Political Economy* 97(5): 1232–1254.

Haselton, Martie G., Nettle, Daniel, and Murray, Damian R. (2015). The Evolution of Cognitive Bias. Ch. 41 in *The Handbook of Evolutionary Psychology*, D.M. Buss (Ed.). Hoboken: Wiley & Sons.

Kahneman, Daniel (2011). *Thinking Fast and Slow*. Farrar, Straus and Giroux (New York,).

Morewedge, Carey K., Monga Ashwani, Palmatier Robert W., Shu Suzanne B., and Small Deborah A. (2021). Evolution of consumption: a psychological ownership framework. *Journal of Marketing* 85(1): 196–218.

7 Building and Commercializing Data Assets

Is data the fuel of the digital economy? Data[1] have many uses, such as reducing information asymmetries, improving resource management, and identifying causal effects of product designs, policies, or strategies using artificial intelligence and statistical analyses. Data can encompass location, behavior, retail, health, administrative, and sensor-based industrial data. In many cases, data are integral to digital innovation. For example, in smart seaports, data about arrivals, departures, location, and cargo must be shared to coordinate the entire port ecosystem. Similarly, in any "smart space" (smart cities, airports, or even cruise ships), data about the location of people and vehicles must be collected to analyze traffic patterns and to predict and suggest services that citizens or travelers may need. In physical operations, analyses of data from sensor-enhanced engines can predict the need for maintenance or replacement of parts. Because of its increasing volume and importance, the data economy has become a central element of new digital policy frameworks such as that articulated by the European Commission.[2] Futuristic scenarios since 2006 have proclaimed data as the new oil.[3]

Although any information good such as text and images can be transformed into data, here we will focus on observational data that have not yet been significantly processed or manipulated, for example, social, laboratory, operations, and measurement data compiled by humans or computers. Evolving communication networks create expanding opportunities to measure real-time economic activity, such as social behavior or performance of production equipment. This chapter explores how to deploy instruments to measure, adjust, and analyze business activities, and how to commercialize the resulting data through internal or external channels. By contributing to a better understanding of the drivers of business

---

[1] In scientific writing, the word "data" is usually used as a plural term. The singular form of data is "datum." Cf. Merriam-Webster dictionary: www.merriam-webster.com/dictionary/data#usage-1 and Krupa, T. (2012). Data is, or data are? APA Style Blog, July 26, 2012. Retrieved from https://blog.apastyle.org/apastyle/2012/07/data-is-or-data-are.html in August 2022.

[2] *The Economist* (2017). Data is giving rise to a new economy. *The Economist*, May 6, 2017. Retrieved from www.economist.com/briefing/2017/05/06/data-is-giving-rise-to-a-new-economy in August 2022. European Commission (2022).

A European strategy for data. Shaping Europe's digital future, June 7, 2022. Retrieved from https://ec.europa.eu/digital-single-market/en/policies/building-european-data-economy in August 2022.

[3] Arthur, C. (2013). Tech giants may be huge, but nothing matches big data. *The Guardian*, August 23, 2013. Retrieved from www.theguardian.com/technology/2013/aug/23/tech-giants-data in August 2022.

performance, data can help improve and innovate new products and services, and potentially generate additional revenue streams.

Instruments are devices, robots, or software that detect and collect data about people, objects, or the environment. We can think of mobile phones or even modern vehicles as instruments because they create a trackable signal about where we are and what we are doing. Our computers are constantly connected to social and communication networks and also perform as instruments because cloud servers track our location, activities, and communication with other people on commercial platforms. In the physical realm, devices such as thermometers, anemometers, gyroscopes, and accelerometers are instruments for detecting the conditions in some environments, and they can be connected to a communication network and tracked remotely.

Instrumentation has been happening for a long time in increasingly automated production systems, and communication networks such as the wireless internet enabled collecting larger amounts of data anywhere and sharing the data for immediate analysis and decision making. As a result, an explosion of data has been taking place: According to the IBM, 90 percent of all data existing in 2012 was created in the previous two years.[4] By 2020, there were over 20 billion connected devices, with IoT devices growing about 20 percent from the previous year.[5] More than 20 exabytes of data – an exabyte has 18 zeros – were generated yearly from transistors.

There is thus a great opportunity to innovate using data collection, analytics, decision making, and sharing. Wireless network capabilities can greatly speed up the collection, dissemination, and analysis of collected data. Firms urgently need to re-imagine their business operations from a data collection perspective to shift toward data-enhanced or even data-driven decision making – a process often called **digital transformation**: using information and communication technologies to enhance an organization to such a significant degree that its value proposition and organizational identity are redefined.[6] One way to get started on this is envisioning how to create a digital twin of critical operations.

Digital twins are digital replicas of assets or activities using modeling and sensors to create digital representations. Digital twins are not new; engineering teams in various industries have used 3D renderings of computer-aided design models, asset models, and process simulations for years. However, faster wireless networks and the resulting availability of real-time data enable much more detailed and dynamic digital representations. When sensors collect data from a

---

[4] Cf. www.livevault.com/2-5-quintillion-bytes-of-data-are-created-every-day/ retrieved in August 2022. The original IBM webpage is no longer available.

[5] Data retrieved from www.statista.com/statistics/1101442/iot-number-of-connected-devices-worldwide/ in August 2022.

[6] Wessel, Lauri, Baiyere, Abayomi, Ologeanu-Taddei, Roxana, Cha, Jonghyuk, and Blegind Jensen, Tina (2021). Unpacking the difference between digital transformation and IT-enabled organizational transformation. *Journal of the Association for Information Systems* 22(1): article 6.

connected device, the sensor data can be used to continuously update the digital twin. The digital twin becomes a real-time accurate copy of a physical object's properties and states.

For instance, digital twins of physical assets such as power-generation turbines, jet engines, and locomotives are becoming common when the assets are very valuable and when downtime would be very costly. In service businesses, digitally tracking user behavior can create a real-time model of the service operations. This enables predicting the performance impact of investments or simulating implications of product or process improvements. Digital twins thus can facilitate better measuring, modeling, predicting, optimizing, and ultimately understanding of business performance. Continuously improving learning models of performance drivers can be valuable for the firm itself and for its ecosystem partners.

7.1 Building Data Value

In many situations, (big) data-driven decisions are of higher quality than heuristic decisions made by individuals based on small data and experience, but there are risks to relying on data and algorithms for critical decision making. Therefore, it is extremely important to collect appropriate data and use it wisely.

We define a unit of data as a "codified observation fixed in a tangible medium."[7] This definition suggests that data are distinguished from information because they consist of individual or streams of observations about the state of something – a person, an object, or an environment. Observations that are not "codified" are not data. If a person simply senses a temperature without articulating somehow in terms of a specific observation such as "warm" or "25 degrees Celsius," that sensation is not codified into a statement. It also needs to be "fixed in a tangible medium" such as paper, a computer drive, or a pelt, in order to be tradeable and thereby economically relevant.

Information goods, in contrast to data goods, can be defined as a "codified expression fixed in a tangible medium." This definition is closely related to the definition of copyrightable content in the United States. Information that is expression not only fixed in a tangible medium but also original can be protected with copyrights. Expression may consist of observations but contains more than just observations. Expression contains a narrative, connection, or interpretation beyond the observations it contains.

The third type of digital good relevant to our analyses is algorithms. Algorithms consist of instructions for achieving a specific outcome. Computer software

---

[7] Thomas, Llewellyn D W, Leiponen, Aija, and Koutroumpis, Pantelis (2023). Profiting from Data: Business Models for Data Products. Chapter 14 in C. Cennamo, G. B. Dagnino and F. Zhu: *Elgar Handbook of Research on Digital Strategy*. Cheltenham: Edward Elgar.

contains instructions for the computer to complete calculations or other actions such as presenting text or images on a screen. As such, software consists of "codified instructions fixed in a tangible medium." If the instructions are not clearly codified or are not fixed in a medium, they are unlikely to be tradeable and therefore economically valuable.

Data and information are closely related goods. The data value chain illustrates the process of turning data first into information and then into knowledge that improves business performance. Instrumentation is the set of actions to enable the gathering of data from the people, objects, or environments involved in products, services, or processes. Identifying the information needed, determining how to collect the relevant data, then analyzing and interpreting the data is critical to success but not a simple set of tasks. Developing a data-driven organization is a challenging process of experimentation, (machine) learning, and continued digitization.

Data building. In the data-building stage, value is created out of raw data (such as observations of financial transactions or the weather) by transforming them into an analytical format, making them structured and available for analysis. There is usually a large initial fixed cost of structuring data from its original format to an analytical format (see Figure 7.1).

Information creation. The creation of information involves identifying insights about the relationships among variables in data, where analytical processes such as statistics, sentiment analysis, or machine learning applied to data generate information that can be shared, adopted, and applied. There is also a substantial initial fixed cost of designing the models and methods of generating insightful information.

Production and operations. In the third stage of data building, knowledge is created from the use of information, and the full economic value of data is realized when insights from information are applied in an organizational context where they inform and enhance the production of goods or services. At this stage, there may be significant fixed implementation costs but the cost of an additional (marginal) analytical insight is low. These insights may enhance the revenue potential of the products and services offered or the production efficiency of the firm. Both increase its profit potential.

In summary, data is a raw material for information, insights, and, ultimately, better decisions and business performance. It can be commercialized via the market for data, the market for information, or the product and service market. Internet of Things technologies enable businesses to collect more relevant and a greater quantity of data about physical, social, and digital activities than ever before. The digital transformation challenge for any business is to discover how the data can best be collected, structured, modeled, analyzed, and used to inform decisions. Data in themselves are rarely valuable without the processes to build information and knowledge to support business performance. Once such processes have been developed, they can provide lasting benefits through improved productivity, quality, and market responsiveness for low additional cost.

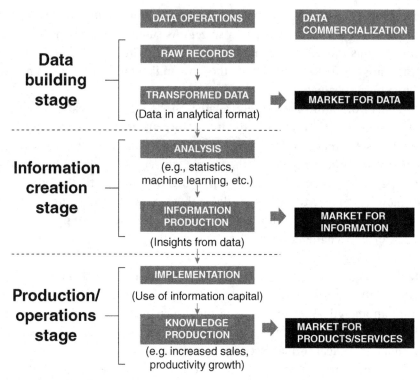

Figure 7.1 Data value chain

Note: Raw data are rarely valuable as is; their value is enhanced by a cumulative process of data building, information building, and, ultimately, knowledge building. Data can be commercialized after transformation to an analytical format, after analyses that generate insights, or after the insights have been implemented in operations to generate better products or more efficient processes.

Adapted based on Chebli, O., Goodridge, P., and Haskel, J. (2015). Measuring activity in big data: new estimates of big data employment in the UK market sector. *Imperial College Business School Discussion Paper*. Imperial College Business School: London, UK. Retrieved from https://spiral .imperial.ac.uk/bitstream/10044/1/25158/2/Goodridge%202015-04.pdf in August 2022.

7.2   Instrumentation: Building the First Digital Twin

Getting started with instrumentation and building the first digital twin of an activity can be daunting. It makes sense to begin by exploring whether there are valuable existing data streams that are reasonably easy to collect, or whether new sensors or APIs will need to be installed to capture and analyze entirely new types of data. In digital communication systems, instruments can sometimes be available for free. The Waze app for mapping and traffic information was an example of that. Waze was a software application available for downloading to mobile phones, so its adoption was voluntary. When the app was active on a phone with a GPS receiver, it constantly sent location information to the Waze central server to be anonymized and aggregated. This gave Waze information about the mobility patterns of all users. Compared against mapping data, the system could detect where users were and how fast they were moving. Users could also upload information about accidents and road construction. Waze then predicted traffic speeds for users of Waze, and later also for users of Google Maps after Google acquired the company. Traffic data was thus crowd-sourced, analyzed, connected with insights, and served back to the community in the form of a navigation system.

A similar idea was behind another mobile app, OpenSignal. OpenSignal collected network coverage information from mobile phones. Similar to Waze, users downloaded the app and allowed their phones to detect wireless telecom signal strength and constantly send the information back to the central server. OpenSignal could then aggregate very detailed information about wireless telecommunications coverage. Their data have been very helpful in demonstrating true wireless coverage around the world.

While Waze and OpenSignal are fascinating examples of instrumentation on the cheap, in most cases, sensor networks need to be purpose-built at significant expense. Wireless sensor networks are spatially distributed autonomous sensors. They can be used to monitor physical or environmental conditions such as temperature, sound, or pressure. They then send the collected data through a communication network to other locations for processing.

For example, sensor networks can help monitor physical structures such as buildings or bridges. In an area with frequent seismic activity such as California, a municipality might want to monitor and evaluate the impact of seismic events on a bridge, because bridge failure is a major risk to the community. This would require combining a network of low-power sensor nodes that continuously supply performance and environmental data. The sensors might measure acceleration to assess vibration, linear displacement to measure a longitudinal movement through thermal cycles, temperature, and strain to measure forces experienced during any seismic event. Time-stamped data can be sent wirelessly to a cloud platform where it can be analyzed. Remote cloud-based visualization and analytic software tools would then allow engineers to analyze and characterize the long-term performance of the bridge components. The bridge monitoring system could also have threshold alerts that automatically notify the municipality when a predetermined condition is met. Wireless sensor networks are also widely used in other valuable but difficult-to-monitor systems such as oil and gas pipelines.[8]

To work out the data needs and the instruments that can be deployed, we can consider three main objects of instrumentation: people, things, and ambient

[8] Aalsalem, Mohammed Y., Khan, Wazir Zada, Gharibi, Wajeb, Khan, Muhammad Khurram, and Arshad, Quratulain (2018). Wireless Sensor Networks in oil and gas industry: recent advances, taxonomuy, requirements, and open challenges. *Journal of Network and Computer Applications* 113(1): 87–97. Retrieved from www.sciencedirect.com/science/article/pii/S1084804518301309 in August 2022.

conditions. People can be instrumented with embedded sensors, including medical devices; devices they carry with them, including mobile phones; and activities they carry out in digital environments where they can be identified through their IP address or registration information. In the future, people may be instrumented via facial recognition, but there are many legal and ethical complications to the wide adoption of these techniques in society.[9] Physical things can be instrumented with sensors as small as RFID (Radio Frequency Identification) tags, or they may have full-blown embedded computers, such as onboard computers in vehicles. Ambient conditions are typically measured by wirelessly connected instruments that track temperature, wind, speed, water flow, air pressure, and so on.

Instruments can also be divided into active and passive sensors. Active sensors, such as radar or ultrasound, send out an electromagnetic signal and detect a response signal that is the basis of inference about the environment. Passive sensors, such as cameras, only absorb information about the surrounding world without interacting with it directly. For example, a connected vehicle acts as an active sensor because it interacts with a wireless communication network to estimate its location. In contrast, a digital and connected thermometer inside a container simply records and transmits the temperature readings without sending any signals into a space.

An important consideration is how frequently the sensors need to upload the information. It can be very infrequent, such as once daily, or a constant reading of the measurement. This choice depends on the data needs and the cost of transfer and analysis. It does not make sense to collect much more data than is useful for the analytical purpose. Another major issue with sensors is their energy consumption. The more frequently data are collected, the more energy is consumed. Changing batteries can be very expensive if the sensors are deployed in remote locations. Some sensors are able to harvest energy from the environment, from light, motion, or heat, which helps to maintain operations, but most sensors will have a finite life.

Parmar et al. (2020) propose a process for getting started with the first digital twin. They focus on organizational digital twins, but the basic approach works for any twinning initiative. The four main steps include identifying a starting point, such as a digital template of an asset; "liberating" data from organizational silos; continuing the digitization of assets and activities; and iteratively enhancing the learning models.

Starting point. To build a digital twin of a physical asset, the digital design (Computer-Aided Design or other software) of the asset can be the starting point. Existing digital artifacts such as data streams, analytical models, and software allow the original design of the asset to be connected with data about its actual

---

[9] See Van Noorden, Richard (2020). The ethical questions that haunt facial-recognition research. *Nature* 587: 354–358. Retrieved from www.nature.com/articles/d41586-020-03187-3 in August 2022.

functioning. Once the key data streams from the physical asset to its digital model are established, then the digital twin can be periodically or continuously updated to reflect the state of the physical asset. Some useful data streams may come from external sources, for instance, data about projected demand and consumers.

Parmar et al. (ibid.) suggest that three models are needed to feed the initial template. The information model identifies data sources in the organization, including sensors and process flows, and available analytical models. The context model describes the expected behavior, such as the various states and ranges in which the measurements can be found. Finally, the impact model establishes any known interactions and correlations between the data streams. For example, the information model of an elevator door will describe its sensors; the context model lists the states and tolerances of those sensors; and the impact model describes the relationships between those states and other sensors in the environment that influence the performance of the elevator.

Data liberation. Allowing a variety of parties to interact with the data can feed the modeling and enhance the template. Parmar et al. (ibid.) describe valuable data as having "gravity" by attracting ideas and innovations. If data are not widely accessible, they cannot connect to other software and analytical models to enable new services and analytics. Nevertheless, the firm can still be selective about who has access, for example, by excluding external parties or by monitoring access. Liberating the data means avoiding data "silos" and only excluding parties who constitute a security risk.

Relentless digitization. An active search for additional digitization opportunities to improve the digital representation helps to align and complement the existing digital artifacts. The operational environment is not static and new opportunities to digitize may arise. For example, the performance models might suggest a bottleneck process that would benefit from additional instrumentation and analysis. Furthermore, collected data may be useful for many purposes and can be easily shared with different models.

Continuous learning and enhancements. The final principle considers the evolution of the digital twin from the initial information, context, and impact models. As the initial models of the operations were necessarily incomplete, they not only need to be maintained but progressively extended to describe more of, and more accurately, the process or the organization.

Recent research finds that digital transformation processes are hampered by the lack of skills and appropriate organizational roles in almost all of the surveyed organizations.[10] Parmar et al. (ibid.) considers five main roles with distinct sets of skills that are required for the successful implementation of a digital twin. Firms need to ensure that each of the five roles is present and well developed in

---

[10] Bean, R. and Davenport, T.H. (2019, February 5). Companies are failing in their efforts to become data-driven. *Harvard Business Review*. Retrieved from https://hbr.org/2019/02/companies-are-failing-in-their-efforts-to-become-data-driven in August 2022.

the organization to accomplish both the incremental development of the digital twin and its successful operation:[11]

1. The **data engineer** understands the creative ways to *capture data* and knows where to look for data inside and outside the organization.
2. The **data scientist** has a blend of *organizational and technical skills* to identify cross-cutting digital innovations. They can describe the digital value in languages that different domains within the organization understand and are often involved in identifying new digital opportunities.
3. The **source system engineer** understands the firm's digital artifacts, such as data, analytical models and software, and knows how to *integrate the artifacts* into the information, context, and impact models.
4. The **software engineer** can *create analytical models and systems* that deliver the digital twin. They understand all the data roles and can develop ideas into reality.
5. Finally, the **digital police** is concerned with the *legal, ethical, and privacy aspects* of the data and the analytical models and can guide the team with respect to the associated risks.

7.3 Commercialization of Data Assets

In this section we focus on the external commercialization of data as a tradeable commodity, as opposed to firms generating value internally by creating, transforming, analyzing, and implementing insights from data assets, ultimately leading to value being realized in the market for products and services (cf. Figure 7.1).

Data are rarely valuable alone. They are usually inputs into analytics (embedded in a software program) to generate insights that can become expressed as content-based information goods (such as a scientific report or an advertisement). Data are thus primarily **intermediate goods**, produced with the intent of being combined and transformed to create other information goods. Furthermore, data are **experience goods**, or even **credence goods**, which gives rise to challenges in verifying the quality and value of data. The value of an experience good is not observable before consumption. Most information goods, such as books or movies, are experience goods: a consumer will not know whether they like the good until they have consumed it. The quality of a credence good is difficult to evaluate even after consumption. For example, a consumer will not be able to assess the efficacy of dietary supplements, except possibly after a longer period of usage. Similarly, the

---

[11] Gartner. (2015). Staffing data science teams. Retrieved from www.gartner.com/en/documents/3086717/staffing-data-science-teams in August 2022.

Saltz, J.S. and Grady, N.W. (2017). The ambiguity of data science team roles and the need for a data science workforce framework. Paper presented at the 2017 IEEE International Conference on Big Data, December 11e14, Boston, MA, U.S.A.

Table 7.1 Complements of data in value creation	
Data complement	Description
Metadata	Data about the data, describing what the data contain and how the variables were constructed.
Provenance	A description of how the data were collected and by whom. The reputation of the collector is often a proxy for the quality of the data.
Inalienability	Data are highly inalienable when their value is inextricably connected with the data subject.
Connected data	Other streams of data that are complementary with the focal data in generating insights.
Analytics	Models, methods, and analytical techniques that facilitate drawing useful predictions from the data.
Context	Where and how the data are used to generate and implement the insights.

Note: The value of data in use depends on multiple, complementary elements that demonstrate and enhance the impact of data.

quality and verity of data can usually only be evaluated by comparing their statistical properties against similar datasets, not directly by viewing or using the data.

The strategic approach to data commercialization requires a close analysis of how data can create value for the external user. It is clear that a single observation of an online purchase or a temperature reading is not very valuable on its own. Its value depends on several additional elements such as metadata, provenance, inalienability, complementary data, analytical tools, and the needs in the context of use itself (see Table 7.1).

As described in the data value chain (Figure 7.1), the value of data grows as it is further refined, transformed, and analyzed. This value is also enhanced when the generated insights can be implemented in a real-world context. However, the insights are more valuable when the focal data are connected and jointly analyzed with complementary data (see Table 7.1). For example, online shopping data are complementary with demographic and occupational data about household members in predicting their voting behavior or their likelihood of buying a new car. Furthermore, sometimes the complementarities can be non-obvious, such as when daily patterns of water consumption in a household can provide information about the health of an elderly resident.

The data being a credence good implies that it is generally difficult to convincingly demonstrate the quality of data to a potential buyer. Providing a sub-sample of the data for inspection before the purchase decision may not fully alleviate concerns about data quality. Instead, comprehensive metadata and provenance can provide assurance that the methods of collection were appropriate and done competently by an organization known for high-quality data and high competence in manipulating data. Additionally, data providers often offer contractual commitments such as a warranty; an obligation to fix any errors or gaps in the data.

The value of data also depends on its connection to an event, a person, or another type of a subject outside of the data. All data are always "about" something – behavior, status, or performance of something or someone. For example, health data are about the health status of individuals at a particular time. Those individuals represented in the data are the data subjects, and health data are often highly inalienable from their subjects. The value of a health status observation depends very strongly on knowing exactly whose health it concerns so that appropriate analyses, diagnoses, and treatments can be applied. The value of health data is greater at the disaggregated level also for a researcher who uses the data to investigate disease patterns in a population. Individual-level data allow the researcher to connect health data with demographic, geographic, and lifestyle data to explore the causal drivers of health outcomes. City traffic data are less inalienable: traffic light optimization doesn't require information about exactly who is driving through "The Octopus" in downtown Ithaca at 5 p.m. on a Friday but about how heavy the traffic is in each direction at that time. In this case, the inalienability concerns the location rather than the owners of the vehicles moving about.

Inalienability is thus an important factor that influences the value of data but it also creates problems related to the rights to control data. Individuals and organizations alike may be concerned about the harms arising from the sharing of their confidential data. Sometimes they may contractually require that the data recipient maintains confidentiality or privacy, in which case leaking the data would be a breach of contract and allow the data subject to pursue legal channels for compensation or remedies. The data may also be kept a trade secret and if the data recipient knowingly leaks secret data they may be legally liable. However, in many cases there are no contracts or trade secrets that allow data subjects to prevent the sharing of data about them. This is why the European Union and some states in the US have instituted regimes for individuals' data rights. For example, the General Data Protection Regulation (GDPR) of the EU and the California Consumer Privacy Act (CCPA) assume that the privacy of citizens and residents is an inherent right and therefore people have rights to know what data is collected about them, decide when data about them is shared or disclosed and to whom, access their own data, request deletion of their data, and not be discriminated against for exercising such rights. Furthermore, GDPR requires explicit consent for any collection and disclosure of personal data (opt in) whereas CCPA only allows consumers to opt out of the sale of their data. GDPR also defines how organizations should protect and manage any personal data they hold. Similar personal data regulations have been adopted elsewhere, including the states of Virginia and Colorado in the US, Brazil, and, most recently, China.

The regulatory turmoil surrounding personal data reflects the difficulties of both data subjects and data holders (e.g., businesses) to control "their" data. In fact, the notion of anyone owning any data is confusing and legally problematic. In general, it is not possible to establish property rights to information, so it is not possible to own data, either. Some information goods can be partially controlled via intellectual property rights such as patents, copyrights, and trademarks or via trade secrets (which are not an intellectual property right). In particular, content and software products can be protected with copyrights, and some algorithms may also be protected with patents. However, copyrights protect only the original expression (the exact sequence of words, notes, or symbols) and not the ideas embedded in the expression. Patents do protect ideas but only technologically novel, non-obvious, and industrially applicable ones. Data can never be protected with patents, but copyrights may provide some limited protection of larger constellations of data.

However, individual observations of data are impossible to protect, and often it is impossible to even demonstrate that another party has used and shared data without permission. In many cases they can claim to have collected the data themselves. For instance, a shopping mall might collect data about shoppers in the facility and use those to attract new vendors to move in. A data business might simply visit the facility to count shoppers and collect similar data. If they did that in a number of regional shopping malls, they might sell the data to vendors evaluating where to establish a new shop. The collected data might or might not align with the data presented by the mall itself, and it would probably not be possible for the mall to keep the data business out of its facility. In fact, this is the business model of OpenSignal referenced earlier. Whereas US wireless telecommunication service providers claim to provide seamless coverage in much of the nation, in practice many wireless consumers are frequently dismayed by the lack of coverage outside of dense urban areas. OpenSignal created a way to collect these data directly from mobile phones to show how inflated those telecom coverage maps tend to be. Such data are valuable for both consumers and businesses dependent on wireless network coverage. From a telecom service provider's point of view OpenSignal is a problem though. However, if someone independently collects the coverage data, telecom companies cannot prevent them from commercializing their data. In other words, telecom companies do not control the information contained in their data, even if they keep their own data a trade secret.

In contrast, if OpenSignal had got hold of the data by a licensing transaction with a telecom provider, the latter would have had an opportunity to contractually define, and legally enforce, how OpenSignal could use and publish the data. Thus, telecom providers can partially exclude OpenSignal from using their data. Furthermore, it is often almost impossible to prevent third parties from using the data. For example, a data customer of a telecom firm might have leaked the data to a third party business who thought they received legitimate data. The telecom firm might not know how the third party got hold of the data, and may not have any legal means to prevent further use, because the third party is not in a contractual relationship with the telecom firm. Indeed, a similar case concerning real-estate data has been assessed in a US court (and settled out of court).[12]

---

[12] Collateral Analytics vs. Xome Settlement Services, Nationstar Mortgate, and Quantarium (2018). Retrieved from https://dockets.justia.com/docket/california/candce/3:2018cv00019/320931 in August 2022.

Commercialization of data assets can thus be challenging because of limited **excludability**. Consequently, much of data trading takes place bilaterally through carefully negotiated contracting. Such licensing arrangements are costly to set up, and, therefore, the assets being licensed must be quite valuable to make the deal worthwhile. Nevertheless, data about consumer behavior are being widely traded in the United States through such bilateral licensing arrangements. There are many large-scale personal data brokers, as described in a Federal Trade Commission report in 2014.[13] Such trading is not possible under the European GDPR, and it is becoming more constrained under state-level regulations such as the CCPA, although in an "opt-out" system, many consumers will not have the attention or knowledge to actually opt out if they prefer that. Nevertheless, concerns about excludability limit data trading in all industries, and there are few, if any, large-scale open platforms for data. Whereas such a platform could mitigate the costs of search, contracting, and distribution, it would accentuate the risks of breach and leakage, and therefore highly valuable data tend not to be made widely available. Provenance and excludability are critical for the preservation of value in data assets, and a large-scale digital data platform might not be conducive to them.

KEY IDEAS

- Data may be freely available or collected through sensor networks but structuring them into an analytical format is costly.
- Value in data is created by refining, connecting, analyzing and implementing data-based insights.
- Digital transformation can be initiated through the creation of a digital twin of an operation or a unit.
- Creating the first digital twin requires cumulative development from product design through production system design to feeding in real-time data for analysis and insights, even after the product or service has been sold to a consumer.
- The value of data can be realized through markets for data, markets for information, or through markets for other products and services.
- Selling or sharing data would leverage its value but markets for data are highly imperfect and inefficient because of the very incomplete excludability of data assets.
- Markets for data are primarily based on bilateral contracting between organizations of strong reputations.

DEFINITIONS

A **credence good** refers to products whose quality cannot be inferred even after consumption, such as nutritional supplements.

Data goods consist of codified observations fixed in a tangible medium.

---

[13] The FTC (2014). Data brokers: A call for transparency and accountability. May 2014. Retrieved from www.ftc.gov/system/files/documents/reports/data-brokers-call-transparency-accountability-report-federal-trade-commission-may-2014/140527databrokerreport.pdf in August 2022.

Digital transformation is a process that combines information and communication technologies to significantly improve an organization, generating a redefined value proposition and organizational identity.

Digital twin is a digital representation of a physical asset, location, or activity consisting of data streams, models, and analytical insights.

Excludability of information goods is incomplete, meaning that it is difficult for vendors to exclude rivals from copying or otherwise imitating the good.

An **experience good** refers to products whose quality can only be inferred after consumption, such as information goods.

Inalienable rights are those that cannot be traded away, such as human rights.

Inalienability of data refers to the inalienable connection between the data observation and the subject.

The market for data enables the selling, sharing, and licensing of data, usually in the structured format.

Wireless sensor networks generate and transfer data streams to digital twins and other analytical purposes of monitoring physical spaces or assets.

DISCUSSION QUESTIONS

1. If there are no property rights to pure information (as opposed to original expression of it), is it possible to sell information?
2. What are the main ways of controlling the sharing of data and how do those influence the business model of data sharing?
3. How could a digital twin increase the efficiency and service quality of a municipal transport network? What about a large airport?
4. What factors might influence whether to commercialize data via the market for data, market for information, or market for products and services?

FURTHER READING

Koutroumpis, Pantelis, Leiponen, Aija, and Thomas, Llewellyn D.W. (2020). Markets for data. *Industrial and Corporate Change* 29(3): 645–660.

Parmar, R., Leiponen, A., and Thomas, L. D. W. (2020). Building an organizational digital twin. *Business Horizons* 63(6): 725–736.

Thomas, L.D.W., Leiponen, A., and Koutroumpis, P. (2023). Profiting from Data: Business Models for Data Products. Chapter 14 in C. Cennamo, G. B. Dagnino and F. Zhu: *Elgar Handbook of Research on Digital Strategy*. Cheltenham: Edward Elgar.

Wessel, L., Baiyere, A., Ologeanu-Taddei, R., and Cha, J., and Blegind Jensen, T. (2021). Unpacking the difference between digital transformation and IT-enabled organizational transformation. *Journal of the Association for Information Systems* 22(1): article 6.

8 | Business Model Design for Information Goods

Having examined the production, consumption, and valuation of information and data, we can start to design business models for information goods. In the previous chapters we have learned about the four fundamental characteristics of information and data goods that we need to consider while doing so.

First, when data and information are digitized and separated from physical packaging, they become nonrival. Nonrivalry means that the same information can be consumed by multiple individuals in multiple locations at the same time, and the consumption experience of one does not detract from those of others. A book or a movie will be equally enjoyable independent of how many other consumers enjoy it simultaneously. However, the economic value of the information may depend on the number of parties who can commercialize it. Nonrivalry is associated with the cost structure of information whereby the fixed cost of creation is large in comparison to the variable cost of producing an additional unit of the good. Making more digital copies of the same information is cheap.

Second, and arising from the nonrivalry characteristic, data and information goods are only partially excludable. Excludability refers to the ability of the producer or holder of the good to exclude others from commercializing the same good. When a car manufacturer sells a vehicle, it is impossible for another firm to sell the very same vehicle. The property right and its transfer can be clearly established and legally enforced in the case of cars. In the case of information, excludability is much more limited and difficult to enforce, leading to information spillovers – unintended transfers of value. Once a copy of the digital good is made available to a customer, it is difficult to prevent them from making additional copies. There are a few strategies one might try. Many information good producers use technical features like file formats and hardware- or software-based access technologies to prevent copying. These are grouped under the heading of Digital Rights Management (DRM) techniques. However, as soon as a new DRM technique is launched, there are usually unlocking algorithms popping up in online discussion sites within minutes. It is a perpetual race. Digital creators can also attempt to prevent copying with legal methods, typically copyright enforcement. We will delve deeper into the copyright regime and its discontents in later chapters. Suffice it to say here that it is costly and difficult to monitor copying and enforce digital rights. Arguably, the most sustainable approach to achieving excludability is to design a business model that does not require constant innovation of DRM techniques or policing and suing users. It involves matching the value proposition and the revenue model with the typical consumption pattern and giving users some degree of freedom to do what they like with the good.

Third, data and information are experience goods, that is, their quality can only be discovered by consuming the good. While many physical goods such as cars have aspects of experience goods (people may have different preferences regarding how a car "drives," and will not know how soon its parts may break or how safe it is in a traffic accident), information goods are entirely about the experience. A book has little value beyond its content, and by inspecting the physical product it is not possible to judge whether one likes it or not. Therefore, it is important for information sellers to design ways for consumers to assess the quality before purchase, to give as accurate or appealing a description as possible to elicit consumption decisions. Sales tactics may include teasers and trailers that reveal a part of the information good. If the shared information is intriguing and of a high quality, the user will still want to pay for the whole product. Branding techniques establish a reputation for a series of goods, such as books or movies by the same author or software by the same developer. Contractual details such as warranties that give users opportunities to reverse the transaction or receive a remedy if the good does not fulfill expectations can facilitate users' purchase decisions because the warranty lowers their risk of not being fully satisfied. Also, digital recommendation systems that collect data about user preferences and recommend other products based on the perceived correlations are commonplace.

Fourth, data, as well as some information goods, may also be credence goods. This means that consumers may not even be able to assess quality upon consumption. Quality may only be inferred over time when performance implications are revealed. The insights offered by many professional services are credence goods. It is difficult to see whether the advice provided by management consultants or lawyers is appropriate or beneficial until it has been adopted and practiced for some time, and the benefits – or lack thereof – are realized. Same applies for data goods. Think about the data from a vehicle that can be wirelessly collected and remotely analyzed. Data can be streams or collections of numbers and words. The quality and value of the data depends on their accuracy and other features which may not be obvious until the data have been structured, arranged, cleaned, combined with other data, and analyzed against a history of performance indicators. Thus, upon initial inspection, especially if the quantity of data is large, its quality is inscrutable.

Data and information being experience goods or credence goods makes it more difficult to apply the pricing techniques discussed earlier. Potential users' willingness to pay tends to be deflated by preference uncertainty. On the other side, because of the Curse of Knowledge, sellers of information tend to inflate the value of the good, leading to a market failure where demand and supply do not meet. For these reasons, it is critical for a digital innovator to design mechanisms that allow users to discover their valuation and preferences, and that allow the innovator to discover users' willingness to pay. Ideally, such mechanisms account for our cognitive tendencies to prefer intuitive, familiar, simple, and quick solutions to our data and information needs.

8.1   Business Model Principles for Data and Information Products

Design product systems for scale. When we combine the nonrivalry characteristic and the cost structure with the buyers' limited and uncertain willingness to pay, we realize that information creators typically need to reach a very large scale to break even. Digital product systems should be designed for rapid and efficient scaling up.

Design versions to discover willingness to pay. Commercialization of information goods also depends on cost-efficient systems for product versioning and market segmentation that allow users to select into their preferred product bundles and that do not consume a lot of resources to capture the most consumer surplus available, helping the innovator to cover their fixed cost.

Design for incentive compatibility with users. To address concerns of excludability, the digital product system needs to provide incentives to keep users paying for access independent of how they utilize the product themselves. The product or service system needs to be "incentive compatible" in the sense of aligning the behavior of consumers with the interests of the innovator. If consumers consistently want to do things that the company doesn't want to support, it will just end up in conflict and even in lawsuits against its customers, which is always a clear sign of a failed business model.

8.2   Redesigning the Business Model at *The New York Times*

Next we re-examine the recent business model redesign by *The New York Times* in the light of the framework developed above.

Design product systems for scale. From the cost-side analysis, we can see that the newspaper needed new digital capabilities particularly in advertising, and it needed to let go of the print production capabilities that were costly and unprofitable. This would have enabled the company to develop a structure with a sizable but scalable fixed cost and very low marginal cost of content dissemination and ad sales. The company needed to make a swift transition to digital and focus on scaling the operations to cover the fixed cost of operations. Unfortunately, print production was the company tradition and many readers and managers struggled to see how digital could ever replace it.

Design versions to discover customers' willingness to pay. With its large and engaged audience, *The New York Times* had a lot of information about readers' preferences and characteristics. Nevertheless it initially decided to offer rather crude mechanisms to version the offerings for different price points. In 2011 it distinguished between different digital devices (e.g., website vs. tablet vs. phone) and between days of the week (Sunday vs. Monday – Friday vs. Friday – Sunday) but not between topics, sections, geographic markets, or many other ways of repackaging the content to bundles that vary in their appeal to different types of readers.

On the other side of the news platform, advertisers were looking to reach the many high-income and highly-educated readers of the paper. However, the lack of sophistication in versioning the product suggests that not much in-depth analysis of readers had been done, meaning that the newspaper was not likely to be able to target advertising very well, either. For example, only in 2018 did the company start to discriminate advertisements based on the content in the news articles.[1] Nevertheless, online newspapers did receive premium ad rates (CPM or "Cost Per Mille," i.e., price per thousand ad impressions), well above those of social networks, for example.[2]

Design for incentive compatibility with users. A big challenge for all digital news organizations is the lack of excludability. Breaking news is unique and fresh for a few minutes, after which it will get copied by thousands of others, online and offline. As the NYT stated in its 2012 risk factors,

> Advancements in technology have exacerbated the risk by making it easier to duplicate and disseminate content. In addition, as our business and the risk of misappropriation of our intellectual property rights have become more global in scope, we may not be able to protect our proprietary rights in a cost-effective manner in a multitude of jurisdictions with varying laws. If we are unable to procure, protect and enforce our intellectual property rights, we may not realize the full value of these assets, and our business may suffer. If we must litigate in the United States or elsewhere to enforce our intellectual property rights or determine the validity and scope of the proprietary rights of others, such litigation may be costly and divert the attention of our management.

Limited excludability is an existential threat to most content-based businesses, and the legal route to address the risks may be extremely costly. Smart businesses, instead, focus on creating incentives for users to keep paying even if the content soon loses its value.

For example, in information businesses, speed and reliability are difficult to provide and, when packaged well, people are willing to pay for access to them. Quick access to information people care about is valuable. The news organization has to be able to both generate valuable news content and deliver it quickly to those individuals to whom it matters. Matching types of news with types of consumers can be a way to enhance willingness to pay. Reliability is a feature of information that is difficult to verify. It requires a reputation built over decades. A reputation can easily be tarnished, but it is slow and expensive to build. Thus, consumers are willing to pay more for information from organizations known to be reliable. In the age of fake news it might seem that a large fraction of the population doesn't care about

---

[1] Edmonds, R. (2019). The New York Times sells premium ads depending on how an article makes you feel. Poynter, April 10, 2019. Retrieved from www.poynter.org/business-work/2019/the-new-york-times-sells-premium-ads-based-on-how-an-article-makes-you-feel/ in August 2022.

[2] Comscore (2010). The New York Times ranks as top online newspaper according to May 2010 US Comscore Media Metrix data. June 16, 2010. Retrieved from www.comscore.com/Insights/Press-Releases/2010/6/The-New-York-Times-Ranks-as-Top-Online-Newspaper-According-to-May-2010-U.S.-comScore-Media-Metrix-Data?cs_edgescape_cc=US in August 2022.

reliability, but recent subscription revenue performance of quality newspapers such as *The New York Times* demonstrate that the opposite is true: a significant number of people will pay for news and investigative journalism that they can trust.

8.3   Business Modeling Digital Twins

Finally, let's consider the business model principles from the point of view of data goods and digital twins.

Design data products for scale. With the inherent cost structure of data networks, whether based on wireless sensors or other communication systems, economies of scale are naturally present in the production of data-based goods and services. Incrementing a digital twin by adding a new data stream or a new analysis to an existing system represents a minor additional expenditure, whereas an additional insight from a slightly tweaked model or an updated dataset may cost almost nothing. Dissemination of digital data or insights will be practically costless. Nevertheless, growing the storage, computing, and analytical capacity has to be a part of the data strategy from the beginning. While these represent fixed costs, such capacity may depend on multiyear agreements with external vendors of cloud computing resources, and, hence, require significant advance planning. However, scaling data systems is generally a relatively uncomplicated proposition.

Design data product versions to discover customers' willingness to pay. Versioning in data systems concerns the ability to quickly offer customized analytical insights that address user needs. Users may be internal users that depend on data-based inputs into their decision making about products and operations or external users that acquire data to be used in their own analyses or information goods to aid decision making. Versioning data-based goods and insights relies on access to a rich set of complementary data streams, sophisticated modeling and machine learning capabilities, as well as skills and experience in generating appropriate and impactful analytical insights. This requires combining digital artifacts, software tools, computing resources, and human capabilities in creative ways.

Moreover, versioning data-based insights is likely to involve constant experimentation to discover hidden structures in data. Digital companies can design entire systems of experimentation with products, services, and operations that use real-time data to test emerging hypotheses about improvements in offerings and processes.

For the users to value the data-based insights, the seller needs to develop long-standing customer relationships and a reputation for quality data and information products to surpass the experience-good property of information and the credence-good property of data. Being quick to customize data-based insights for the users' evolving needs helps to establish a track record of valuable insights that improve product features or process efficiency.

Design data for incentive compatibility with users. Licensing valuable static data can be dangerous because of the lack of excludability. To reduce the potential harms from unauthorized data sharing, the data vendor can add value through dynamic data, modeling, and constant improvement of the generated insights. Then, the freshness and constant improvement of the service creates a barrier to entry. This type of dynamism requires the dynamic capabilities of ever-expanding data collection, constantly incremented models, and data skills improved through learning and training. With the help of dynamic capabilities to constantly evolve the offering, data-based insights become a dynamic and ongoing service rather a static product, making it difficult for rivals and potential entrants to catch up and imitate.

This analysis reveals that the process for creating and maintaining a digital twin maps well for commercializing data-based goods and services. The cost structure of data systems, especially through data liberation and expanding digitization, supports efficient scaling; experimentation to improve the models bodes well for versioning to discover users' willingness to pay; and the resulting ongoing service relationships align the users' incentives with those of the service provider, facilitating excludability and long-term revenue performance. In contrast, provision of static data products is unlikely to allow designing business models that resolve the last challenge, incentive compatibility between users and sellers. A static approach also limits the dynamic versioning of data products, making it more difficult to practice price discrimination and discover willingness to pay.

KEY IDEAS

- Digital business operations need to be designed to facilitate scaling. Both information and data goods have cost structures that feature high fixed costs and low marginal costs. These goods also are difficult for buyers to value so the average user's willingness to pay will often be small. Most businesses will need to operate on a large scale to reach profitability.
- Product design should be oriented toward discovering users' willingness to pay for the product. Whether using freemium, versioning, or other nonlinear pricing strategies, finding the right features and bundles takes a lot of experimentation and design thinking.
- Digital goods are difficult to control, and in many cases it is not even useful to try. The best business models focus on making it costly or difficult to break the service terms and conditions and share the data or information. Aligning users' anticipated behavior with the growth of the company leads to mutually reinforcing behaviors and long-term customer relationships.

DISCUSSION QUESTIONS

1. How are variable costs related to "scaling" of the business model? Should a company attempt to scale its business if its current variable costs exceed sales?
2. What should an innovator of a new micro-mapping service do if it discovers that its users are not willing to pay anything for the digital service, even though they consume a lot of it and share it in their social networks?

3. Stock price data is a public good. How can a digital business sell stock price data? Explain when stock prices can be sold for a positive price and how this relates to the principle of aligning users' needs and behavior with the business model.

FURTHER READING

Weill, Peter and Woerner, Stephanie L. (2013). Optimizing your digital business model. *MIT Sloan Management Review*, Special Collection "Top 10 Lessons on Strategy." Retrieved from https://strategygurus.com/wp-content/uploads/2020/05/STR0715-Top-10-Strategy.pdf#page=30 in October, 2022.

CASE 2: *THE NEW YORK TIMES* IN SEARCH OF A REVENUE MODEL

Case 2.1 Digital Transformation of News

Newspapers are an archetypal information business. They have been struggling to transition to the digital marketplace. Around the year 2000, newspaper revenues consisted primarily of advertising revenue. Classified ads were a particularly lucrative market where major newspapers practically held monopolies in their primary circulation region, such as the New York City metro area for *The New York Times* (see Figure C2.1).

After the internet took off, advertising revenues of the newspaper industry declined rapidly because of competitive entry into online advertising. All categories of advertising shrank, but classified ads declined the most substantially.

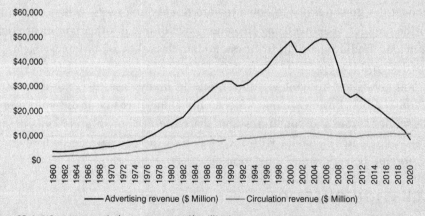

Figure C2.1 US newspaper industry revenues ($ million)
Note: Ever since the 1970s, advertising was a lucrative business for US newspapers. The internet enabled increased competition that started to impact advertising revenues in 2007, and the subsequent decline was precipitous. Subscription revenues held steady but exhibited no growth.
Data source: www.pewresearch.org/journalism/fact-sheet/newspapers/. Retrieved in September 2021.
Data are estimated for 2013–2020.

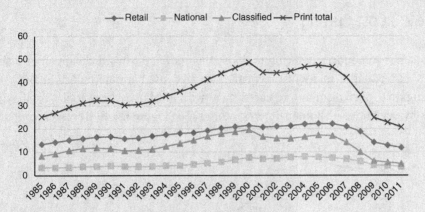

Figure C2.2 US print newspaper revenues by category ($ billion)
Note: All categories of print newspaper advertising declined after 2007 but classified ads shrank the most rapidly.
Data source: www.pewresearch.org/wp-content/uploads/sites/8/2017/05/State-of-the-News-Media-Report-2012-FINAL.pdf. Retrieved in September 2021.

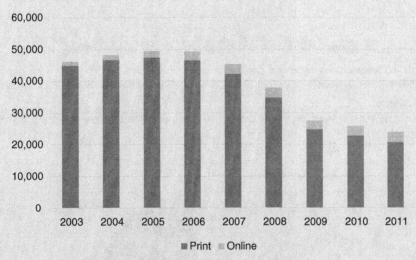

Figure C2.3 US newspapers' print and online advertising revenues ($ billion)
Note: While print advertising collapsed, digital advertising took off very slowly.
Data source: www.pewresearch.org/wp-content/uploads/sites/8/2017/05/State-of-the-News-Media-Report-2012-FINAL.pdf. Retrieved in September 2021.

Commentators have blamed this on online businesses such as Craigslist and Monster.com taking over regional classified markets. However, another major explanation is simply that newspapers were slow to switch to digital operations, and in the process, they lost the local monopolies. Furthermore, when retail advertising and national brands started to switch to digital delivery, newspapers were slow to adopt sophisticated advertisement delivery technologies that would effectively compete with specialized advertising markets created by Google and other digital platforms (see Figures C2.2 and C2.3).

Case 2.2 Cost Cutting

Newspapers responded by trying to revise their content toward cheaper and easier topics. For example, many of them cut expensive international reporting and investigative journalism and replaced them with local and cheap topics such as blogs by celebrities or human-interest stories (See Figure C2.4). However, content

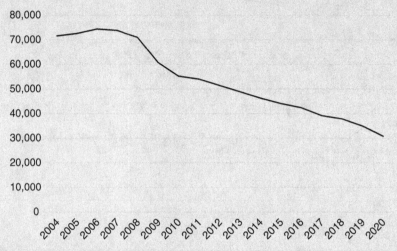

Figure C2.4 US newspapers' newsroom employees
Note: When advertising revenues collapsed, newspapers responded by reducing their human resources in news production.
Data source: www.pewresearch.org/journalism/fact-sheet/newspapers/#newsroom-investment. Retrieved in September 2021.

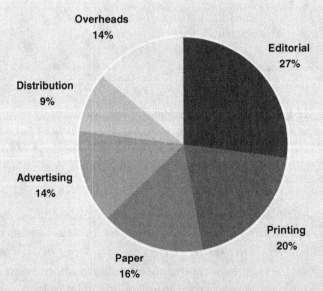

Figure C2.5 Print newspapers' operating expenditures
Note: In 2010, physical manufacturing represented almost half of newspapers' operating costs. The other half was comprised of editorial, advertising, and administrative overheads.
Data source: Enders Analysis, 2011. Retrieved from https://discoverleveson.com/evidence/Claire_Enders_Competitive_pressures_on_the_press/7687/media in September 2021.

production still represented a large fixed cost, even though much of the variable cost of physical production had disappeared in the transition to digital distribution.

Almost half of the total cost of a print newspaper consisted of physical production: paper, printing, and distribution. Editorial costs related to content creation were also a very significant element (see Figure C2.5). However, when newspapers switched to digital production, much of the physical production cost disappeared and editorial as well as advertising sales and delivery became more prominent parts of the total.

Case 2.3 Digital Business Model Discovery

With both revenues and production costs declining rapidly, newspapers struggled to reach profitability during their digital transformation. Cutting costs, gearing up to rapidly growing digital advertising markets, and seeking types of content and delivery modes that are more likely to attract readers and advertisers seem straightforward strategies, but they were challenging to implement.

Companies such as *The New York Times* remained unprofitable for years, and many less prominent newspapers went bankrupt. Why was the transition so challenging for them? One explanation is that there were substantial adjustment costs and behavioral uncertainty that took time to perceive and address. Adjustments were particularly painful in physical production and distribution of print newspapers where long-standing operations and facilities had to be shut down and unionized employees laid off. Behavioral uncertainty affected the discovery of new revenue models and content delivery innovations. Paper-based customer insights were of little use in the digital realm and new models had to be developed, tried out, and improved through experimentation. People were reading content and engaging with advertisements differently in the digital environment, and it took time to understand the reasons for and implications of this. Furthermore, building digital technologies required new capabilities that had to be built from the ground up. Content management systems and customer analytics were not available off the shelf and newspapers had to develop those critical resources. Still, why did it take more than 10 years to turn around *The New York Times*?

The New York Times explored a number of strategic options that could boost the shrinking revenues. Initially the company assumed that the online content would complement the offline content and make it more valuable for subscribers and advertisers. *The New York Times* launched a news website in 1996,[3] with most of the newspaper content freely available. Arthur Sulzberger Jr. commented: "We see our role on the Web as being similar to our traditional

---

[3] Lewis, P.H. (1996). The New York Times introduces a web site. *The New York Times*, January 22, 1996. Retrieved from www.nytimes.com/1996/01/22/business/the-new-york-times-introduces-a-web-site.html in August 2022.

print role – to act as a thoughtful, unbiased filter and to provide our customers
with information they need and can trust." The company also noted: "With
its entry on the Web, The Times is hoping to become a primary information
provider in the computer age and to cut costs for newsprint, delivery and
labor." Initially the website may have driven traffic to the paper product and
generated new advertising revenue, but soon both subscription and advertising
revenues started declining. By the early 2000s it was clear that free digital
news was not a sustainable model for quality newspapers. In 2006–2007
the company experimented with paid content by launching the Times Select
premium package that bundled high-profile columnists and other content
assumed to be particularly highly desirable. None of the early experiments
worked well.

Finally, in 2011 the company decided to try a paywall that would restrict
access to the online content. At the time of the paywall launch, the www.nytimes
.com was the most popular news website in the US. It had a large and engaged
audience but it struggled to monetize the visitors. *The New York Times* paywall
offered the following subscription options:

a. 20 free articles per month via the website
b. free referral access from google and social media
c. $15 per 4 weeks for full website access and smartphone app
d. $8.75 per week all digital access ($455 per year).

Arthur Sulzberger Jr. commented again:

> Today marks a significant transition for The Times, an important day in our 159-year
> history of evolution and reinvention. Our decision to begin charging for digital access
> will result in another **source of revenue**, strengthening our ability to continue to
> **invest in the journalism and digital innovation** on which our readers have come to
> depend. This move will enhance The Times's position as a source of **trustworthy news,
> information and high-quality opinion** for many years to come. (*The New York Times*,
> March 17, 2011, my emphases)

As a result of the paywall, the NYT gained 390,000 new digital subscribers.
Webpage views declined from 700,000 per month to 600,000 per month while
digital subscription revenue grew to $81 million. However, total subscription
revenue increased only by $21 million due to cannibalization of print revenue.
Overall, despite the page view decline, digital ad revenue increased by 5.3
percent in Q4 2011.

While digital subscription revenues were growing modestly, *The New York
Times* company was not yet out of trouble (see Table C2.1). Revenue was flat and
well below that just 10 years earlier, and the cost structure remained heavy in
2012. The company listed the following as its major risk factors:[4]

---

[4] Source: Annual Report 2012.

Table C2.1 *The New York Times* Company financials (in $ millions)

Statement of Operations	2012	2011	2010	2009	2008		2002
Revenues	1,990	1,953	1,981	2,022	2,440		3,079
Operating costs	1,830	1,791	1,813	1,964	2,377		2,534
Net income (loss)	133	(40)	108	20	57		300

Note: The revenues of *The New York Times* declined for over a decade during the company's digital transformation.
Data source: various annual reports. Retrieved from https://investors.nytco.com/reports-and-filings/sec-filings/ in September 2021.

- We have significant competition for advertising, which may adversely affect our advertising revenues and advertising rates.
- If our efforts to retain and grow our digital subscriber base and build consumer revenue are not successful and if we are unable to maintain our digital audience for advertising sales, our business, financial condition and prospects may be adversely affected.
- To remain competitive, we must be able to respond to and exploit changes in technology, services and standards and changes in consumer behavior, and significant capital investments may be required.
- Decreases in print circulation volume adversely affect our circulation and advertising revenues.
- If we are unable to execute cost-control measures successfully, our total operating costs may be greater than expected, which may adversely affect our profitability.
- The underfunded status of our pension plans may adversely affect our operations, financial condition and liquidity.
- A significant number of our employees are unionized, and our business and results of operations could be adversely affected if labor negotiations or contracts were to further restrict our ability to maximize the efficiency of our operations.
- We may not be able to protect intellectual property rights upon which our business relies, and if we lose intellectual property protection, our assets may lose value.

In 2013 the company attempted another revision of the paywall design (Aral and Dhillon, 2021). The number of free articles on the mobile app was reduced to three per day but now readers could access all types of content. Previously the mobile app allowed unlimited number of articles but only from the Top News and Video sections. Thus the quantity of content was reduced, and the diversity of content increased. As a result, total article views decreased by 0.26 per individual per day. On average there were two ads per article and the ad revenue was about $10.50 CPM, meaning the company earned $10.50 for 1,000 ad impressions. Within a seven-month period observed, Aral and Dhillon (2021) suggest that the company lost $940,000 in ad revenue.[5] However, it also gained 28,000 new digital subscribers, because a fraction of those who were locked out due to the more restrictive paywall chose to become subscribers instead. From these new subscribers, *The New York Times* collected $2.24 million in extra revenue. Overall, thus, the paywall redesign was highly successful. The revenue model design can be very influential, and because it is very difficult to predict how digital consumers behave in a new digital environment, the optimal design can only be discovered through repeated experimentation and learning.

DISCUSSION QUESTIONS: CHALLENGES OF REDESIGN

1. How would you (re)design *The New York Times* digital newspaper to achieve greater economies of scale?
2. What would be the implications for pricing the content?
3. What were the challenges for *The New York Times* of discovering customers' willingness to pay?
4. How can *The New York Times* prevent rivals from copying its content, or mitigate the business implications of copying?

---

[5] S. Aral and P. S. Dhillon (2021). Digital paywall design: implications for content demand and subscriptions. *Management Science* 67(4): 2381–2402.

PART III
Networks

··

While digital technologies can be adopted and exploited in all markets, a much smaller set of industries can truly operate as digital markets. Nevertheless, digital markets present quite distinct and valuable features that cannot be fully emulated by offline markets. Digital markets operate through technology-based intermediaries, such as digital platforms or auctions. Whereas both platforms (multisided markets) and auctions have counterparts in the offline world, their digital versions enable unprecedented scale and speed. Compare, for instance, eBay's gross merchandize volume of $88 billion[1] against the major offline auction house Christie's $6.6 billion in 2017.[2] Even eBay's net revenue consisting of transaction fees and other services exceeded $10 billion in 2018. Christie's venerable history goes back 250 years, eBay's history, just 25 years.

eBay is a multisided platform like many digital markets, connecting two or more distinct "sides" or groups. eBay has sellers (often small businesses) and buyers (often individual consumers). However, a digital platform can connect many more types of parties and do so very efficiently. For example, a music platform such as Spotify can connect listeners, music labels, musicians, music stores, and advertisers. Digital technologies are enabling such diverse parties to exchange ideas, content, data, or monetary value in unprecedented efficiency, scale, and precision. Thus, if a digital market takes off and grows large, offline rivals will have a hard time displacing it.

At the same time, digital markets and platforms are technological systems. Their central service is mediating connections and exchange. Connected devices and users form a network, and analysis of digital markets as networks provides many crucial insights into their growth and performance.

---

[1] eBay company website (2018). First quarter 2018 results. Retrieved from www.ebayinc.com/stories/news/ebay-q1-2018-results/ in August 2022.

[2] Neuendorf, H. (2018). The auction house Bonhams has been purchased by a London-based private equity firm. Artnet News, September 4, 2018. Retrieved from https://news.artnet.com/market/bonhams-sold-to-epiris-1342580 in August 2022.

9 | Networks and Systems

> On the one hand you have – the point you're making Woz – is that
> information sort of wants to be expensive because it is so valuable – the
> right information in the right place just changes your life. On the other
> hand, information almost wants to be free because the costs of getting it
> out is getting lower and lower all of the time. So you have these two things
> fighting against each other.
>
> (Stewart Brand to Steve Wozniack in 1984)

Information is valuable and the cost of disseminating information is tending to
zero. But realizing the value of information by getting it to the right place at the
right time requires sharing and exchanging it. Its societal value is unleashed by
networks of communication. Communication networks can be small or large technical systems that connect different types of devices to one another. Of course,
they can also involve just human messengers or pigeons, but in the digital economy, we are interested in systems that connect information and communication
technology devices. Such communication networks require physical connections
(optical cable; Ethernet cable; radio antennae and receivers) and social connections (a person or a group of people communicating to another).

The power of modern communication networks is amplified by their capacity to
expand in a decentralized fashion. This is to a great degree facilitated by modular
design choices made in the very early stages of the internet. A **modular system**
entails a set of components, or modules, that are connected using **technical standards** to other components, devices, computers, or services. Modularity typically
implies that systems or devices can accommodate components from many different providers. Over time, the power of modularity is generativity, enabling decentralized innovation activity in each of the components, as long as the interface
standards are maintained and respected. Modular systems can thus often innovate
and evolve more rapidly than monolithic systems.

The Internet is an **open system** where individual computers (or nodes in the
network) are connected by interface standards designed and maintained by the
Internet Engineering Task Force (IETF). Similarly, "IBM-compatible" personal
computers were designed to accommodate components from many vendors after
IBM decided to open up its architecture.[1] Most telecommunication systems are also

---

[1] PCMag (2011). Why the IBM PC had an open architecture. PC Mag, August 8, 2011. Retrieved from
www.pcmag.com/archive/why-the-ibm-pc-had-an-open-architecture-286065 in August 2022.

standardized, usually by government agencies participating in technical groups of the International Telecommunications Union. Each of these communication systems facilitated intense innovation and competition because the open and decentralized designs gave access to a diverse group of innovators and entrepreneurs trying to develop their ideas and products. Such open systems can become breeding grounds for rapid technological change.

Computers themselves are complex **technical systems** with hundreds of components. However, the original computers such as the Colossus, world's first digital programmable computer that the United Kingdom used to decipher German messages during the Second World War, were one of a kind. Even in the 1960s, computers were purpose-built in small numbers. The Burroughs 201 computer that the University of Virginia purchased for over $1 million (worth more than $8 million in 2019) had 1,800 vacuum tubes. Only 50 computers of this kind were ever built. These early computers were not standardized or modularized in any meaningful way.

Modern computers are much more complex machines, but they are also much more standardized. In personal computers and laptops, many of the key components inside the computer are not manufactured or even designed by the maker of the computer. The decision by the then-leading firm IBM to open up the architecture of personal computers for components made by other firms in the early 1980s was key to the explosion of the market – and, ultimately, to IBM losing control of the market and eventually its leadership.[2]

Similarly, more recent (and vast) technical systems of communication and exchange such as digital platforms for applications (App Store, Play Store), social networks (Twitter, Snapchat), and blockchain platforms (Ethereum, EOS) are fundamentally based on the same principles: openness and modularity. They feature standardized application programming interfaces for software developers and standardized ways to interact or transact for users and advertisers. There is often minimal control of who joins and what they offer, as long as they abide by the design rules governing the system (Baldwin and Clark, 2000). However, such standards and interfaces do not arise by accident or on their own; they are painstakingly developed, often cooperatively by many organizations via working groups in organizations such as the IEEE, the American Institute for Electrical and Electronics Engineers. Also, decisions to open and modularize communication systems are not automatic or self-evident; they should be made based on a thoughtful analysis of the market. For example, Apple did not adopt the open PC architecture. It made all the components in-house, including microprocessors, for many years. While in 2020 this may have looked like a wise strategy, the company nearly went bankrupt in the 1990s. At its lowest, Apple held a personal computer market share of about 2 percent in 1997. A closed architecture made Macintosh computers niche products that almost went extinct. Subsequently, Apple adopted

---

[2] Reilly, Edwin (2003). *Milestones in Computer Science and Information Technology*. Westport, CN: Greenwood Press.

a significantly more open strategy regarding hardware components and software applications although it remained more closed than most rivals.

There are also much smaller technical systems such as combinations of hardware and software or content. These include computer game stations + games and DVD players + discs. In each of these markets, firms need to decide about the architectural openness of their products and how to design the interfaces that facilitate connections. This chapter and the next are focused on such **network strategies**.

9.1 Network Effects

Technical systems are critically influenced by dynamic forces called **network effects** that are positive demand-side externalities. Let's first consider communication networks. When one person joins the network, the benefits from the network are increased for many if not all existing network participants. For example, when Coco joins the instant messaging service used by her teammates Taylor, Serena, Madison, and Sloane, not only can she connect with her teammates who are already in the network, but those teammates' valuation of the service is enhanced by Coco also being on it. Because the friends did not compensate Coco for joining, they enjoyed a positive externality – an unpaid beneficial effect. She thus made the service slightly more valuable for everyone who can now potentially connect with her. This is a **direct network effect**.

The network effect can be described in more formal terms with what is called **Metcalfe's Law**: the value of a network V can be *approximated* by the square of its size S: $V = S^2$. When Coco joins the network that already has 4 members, 4 new connections can be formed. The network now has 5 members, with a maximum number of (two-way) connections of 5*4/2 = 10 (see Figure 9.1).

The number of two-way connections is thus $C = S(S-1)/2$.

Asymptotically the number of connections, which is related to the value of the network, approaches the square of the size. Metcalfe's Law is therefore a simplification of the network effect.

We can also distinguish an **indirect network effect**. This also involves a communication network that becomes more valuable with the number of connected devices, but these devices are system goods, and the network effect operates through the complementary goods market. For example, a game console and games make up a system good – game consoles and games are strongly complementary because the console requires content to be enjoyable. Most gamers don't necessarily care about how many other gamers are also using the same system (unless they play multiplayer games online), but they do care about the number of games available for them to play. For example, the value of Nintendo's Switch console is much reduced if you can only play Mario Kart with it. Then, the network effect in such a **two-mode network** operates through the game content market: the more content is available, the more valuable is the game station to the player. The more content becomes available, the more benefits accrue to all players.

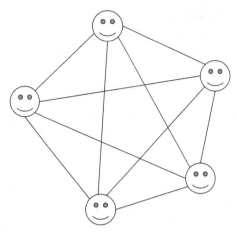

Figure 9.1 Network of five nodes
Note: A network of five nodes has 10 two-way connections, or 20 one-way connections. If one more individual joins this network, 5 new connections can be formed. Thus, the number of potential new connections with a new participant grows as the network grows: The 100th new participant enables 99 new connections.

Many other systems also feature this positive feedback loop between a hardware device (music player, video player, smartphone, e-reader) and software or content goods (music, movies, applications, e-books). The more people buy the device, the more complementary goods will be offered, and, consequently, the more people will buy the device because the value of the system has increased due to a larger number of complements. Consumers then *indirectly* care about other consumers' choices, and their adoption processes become correlated. However, the feedback loop also works in reverse: few choices in the content market are available → fewer people buy the device → even fewer choices are available. There can thus be both virtuous cycles (more begets more) and vicious cycles (less begets less). Such cycles are difficult to break without substantial effort or investment. Figure 9.2 illustrates the indirect network effect in a two-mode network in the e-reading market.

Because network effects create a positive feedback loop, we need to consider the concepts of installed base and critical mass. **Installed base** refers to the number of consumers that have invested in the device that is usually significantly more expensive than the content that it supports. The greater the initial investment, the greater is the commitment to the network. And the greater the installed base, the more lucrative is the market for content providers. However, when there is no content available, and no user has yet purchased the device, there is no point in buying a device that has no complements that make it enjoyable. The early buyers thus have to be convinced that there will be a lot of content in the future. If enough consumers have joined the network and made it attractive to other consumers to join, too, then the network has reached its critical mass. The network has to grow beyond its critical mass to "take off," that is, to grow spontaneously.

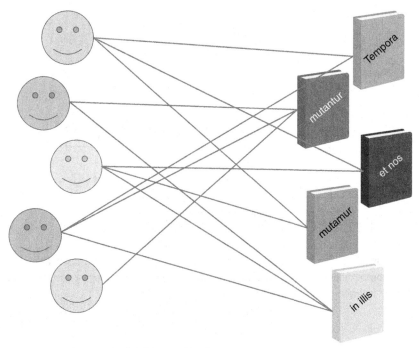

Figure 9.2 Two-mode network of children and books
Note: In a two-mode network, each node on one side can only connect to nodes on the other side.
Hence, 5 kids can each connect to 5 books, making the maximum number of connections 25.

9.2 Demand for Network Goods and Critical Mass

When consumers care not just about the product or service itself (e.g., instant messenger), but also the number of consumers they can connect with (i.e., the size of the installed base), the demand analysis becomes more complicated with a nonlinear demand curve.

Following Varian's (2009) simple model of network growth, let's assume there are heterogeneous customers, some of whom are very excited about a new messenger app ("geeks") and others who are less thrilled but might join if their friends use it ("followers"). The valuation V_i of geeks is higher than that of followers. We can assume that this valuation is uniformly distributed, with a density of one, between zero and some number A that reflects the valuation of the most enthusiastic potential user. However, the actual willingness to pay also depends on the number of friends to connect with:

$$P = WTP_i = V_i N$$

$$V \in [0,A]$$

Then the total quantity demanded by all consumers up to the marginal consumer *i* equals:

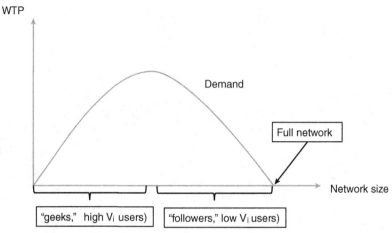

Figure 9.3 Network demand when customers have heterogeneous preferences
Note: When network participants value the network technology and the connections it enables, the demand function becomes quadratic. Initially it is populated by users who strongly value the technology itself, and later followers respond primarily to the growing size of the network.

$$Q = N = A - V_i$$

$$=> V_i = A - N$$

In other words, all "geeks" with a higher WTP than *i* will pay the price, and we are trying to determine who is the marginal consumer *i*, the one with the lowest WTP to still buy the product for price P. Combining the demand function with the WTP formula generates:

$$P = N(A - N) = AN - N^2$$

As a result, we can describe the marginal consumer *i* with a *quadratic* demand function that depends on the range of preferences A and the size of the installed base (see Figure 9.3). If the installed base N = 0, the WTP of consumer *i* is also zero. When N grows, the WTP of the marginal buyer grows up until the inflection point where all geeks have already bought the system and the remaining followers are less and less enthusiastic and require a larger and larger network to join (because their V_i is so low).

Under these circumstances, for any positive price P_1, there may be three equilibria. If the number of users N is below critical mass C_1, the market has not reached critical mass and will collapse to zero because the WTP of the next most enthusiastic user is still below the price P_1. Point $N = C_1$ is an unstable equilibrium and just a tiny push beyond this point will help the market to take and grow until it reaches F_1. F_1 is the other stable equilibrium for this set-up, the largest market attainable with price P_1. For the remaining consumers, their willingness to pay is below the price demanded P_1. Thus, to reach more customers, the network provider would need to reduce the price. The full network can only be reached if it is free. Figure 9.4 illustrates these equilibria.

Thus, the network innovator will need to create expectations or build the market to reach critical mass, or else the network will fail. Only beyond critical mass will

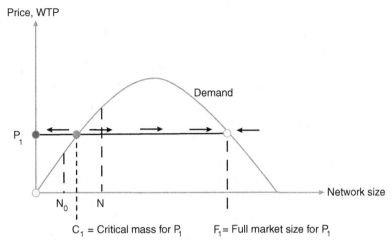

Figure 9.4 Network growth and multiple equilibria
Note: When network demand is nonlinear, for any positive price there are two stable equilibrium outcomes. If the size of the network stays below critical mass, it will collapse to N = 0. If the network grows above critical mass, it will expand until N = F_1.

the positive feedback effect (virtuous cycle) take over. The critical mass typically consists of consumers with the greatest enthusiasm for the product. The higher the price, the higher the critical mass threshold.

9.3   Network Strategies: Reaching Critical Mass

Considering that reaching critical mass is a challenging hurdle in launching new networks, we next focus on what can be done to overcome it. Pricing is a natural lever to encourage adoption when entering a new market. Sometimes sellers of highly desirable products engage in "cream skimming" strategies to attempt to absorb as much of the consumer surplus as possible. Launching networks requires the exact opposite: providing the service free of charge or even subsidizing users in adoption. This is often the purpose of "freemium" strategies: initially build the network with the free service and then attempt to upgrade users to premium services to generate a profit. Various other price discrimination strategies can also facilitate recruiting users and reaching critical mass.

An example of a successful freemium network strategy is Skype. The pioneer of IP (Internet Protocol) telephony was initially a peer-to-peer (P2P) software product that was (and still is) free for Skype-to-Skype users. Later, the "Skype-out" feature was added, building a one-way connection between the Skype network and fixed-line telephone networks. These services were for fee and contributed to making the business profitable and viable in the long term. The original P2P architecture economized on computer resources needed to run the service and also facilitated commercialization.

Consumers' expectations about the ultimate market size can also influence the timing of their adoption decisions. Therefore, a big part of any network launch strategy is marketing – influencing those expectations. If a large part of the market believes in the network being successful, consumers may adopt based on their expected valuation rather than their valuation based on current network size. Thus, if a network start-up manages to convince potential users about its ultimate success, consumers' expectations can become self-fulfilling.

Expectations play such a central role in digital networks that there is a term for excessive marketing without actual fulfillment or even launch: vaporware. These products are announced and possibly developed but never launched. The innovating companies behind vaporware may use the announcements to test and drum up demand and obtain feedback on demo versions, but eventually decide that the product will not be successful. It is telling that such important systems as 3G, Bluetooth, Windows Vista, and IBM Watson were considered vaporware for a long time.[3]

The growth of a new network business can also be accelerated by tapping on an existing network or allowing other networks to interconnect. In the next chapter we delve deeper into decisions related to network openness and compatibility with other products and services. Connecting to and building off of an existing network can help jumpstart the network effects and gain critical mass. However, dependence on an external network can also bring about strategic conflicts and risks.

9.4   Network Strategies: Switching Costs and Consumer Lock In

Communication networks and other technical systems tend to create incentives for users to stay connected and raise the costs of switching to other systems. Buying a costly device that only works with the content of a specific system makes it difficult to switch to another system that later on might have more or better content. Therefore, once the consumer has bought the device, they tend to keep it for a while. Same for communication networks: even in case a newer instant messaging network provides better features than the incumbent, users tend not to switch if they have all their friends in the old network and only a few friends in the new network, unless the features of the new network are much more valuable for them.

These are examples of **switching costs** that are very common in digital markets and can substantially influence competition – and strategy. In addition to investments in durable goods like expensive devices or equipment or the coordination cost of switching to new communication networks, switching costs can be contractual such as those specified in telephone service contracts or in airline loyalty

---

[3] Wikipedia: List of Vaporware. Retrieved from https://en.wikipedia.org/wiki/List_of_vaporware in August 2022.

programs. Wireless service contracts may define penalties for switching before the specified term (such as two years), whereas frequent flyer programs impose a loss of a benefit if one flies other airlines. There can also be switching costs due to learning a skill specific to a device or a system, or due to file or data formats specific to a software program. These do not arise randomly but by design.

Switching costs may "**lock in**" consumers to a particular system, which gives the system provider additional market power and enhances their ability to price the product higher. More precisely, the value provided by a competing system must exceed the value provided by the incumbent plus the switching cost. Let's assume that a user is already locked in product Alpha (that has value V_a). A new product Beta is launched and associated with value V_b and price P_b. If there is a cost SC for switching from Alpha to Beta, the user will keep buying Alpha if:

$$V_a - P_a \geq V_b - P_b - SC$$
$$\Leftrightarrow P_a \leq P_b + SC + (V_a - V_b)$$

In other words, as long as the consumer surplus from product Alpha exceeds that from product Beta, the user will not switch. The switching cost SC thus detracts from the surplus generated by Beta. However, for very large values of V_b, the consumer will switch. Thus, if Alpha is fixed-line telephony and Beta is wireless, even though SC is quite substantial, users may be willing to switch because Beta offers so much more value with the added feature of mobility.

In some situations, switching costs may create a lot of market power. For example, if a consumer is willing to pay $3 for a bag of peanuts when they are in a store, they may be willing to pay much more for the same bag of peanuts when they are in a hotel room at night. The cost of switching from the hotel minibar to a convenience store on the street is significant, perhaps up to several dollars. Hence, guests may pay $8 for a bag of peanuts when they are "held hostage" by the hotel.

Therefore, switching costs and resulting consumer lock in change the nature of competition. Now the emphasis becomes building the installed base. To get a user to adopt the system, vendors will compete very hard and may even subsidize new adopters. However, after the users are locked in, firms will have strong market power and are able to extract significant profits. From the firm's perspective, profits will depend on the total switching cost over all customers: the value of the system equals the installed base multiplied by the switching cost per customer. Thus, even if the cost of switching is small but there is a large installed base, the company may benefit greatly. On the other hand, there can be very large lock-in effects even with a small market share, as in the case of Apple, the Jedi master of lock-in strategies. Switching costs often allow firms to significantly enhance their profit margins. Nevertheless, firms cannot become complacent and only rely on switching costs as a strategy, because eventually rivals will innovate and provide a product that is so much better that its value will exceed the switching cost – the story of Apple in the 1990s. This new product may then take over the market.

Network effects also generate switching costs because they impose a difficult coordination problem on users. Although setting up a user account in another social network or messenger is fairly easy, it is difficult to get friends to switch over to the new network because all of their other friends are also on the old network and would need to be moved over. In the case of indirect network effects such as the kids and books example, the switching cost arises from the lost benefit of complementary goods such as content. For example, if a kid had already invested in a library of e-books in one system, they might have to forego the library if they decided to switch to a new e-reader that does not support the file format of the existing books. Thus, whenever there are direct or indirect network effects, there will also be switching costs that influence consumer behavior and competitive strategies.

KEY IDEAS

- Communication networks connect individuals or organizations, and the more potential connections there are, the more valuable the network.
- The value of the network depends on the number of possible connections and is proportional to the square of the network size.
- Technical systems are networks consisting of individuals with devices and their complements, such as software or content. Technical systems exhibit indirect network effects because individuals don't want to connect to many other individuals but to many complements. Then, the value of the network depends on the number of available complements.
- Network participants have heterogeneous preferences regarding the network services, but they also care about the number of other participants or complements. This gives rise to a nonlinear demand curve and multiple equilibria.
- One of the stable equilibria is an empty network, and the other stable equilibrium is a full network that depends on the price of the service.
- The network has to grow beyond its critical mass to become sustainable, but once large, there are substantial costs of switching to other networks. Switching costs lock consumers into the network.

DEFINITIONS

Installed base consists of the hardware investments or other significant commitments such as subscription fees to join a multi-mode network.

Interfaces of a system connect the components of the system to each other. They can be standardized or idiosyncratic, and they can be open, controlled by one party, or closed.

Lock in happens when switching costs are high and users find it difficult to leave the system.

Metcalfe's Law states that the value of a network grows approximately with the square of its size.

Modular system is a technical system consisting of modules that are connected with standardized interfaces. Modularity allows each module to innovate without interfering with the rest of the system.

Network effects can be direct or indirect. **Direct network effects** arise from the benefits created by a new network participant for the existing participants. **Indirect network effects** arise from such benefits for others created by a new network participant in a two-mode network. Benefits are received by the network participants of the other type.

Network strategies concern strategies to build a communication network or a technical system that consists of multiple components or participants. The most important network strategies include choices regarding network compatibility with earlier networks and openness for others to innovate additional products.

Open systems provide interfaces that are widely available for interconnection by new components.

Switching costs arise when a user switches between two systems and has to incur either monetary costs or expend effort to switch.

Technical standards define how components in a system are designed and interconnected.

Technical system is a technology consisting of multiple components or products jointly producing some service. Systems can be small such as a computing device consisting of many different standardized components or large such as telecommunication systems consisting of fixed networks, wireless networks, and terminal devices. Any multicomponent product can be analyzed as a system. Many technical systems consist of hardware, software, and content.

Two-mode (multi-mode) network includes nodes of two (multiple) types. Each node type can only connect to nodes of the other type(s). Many two-mode networks include devices and software-embedded content in specific file formats.

DISCUSSION QUESTIONS

1. The Facebook social network has 2.8 billion users. What is the network effect associated with this network size?
2. Regulatory agencies decide to split the network along continental lines, preventing connections and sharing of data across continents. Assuming each of the six continents (excluding Antarctica) has equal numbers of users, what is the combined network effect of the new social network?
3. If Facebook's market capitalization is $900 billion before the regulatory action, how much is its new value after the new regulation?
4. How do you think the new regulation will influence the firm's ability to generate revenue by showing advertisements to the users?
5. Before the regulation, the median (North American) user of Facebook valued the service at $42 per month.[4] How does the regulation influence the perceived costs of switching and the resulting lock in?

---

[4] Brynjolfsson, E., Collis, A., Diewert, W.E., Eggers, F., and Fox, K. J. (2019). GDP-B: Accounting for the value of new and free goods in the digital economy. NBER Working Paper 25695. Retrieved from https://www.nber.org/system/files/working_papers/w25695/w25695.pdf in August 2022.

6. If A = 10 in the demand model for Facebook, what is the full size F_1 of the social network? If the company decides to switch to charging users $5 per month, then what would be the critical mass C_1 and the full size F_1 of the network?

FURTHER READING

Baldwin, C. Y. and Clark K. B. (2000). *Design Rules: The Power of Modularity.* Cambridge, MA: The MIT Press.

Farrell J. and Klemperer P. (2007). Coordination and Lock-In: Competition with Switching Costs and Network Effects. Chapter 31 in M. Armstrong, R. Porter (eds.). *Handbook of Industrial Organization.* Amsterdam: Elsevier, Vol. 3, pp. 1967–2072.

Varian, H. (2018). *Use and Abuse of Network Effects.* Social Science Research Network working paper. Retrieved from https://papers.ssrn.com/sol3/papers.cfm?abstract_id=3215488 in August, 2022.

10 Network Competition

Competition under network effects takes on interesting dynamics for which any digital innovator will need to plan. As described in the previous chapter, network adoption is likely to proceed in a nonlinear fashion. Initially it is very difficult to attract paying users, but, if successful, after the threshold of critical mass, suddenly the desirability of the service (its technological value and the size of the existing network) exceeds its price for a large number of users. The network "takes-off." Ultimately, it will reach its full size and any remaining non-adopters are simply very reluctant to adopt so even a large network size will not entice them to buy in. Facebook is not for everyone!

In the early days of the network, it is very challenging to gain visibility and legitimacy in the market, but strategies such as penetration pricing, marketing, or enhancing network effects that were described in the previous chapter can help. All these make it easier for potential users to believe in the ultimate growth of the network even though initially the community is small and the network effects negligible.

If there is more than one competing network battling to reach critical mass, the marketplace can be even more volatile and the outcome very unpredictable. If network effects are strong, meaning that the users care relatively more about the connections (N) rather than about the inherent features of the product (V_i), the market may "tip" and feature "winner take all" dynamics. **Market tipping** means that one network will take over the market and the losing network will collapse. This follows directly from the demand model for network services:

$$P = WTP_i = V_i N$$

When consumers value both the features of the network (V_i) and the size of the network (N), there may be a market share threshold after which the network size dominates consumers' choices, and one contender takes over all users in the market. The figure below illustrates this dynamic. With two competing networks that were launched at the same time, initially each network has about half the market (market share about 50 percent) and they battle it out in the "battle zone." Over time, however, possibly even due to random events such as the lumpiness of large customers adopting a network, the market shares could slip beyond the "absorbing barriers" and then one of the networks will take over the market. While in the battle zone, either network has a good chance of winning over the market, but beyond the absorbing barrier, the market will tip and force one of the contenders to exit (Arthur, 1989).

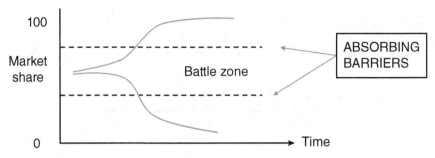

Figure 10.1 Network competition with two competing technologies
Note: If network effects are strong when two similar network technologies are simultaneously launched and compete for the market, it is likely that one of them will take over the market. Even just a random disturbance might push the networks beyond the "absorbing barriers" which prevent them from re-entering the battle zone.
Source: Adapted from Arthur, W.B. (1989). Competing technologies, increasing returns, and lock-in by historical events. *Economic Journal* 99(394): 116–131.

Within the battle zone, each network will use its competitive arsenal to try to attract more users, gain visibility and legitimacy through marketing, and convince users and providers of complementary goods about the future size and viability of the network. Often the network that reaches critical mass first will win, because they can gain such a large boost from the network take-off that the rival service will fall behind permanently (see Figure 10.1).

A famous example of battling networks was the high-definition optical disc (DVD) player market. On one side, Sony, Phillips, and a consortium of their partners promoted the Blu-ray technology, and on the other side, Toshiba, NEC, and their partners promoted the HD-DVD standard. Each technology was fully functional, although with slightly different strengths and features, and they were launched in the global market around 2006. Blu-ray was billed as the slightly more advanced (and more expensive) technology, preferred by the movie studios for its better Digital Rights Management features, whereas HD-DVD was preferred by computer makers and game developers because of its lower price and easier manufacturing process. Ultimately, however, after two years of market battle, and each side being alternately ahead or behind, the battle was decided by Universal Studios, Warner Bros. and Walmart switching from HD-DVD to Blu-ray in 2008. Toshiba soon announced it was ceasing its support of HD-DVD players and admitted defeat. However, the "battle" extended over two years, plus several years of development before product launches, and was extremely expensive for the parties. In 2008, Toshiba revealed it lost almost a billion US dollars in the long and difficult process of product development and market rivalry.[1]

---

[1] See Reuters (2008). Toshiba faces $986 million loss on HD DVDs. Reuters Technology News, March 12, 2008. Retrieved from www.reuters.com/article/us-toshiba-idUST28076020080313 in August, 2022.

10.1   Performance versus Compatibility

As described by the network demand model, network businesses compete on technological performance and network size. A new entrant can offer a substantial innovation in terms of product performance (V_i) or promise of a greater network effect (N) through connected users, complementary products and services, and related, compatible services. It can also pursue strategies that expand the expectations about the ultimate market size by offering the service compatible with existing networks or by allowing others to build off of it through open interfaces. These network strategies establish **interoperability** between two or more systems.

Incremental innovations tend to more readily fit into and complement existing networks. For example, 4G wireless communication devices were compatible with the existing 3G networks to induce a large network effect; 4G phones would work in the existing 3G networks; and 3G phones would work in 4G networks. However, with the emergence of 5G wireless technologies, an entirely new air interface was launched, "5G New Radio." This radical innovation enabled an order of magnitude greater speed and lower latency. Nevertheless, the collective goal of the industry was to build 5G "on top" of 4G and enable a gradual transition for existing wireless networks and devices.[2]

This type of **compatibility** with earlier networks is a strategic choice. While a larger network is always more desirable for consumers, it is not always in the interest of the innovator to offer compatibility. For example, instant messaging on Apple's iPhones was designed to enhance the network internal to the Apple universe, and not facilitate connection to the wider smartphone ecosystem. When Apple entered wireless communication in 2007 with the iPhone, it had no installed base in earlier generations of smartphones or communication networks and was not attempting to create a transition path or broader interoperability across different devices. Apple thus entered instant messaging with a high V_i (significant feature innovation) and small N (incompatible with existing systems).[3]

In contrast, Twitter was launched as a service compatible with SMS text messaging. The original character limit of 140 was defined such that when mobile phone users wanted to tweet, they could use the text messaging system to send it out. This compatibility facilitated the initial growth of the network, although the service itself had limited technological novelty or features. Twitter thus launched with low V_i (few advanced features) but a path to achieve a high N quickly.

---

[2] Cf. the wireless industry's shared vision of generational compatibility: 3GPP website. Retrieved from www.3gpp.org/about-3gpp/about-3gpp in August 2022.

[3] Voice communication of the iPhone was compatible with other mobile and fixed-line phones, of course.

10.2   Openness versus Control

In addition to backward compatibility, network strategies involve choices about the **openness** of the new network itself – whether it will allow other networks to become compatible with it. Once the network is launched, it will be important to consider whether to open up its boundaries such as Application Programming Interfaces (APIs) to other developers, or whether to tightly control interfaces and keep the system closed. For example, the application platforms in the Apple and Android systems followed very different strategies of openness originally. Apple was much more selective about allowing apps into App Store, whereas Google was very liberal regarding access to Play Store. As a consequence, the Android app market grew much more rapidly, whereas the Apple app market developed a reputation for higher-quality applications. As late as 2019, there were almost 2.5 million apps in Google's Play Store, and just under 2 million apps in Apple's App Store. Similarly, Facebook made the social network much more entertaining by opening up APIs for online games such as Farmville by Zynga. Facebook became a multisided platform, attracting and orchestrating not just users connecting to other users but also complementary service providers connecting with users. Such strategic decisions about openness can accelerate the growth of the network by generating indirect network effects and making the whole system more valuable. However, there are also risks to opening up the system to all comers, as the scandal surrounding the Facebook app "This Is Your Digital Life" that was linked to the political consulting firm Cambridge Analytica demonstrated: Facebook was not able to control the extent and usage of data harvesting by apps connected to its platform.[4]

Openness thus comes with its own trade-offs. Competition is a major downside for network complementors and a major upside for consumers. When a digital network is open, it will attract many entrants who extend and complement the system in their own ways. Entry barriers are low and as long as there are profit opportunities, and sometimes even if there are none, new firms continue to enter. This leads to lots of innovation and new services, and low prices. Great for consumers; tough for firms.

An example of an open system with much competition is wireless telecommunication networks. Starting from the second-generation (2G) systems, major wireless communication systems have been governed by open technical standards. The GSM (Global System for Mobile) standard evolved through cooperation by major European equipment companies such as Ericsson, Nokia, Siemens, and Alcatel. The resulting open standard was available for all companies globally.

---

[4] See Cadwalladr, C. and Graham-Harrison, E. (2018). Revealed: 50 million Facebook profiles harvested for Cambridge Analytica in major data breach. *The Guardian*, March 17, 2018. Retrieved from www.theguardian.com/news/2018/mar/17/cambridge-analytica-facebook-influence-us-election in August 2022.

The alliance was so successful that the third-generation (3G) systems attracted participation by Asian and North American companies such as Lucent, Nortel, Qualcomm, Samsung, LG, Huawei, and others. The 3G wireless system was cooperatively standardized through an international alliance called Third Generation Partnership Project (3GPP) that became the central standards development organization for 3G, 4G and later 5G wireless communication systems. The global adoption and success of these systems attests to the benefits of network openness. As a counterexample, Qualcomm attempted to develop competing standards by tightly controlling the system. It had had some success with 2G systems owing to its radical innovation, the CDMA air interface technology. But the 3G networks that Qualcomm attempted to globally commercialize flopped, because telecom operators around the world preferred the open and more competitive UMTS standard by the 3GPP alliance. Users and clients hate to be locked in by a monopolist. But luckily for Qualcomm, the company's air interface technology was so superior to rival technologies that 3GPP also decided to adopt it in the UMTS standard. Over the years it has collected billions in patent licensing royalties, especially when it was able to tie the sales of chipsets and licensing.[5]

Whether networks are open or controlled, and whether they are compatible with previous networks or start an entirely new network, competitive strategies will revolve around the familiar concepts of switching costs, lock in, and network effects. For high V_i systems that decide to go it alone (rather than interoperate with existing systems), convincing users that they will not be locked in to a monopoly, and that incurring the switching cost is worth it, are key issues. The network innovator may try to commit to low price schemes (e.g., freemium), and even subsidize switching costs for users. They may also build alliances with other companies to enhance their legitimacy and mitigate the expectation of a future monopoly. Such strategies were followed by the developers of the high-definition DVD system Blu-Ray.

For relatively lower V_i systems that are launched as compatible with existing networks, the challenge is to differentiate themselves and create unique competitive advantages. For example, an online social game creator may enter the market through Facebook and find a large potential audience, but in that kind of an open system, there will be many other entrants, too. How to distinguish your game from thousands of others? Similarly, by opening up network interfaces to many other developers, the whole system will become more valuable but the core network may lose control over its evolution. IBM selected such an open architecture for its innovative personal computer in the 1980s. Many clones entered the market, and a few of the key components managed to maintain their dominant market positions – microprocessors by Intel and the operating system by Microsoft. Ultimately, IBM

---

[5] Lee, T.B. (2019). How Qualcomm shook down the cell phone industry for almost 20 years. Ars Technica, May 30, 2019. Retrieved from https://arstechnica.com/tech-policy/2019/05/how-qualcomm-shook-down-the-cell-phone-industry-for-almost-20-years/ in August 2022.

was not able to maintain its distinctiveness and market leadership and sold the business unit to the Chinese company Lenovo in 2004. Interface design and control can be critical for the success of the system.

10.3   Communication Standards Development

Communication standards moderate the openness of the system. They can play a major role in the evolution of a communication network. Standards are technical specifications that define how the interfaces between the components of a system should be designed so as to achieve interoperability between the various devices participating in the network. For example, railroad gauges are always standardized in a rail network. As the American history illustrates, discrepant railroad gauges can inflict great societal costs, and switching can be expensive. In 1860, there were as many as six gauges in the United States. When a train arrived to a station where the gauge changed, all freight and passengers needed to be unloaded and reloaded to new cars. However, switching costs were so huge, too, that a civil war was needed to convince the North and the South to convert to the same gauge.

Just like the early railways, telecommunication systems were initially developed by individual companies who bought the components from electronics manufacturers and commissioned custom-built networks that were each unique. However, the global movement for standardization in the early twentieth century brought national telecommunication operators such as AT&T in the United States or PTTs that were governmental agencies running Postal, Telecommunication and Telegraph networks of each country to get together to coordinate and enable international telecommunications in the period after the Second World War.

The first transatlantic cable for telegraph was laid in 1858 but at that time the messages had to be translated at national borders from one system to another, significantly slowing down communications. The International Telecommunications Union (ITU) was originally founded as the International Telegraph Union in 1865 to coordinate international agreements about transmission technologies.[6]

Wireless radio communications were first demonstrated in 1880 and during the 1890s several inventors with famous names such as Tesla, Bose, and Marconi started to experiment with the new technology. Marconi made the first transatlantic transmission in 1901. Nevertheless, challenges of incompatibility hampered early radio communications and international standards started to develop in the early 20th century. For example, the "SOS" message was standardized as the international maritime distress call. This did not help the *Titanic* which didn't receive timely information about the iceberg sighting or help after hitting it because of intermittent, poorly coded, and chaotic radio communications. Another ship, the *Californian*, was within eyesight of the *Titanic* when it hit the iceberg, but the ship

---

[6] ITU History. Retrieved from www.itu.int/en/history/Pages/ITUsHistory.aspx in August 2022.

did not receive the distress call.[7] Hence the ITU, and subsequently the Radio Act of 1912 in the United States, created agreements for common frequencies to be used for emergency communications only, and regulated the frequency spectrum to be licensed for specific purposes.[8]

The American company Motorola was the first one to miniaturize radio communications into one mobile phone in the early 1970s. This set off a race to develop phones and networks for commercial use. These first-generation analog networks were launched in Japan and in the Nordic countries in 1981. The Nordic electronics companies, including Ericsson from Sweden and Nokia from Finland, joined forces with national telecommunication carriers to create a new international standard called NMT (Nordic Mobile Telephony). Both the collaborative development approach and the technology behind NMT turned out to be outstanding commercial and technical successes. Nokia, Ericsson, and the Nordic telecom operators continued to cooperate, bringing along major European tech companies such as Siemens and Alcatel to work on the next-generation networks. The first digital network was 2G, which was launched in 1991 in Finland, and 3G was the first network with mobile internet capabilities, launched in 2001 in Japan but soon thereafter in Europe and in the US thanks to the now global cooperative effort to standardize the frequency bands, air interface technologies, and other features of these increasingly complex communication systems.

In communication networks, standards are as critical for information exchange as gauges are in rail networks. Without standards, documents or files circulating in one system need to be downloaded, reformatted, and uploaded in another system at great cost. In fact, still in 2020 there were industrial communication systems such as seaports where one computer system did not interoperate with another computer system, and, as a result, information was printed on paper, transferred manually to operators of the other system, and retyped into the other system. This was incredibly inefficient, but sometimes operators in the two systems are unable to agree on the transition path to a more interoperable system. Key issues are often data security and control of the content. None of the parties wants to relinquish its control over its proprietary information resources.

Communication **standard development** may be competitive or cooperative. **Competitive standard development**, or a "**standards war**" means that multiple rival standards are being developed and launched simultaneously. If network effects are strong, this will probably mean that one of the standards will fail, as explained in Section 10.1. An early standards war was the war of the currents. Thomas Edison was the proponent of the direct current (DC) and held a number

---

[7] Danigelis, A. (2012). Wireless could have saved lives on Titanic. NBC News, April 11, 2011. Retrieved from www.nbcnews.com/id/47018360/ns/technology_and_science/t/wireless-could-have-saved-lives-titanic/ in August 2022.

[8] Lasar, M. (2011). How the "Titanic" disaster pushed Uncle Sam to "rule the air." Ars Technica, July 7, 2011. Retrieved from https://arstechnica.com/tech-policy/2011/07/did-the-titanic-disaster-let-uncle-sam-take-over-the-airwaves/ in August 2022.

of patents in generation and distribution technologies. George Westinghouse and Nikola Tesla were the main proponents of the alternating current (AC). DC was safer but generated at lower voltage so its transmission network was less efficient and limited in size. AC was deemed more dangerous at high voltages, but Tesla had developed a transformer that allowed manipulating the voltage levels, making AC more versatile and suitable for larger distribution networks. The two rival sides of the battle developed their own technologies and attempted to convince the public and decision makers about the advantages and disadvantages of each. Edison, in particular, is known to have publicly electrocuted animals and even a death-row inmate to demonstrate the dangers of AC.[9] Nevertheless, AC was selected to electrify the Chicago World Fair in 1893, and subsequently it won other large contracts that tipped the market in its favor. Since then, AC generation and distribution has dominated the marketplace. However, DC may be making a comeback by providing higher efficiencies in extremely high voltage transmission, and in computing and renewable electricity![10]

Cooperative standard development often takes place in industry organizations such as alliances, consortia, or formal **standard development organizations** such as 3GPP. These can range from a small group of companies getting together to coordinate and promote a specific technology, such as the original Bluetooth Special Interest Group to very large international organizations such as the International Telecommunications Union (ITU) and the Institute of Electrical and Electronics Engineers (IEEE) or national organizations such as the Alliance for Telecommunication Industry Solutions (ATIS).

Bluetooth SIG was founded in 1998 by five companies: Ericsson, IBM, Intel, Nokia, and Toshiba. The short-range radio technology originated from Ericsson, but the company decided to open it up using this industry forum to collaboratively maintain and further develop the technical specifications. In 2019, membership fees for companies ranged from $7,500 for small firms to $35,000 for large firms. Membership in the forum gave access to the Bluetooth trademarks and product certification and to the technical working groups that developed enhancements to the specifications. However, users of the standard still needed to separately license relevant patents from the patent holders, primarily Ericsson.[11]

IEEE, founded in 1884, was a large professional organization with about 400,000 individual members in 160 different countries. It hosted many technical communities that developed and learned about emerging technologies and scientific

[9] King, G. (2011). Edison vs. Westinghouse: a shocking rivalry. Smithsonian Magazine, October 11. Retrieved from www.smithsonianmag.com/history/edison-vs-westinghouse-a-shocking-rivalry-102146036/ in August, 2022.

[10] Finkel, A. (2017). Nikola Tesla: The AC/DC current wars make a comeback. Cosmos, September 14. Retrieved from https://cosmosmagazine.com/technology/tesla-vs-edison-the-ac-dc-current-wars-make-a-comeback in August 2022.

[11] Brachmann, S. (2015). Evolution of technology: Bluetooth, the once and future king. IP Watchdog, May 10. Retrieved from www.ipwatchdog.com/2015/05/10/evolution-of-technology-bluetooth-the-once-and-future-king/id=57473/ in August 2022.

discoveries. It also had a portfolio of nearly 1,300 standards under development, ranging from aerospace and antennae to smart grid and wireless communication technologies. IEEE had been the central venue for standardization of computer architectures and interfaces. Individuals or companies could join the IEEE Standards Association to participate in specification development, vote in technical projects, and potentially become working group leaders and agenda setters.

Standard development in cooperative organizations tends to be highly structured with committees and formalized work procedures to initiate, develop, modify, and certify technical specifications. All this takes time and expertise on the part of participating individuals and firms. Cooperative standard setting therefore tends to be lengthy and bureaucratic, but eventually generates standards that have wide acceptance in the marketplace.

One of the enablers of open and global standardization is the market for **intellectual property**. Computer and communication technologies involve a large number of patents that provide the right for the inventor or their assignee to exclude others from using the patented technologies. If maintained, patents may be valid for 20 years and provide fairly strong protection against direct imitation of hardware or software inventions. Most electronics and communication standard development organizations have policies about essential intellectual property rights that allow patent holders to collect "Fair, Reasonable, and Non-Discriminatory" (FRAND) royalties for their rights. If a patented technology is "essential," meaning the standard cannot be implemented without it, and the standard is adopted globally, a patent can be hugely valuable just because of the royalty revenue. It has been estimated that about 10 percent of the price of a smartphone goes toward patent royalty payments to other companies. Standards thus facilitate access to innovative features through the institutionalized process of coordinating and selecting technological solutions and providing opportunities to license technologies from other firms. Each firm has less control over the evolution of the industry, and more competitors can enter, but consumers are better off when innovations get widely implemented and many vendors and service providers compete in the market.

KEY IDEAS

- When multiple networks or standards compete in a market with strong network effects, the market is prone to tipping. Market tipping can take a long time and is often extremely costly, especially for the losing parties.
- Strategic decisions regarding compatibility and network openness determine how large the network will grow. Compatibility facilitates migration into the network from pre-existing networks, and openness enhances the complementary services, making the network more appealing to a larger number of people. The downside of compatibility and openness is becoming dependent on external providers of services.
- Communication network providers may need to consider whether and how to engage in formal standard development. A standards war ensues when two companies or groups of companies battle in the market for dominance. Cooperative

standard development takes place in national or international standard development organizations. Cooperative development takes a lot of time and resources, but the outcome is often a larger market with more adoption by end users.

- As electronics and software technologies can be protected by patents, patents have become an adjacent market of their own. When patented technologies are used in standardized systems, the patent holders often agree to license their patents to everyone adopting the standard. This sets up a market for standard-essential intellectual property. Many of the standard-essential patents are very valuable and they are frequently challenged in court as the patent holders' rivals are hoping to eliminate or reduce their royalty payments.

DEFINITIONS

Compatibility and **interoperability** refer to the ability of components of a system to interconnect.

Intellectual property includes a variety of intangible technology assets such as patents and copyrights. IP related to technical standards are often referred to as essential IP. SDOs usually have explicit policies regarding how essential IP should be licensed under Fair, Reasonable, and Non-Discriminatory terms.

Market tipping may happen when network effects are strong in a market with multiple competing systems. If a market tips, after some threshold, no amount of innovation by the losing side can entice users to not switch to the larger system.

A **network** or a **communication system** is **open** when anyone can connect.

Standard development is the process through which technical standards are developed. While **cooperative standard development** is very common in computing and telecommunications, firms occasionally end up in **competitive standard development** or a **standards war** where two standards compete for the market.

Standard Development Organizations (SDOs) are set up to orchestrate and manage industry-wide cooperative standard development.

DISCUSSION QUESTIONS

1. You are planning to develop a new game for mobile devices. Would you choose to make it compatible with an established gaming platform? What does the decision depend on? Describe the benefits and drawbacks of your selected compatibility strategy.

2. Your game is a new type of a social network and there is one other very similar application for mobile devices. What would you do to gain users more rapidly than your rival?

3. A developer contacts you and offers to develop "mods" and other virtual goods for your game, in exchange for a share of associated revenues. Do you think it's a good idea? What information would you need to decide?

4. When would you agree to develop standardized technologies for your game with providers of similar games? Under what conditions would you offer the core technologies of your game as an open standard to other developers?

FURTHER READING

Arthur, W. (1989). Competing technologies, increasing returns, and lock-in by historical events. *The Economic Journal* 99(394): 116–131.

Besen, S. M. and Farrell J. (1994). Choosing how to compete: strategies and tactics in standardization. *Journal of Economic Perspectives* 8(2): 117–131.

Corts, K.S. and Lederman, M. (2009). Software exclusivity and the scope of indirect network effects in the U.S. home video game market. *International Journal of Industrial Organization* 27(2): 121–136.

Katz, M.L. and Shapiro, C. (1994). Systems competition and network effects. *Journal of Economic Perspectives* 8(2): 93–115.

Rysman, M. (2004). Competition between networks: a study of the market for yellow pages. *The Review of Economic Studies* 71(2): 483–512.

11 Platform Strategies

Digital platforms are marketplaces where a variety of participants gather to exchange goods, information, or services. We know a lot about marketplaces from both personal experience, history, and economics. What makes digital platforms different?

Platforms, like marketplaces, consist of a structure for interaction where the core components are relatively fixed and stable, and other components change over time. In a traditional marketplace like the grand bazaar in Istanbul, the physical structure can stay more or less the same for centuries (over 500 years in this case), whereas the individual shops and their merchandize will change on a monthly or even daily basis. Same for digital platforms: the core architecture stays stable for extended periods of time (though probably not 500 years) and applications, users, vendors, and service providers come and go.

Platforms create value by allowing users to connect with each other and interact or transact in some way. The additional benefits provided by digital platforms include improved matching, trust, and liquidity, and lower costs of search and transaction. Connectivity among users based on digital communication technologies reduces **search costs** when one can easily search over many providers or users. As a result, **matching** of buyers and sellers is improved because of the better search technologies and the larger market. High-quality platforms also offer mechanisms to accumulate and verify a participant's reputation through their transaction history and associated analytics. There may also be mechanisms of quality assurance that allow buyers to return or get their money back for poor-quality items. These service features are easier to develop in digital environments, enabling the platform to build **digital trust** and goodwill in the trading community. Digital platforms may also reduce **transaction costs** by standardizing interfaces, automating payments, securing transfers, monitoring transaction patterns, and generally creating **liquidity** in the market. Liquidity means that a willing seller of an item is likely to find a willing buyer for a reasonable price and arises from improved search, matching, and scale of the marketplace. While earlier marketplaces could provide many of these service features, digital platforms are able to provide them all, and also enable unprecedented economies of scale. A digital platform such as eBay can facilitate commerce not just within a city, like the market hall or bazaar, but across the nation. They may thus create exceptionally efficient markets. However, the market for platforms themselves is anything but competitive and efficient.

Digitalization enhances competition in many markets. For example, the market for books is now almost entirely online and Amazon has reduced book prices significantly. Same for electronics, music, and all sorts of knick-knacks. However, in each area, there is usually one dominant platform. Amazon dominates books and now much of electronics. Spotify is beginning to dominate music, although other streaming platforms such as Apple Music are fighting back. eBay dominates markets for used goods. Such markets with strong network effects – substantial benefits from connecting to the larger market – tend to tip and become monopolized. Few people care much about the software features of eBay, but it is the largest market for the "DuroMax XP4850EH Hybrid Portable Dual Fuel Propane/Gas Camping RV Generator" (over 20,000 items sold in a seven-day period in June 2019 for a total revenue of almost $12 million).[1] This means that anyone in the market to either buy or sell this item is the most likely to have their needs met for a competitive price by going to eBay rather than some other digital marketplace.

The benefits of scale in markets are not surprising, but the ability of digital markets to scale globally is much more recent – and striking. After platforms achieve critical mass, there is often no point for a rival to enter because catching up to an exploding platform generally is a losing proposition, at least if the entrant offers no radical innovation. As a result, network effects allow platforms to concentrate vast market power. In fact, by 2021, seven of the 10 world's most valuable companies by market capitalization were not only digital companies, but digital platforms (see Table 11.1). The only non-digital company remaining on the list was the Saudi oil company that had found a way to accumulate exceptional market power in a different manner.

Such concentration of market power potentially creates a significant monopoly cost to society. Platforms such as Google and Apple may have access to everyone's information through their ability to leverage search, email, and mobile software services. Facebook may have access to everyone's social networks and other sources of information, and Uber or Google (via Waze) may have a complete profile of everyone's mobility. These types of networked services thus tend toward market tipping and domination, creating headaches for governmental regulators.

In traditional markets, dominant companies providing "essential facilities," such as telecommunication networks, electric utilities, or railroads, may be regulated (cf. Lipsky & Sidak, 1999[2]). However, in digital markets where consumers have free access to the services but then are subject to the collection and monetization of private information, the regulatory framework has not evolved rapidly enough to address monopolization of information exchange. However, calls for breaking up the major digital platforms in Europe and in the United States have grown louder.[3]

---

[1] These data were retrieved from https://crazylister.com/blog/top-selling-items-on-ebay/ in August 2022.

[2] Lipsky, A.B. and Sidak, J.G. (1999). Essential facilities. Stanford Law Review 51(May): 1187–1248. Retrieved from www.criterioneconomics.com/docs/essential_facilities1.pdf in August 2022.

[3] See, for example, *The New York Times* (2019). Retrieved from www.nytimes.com/2019/05/09/opinion/sunday/chris-hughes-facebook-zuckerberg.html in August 2022.

Table 11.1 The world's most valuable companies by stock market capitalization and their main services, 2021

Ranking	Company	Stock market value ($ million)	Main products and services
1.	**Apple**	2050	Digital platform (App Store)
2.	Saudi Aramco	1890	Oil
3.	**Microsoft**	1778	Digital platform (Windows)
4.	**Amazon**	1558	Digital platform (marketplace)
5.	**Alphabet**	1395	Digital platform (Google, Android)
6.	**Facebook**	839	Digital platform (social network)
7.	**Tencent**	767	Digital platform conglomerate
8.	Tesla	641	Electric cars
9.	**Alibaba**	615	Digital platform conglomerate
10.	TSMC	613	Semiconductors

Note: Digital platform companies in bold.
Data retrieved from https://en.wikipedia.org/wiki/List_of_public_corporations_by_market_capitalization#2021 in August 2022.

11.1   Multisided Markets

A **multisided market** consists of a digital platform that brings together two or more distinct "sides," or types of parties, who depend on each other in some important way, and whose interaction makes the platform more valuable. There are thus indirect network effects between the different groups.

Keeping with the bazaar theme, the "sides" within a shopping mall include consumers and shops. The platform here, the shopping mall, hosts both shops and consumers who visit. Similarly, eBay hosts buyers and sellers of everything under the sun. Online news services usually host readers and advertisers.

The difference between a multisided market and a traditional "merchant" is that the latter buys and sells stuff. For example, Walmart is not a platform but an intermediary that buys goods from suppliers and then sells the goods to consumers. It doesn't facilitate direct transactions between suppliers and consumers. Although a larger selection of items makes it more likely that consumers find what they need and are more satisfied, a Walmart buyer does not know where the goods were sourced. This difference matters because a business such as Walmart does not involve network effects. While there are strong economies of scale, consumers do not specifically benefit from a large number of suppliers, as long as the product range is broad and the prices are low. In the digital platform environment, in contrast, there are sizable benefits from large numbers of parties on each side, because it is not known ahead of time which one will be the ideal match for a particular purpose. The power of eBay comes from its ability to connect individuals with unusual items with those who have unusual preferences. The power of Twitter came from its ability to connect (and amplify) individuals with exceptional view-points with those who appreciate the information or the perspective. The power of Walmart, in contrast, comes from its ability to buy products in very large quantities for very cheap prices, and then sell them through its large network of stores for only slightly higher prices.

Analyzing the structure of network effects is critical for understanding how they might evolve. A multisided market may have multiple network effects that can be positive or negative. For example, Google's search engine platform has two sides: searchers and advertisers. The platform is more valuable to advertisers when there are more searchers. This is thus a positive effect. However, searchers usually do not care about advertisers, and some searchers even find advertisers a negative good (a "bad"). There is thus a positive **cross-side network effect** only in one direction, from searchers to advertisers. There can also be positive or negative **same-side network effects**. For example, players usually prefer massively multiplayer online games where there are many other players – a positive same-side network effect. However, in some situations parties on the same side may be competing against one another. An example is a dating site, where most men prefer to have many women on the other side (positive cross-side effect) but few men on their own side (negative same-side effect). But, there could also be a positive same-side network effect on a dating site. Such effects thus need to be carefully examined and mapped out in order to understand which parties bring the most value to the platform: What is the nature of the interactions among the different types of participants? This is particularly important for choosing appropriate launch and early-stage growth strategies.

11.2 Chickens and Eggs

As with two-mode communication networks generally, the trickiest strategic challenge for platforms is to achieve critical mass. The extra challenge with multisided markets is to get sufficient numbers *on each side* that are subject to positive network effects. This requires that the platform innovator pay careful attention to the structure of network effects and the incentives for each side to join the platform. The analysis of network effects will show which parties are critical to attract to the platform. **Platform strategies** that the innovator can pursue consist of designing incentives for these parties to join by using pricing, service design, and integration strategies. **Network strategies** of openness and compatibility that were discussed in Chapter 10 can also be used to facilitate the user acquisition of the platform.

Platform pricing is a strategy economists have studied thoroughly. The key issue is to help individuals on the different sides coordinate their actions in order for both (or all) to adopt the platform around the same time. Otherwise, the **chicken-and-egg** problem will simply lead to a collapse. If sellers adopt the platform but

Buyer

		Go	Not
Seller	Go	5,1	-1,0
	Not	0,-1	0,0

Figure 11.1 Game-theoretic illustration of attendance at a trading event
Note: There are two equilibria in this game, the (Go,Go) equilibrium (preferred) and the (Not,Not) equilibrium. If the seller believes the buyer will not attend, there is no reason for the seller to attend, either. Both parties are the least happy if they attend without the other party. The platform's challenge is to convince both parties to attend.

there are no buyers, they will soon leave. If buyers adopt the platform but there are no sellers, they will soon leave. It is thus not helpful to ask "which one should come first, chicken or egg," but to attract both at the same time if there are positive cross-side network effects between them.

An example may be helpful to illustrate platform pricing. We will explore the preferences and incentives, and resulting optimal prices, to visit a comics trading event. There are sellers and buyers in the market, and sellers' preferences are significantly stronger as illustrated in the game matrix in Figure 11.1:

Simplifying to just a two-person game, if both the seller and the buyer attend, the seller's utility (e.g., profit) is 5 and the buyer's utility (e.g. consumer surplus) is 1. If the seller attends but the buyer does not show up, the seller experiences the utility of -1 (e.g., transportation cost to the site) and the buyer's utility is 0. If the buyer attends and the seller doesn't, these utilities are reversed. If neither attends, neither gains any utility. It is thus socially optimal that both parties attend the event (total utility of 6), but there is a second equilibrium when neither attends which can be tricky to avoid. This is thus a chicken-and-egg problem of coordinating the responses of the parties. Neither party wants to be the only one showing up and may simply stay at home to avoid that outcome if they are not sure their counterpart will attend. How to convince both parties to attend?

One option is to use pricing to entice sellers and buyers to attend the event (see Figure 11.2). We assume the platform will charge P_S for sellers and P_B for buyers. How much should each be?

If the platform applies monopoly pricing, we know that the maximum value for $P_S = 4.99$ and for $P_B = 0.99$. However, even this type of straightforward (and perfect) price discrimination will not solve the chicken-and-egg problem. There is still a good equilibrium (Go, Go) and a bad equilibrium (Not, Not), but if the parties are stuck in the bad equilibrium they will not be able to get out; there is no incentive for either party to change out of (Not, Not) if they know their counterpart is not

Figure 11.2 Platform pricing strategies to induce attendance
Note: The total utility from trading equals the utility from trading minus the price of entry. What prices P_S and P_B can make the (Go,Go) equilibrium the only equilibrium, meaning that the parties will attend even if they believe the other party may not attend?

attending. How can we make it appealing for the parties to attend either way? The solution is to "divide and conquer." By choosing a negative price for the buyer (i.e., a subsidy), it is possible to make "Go" their dominant strategy. When the buyer attends independent of the choices of the seller, the seller knows the buyer will be there. How much should the prices be for each side?

Pricing can thus be used to coordinate the different platform sides. The higher the willingness to pay, the higher the price. The platform may even subsidize one side (apply a negative price) that has a low willingness to pay but that contributes to network effects for another side. The key insight is that pricing based on either marginal cost or price discrimination is unlikely to motivate potential participants to join the platform. The greatest strategic challenge for platform innovators is to reach critical mass, therefore pricing should initially focus on maximizing adoption. Indeed, there is great variety of possible platform pricing schemes, and successful schemes carefully assess each side's willingness to pay and motivation to join. For example, some online newspapers (usually high-quality or timely information) charge both readers and advertisers, and others charge only advertisers (usually lesser-quality or less-critical information). Microsoft built an ecosystem of software developers and gave them free access to the Windows platform, while users paid for the platform. In contrast, Apple and Google charge app developers a fee to be added on the platform, whereas users do not pay for platform access (they may pay for apps, though).

In addition to pricing, platform innovators may consider offering some critical complementary services internally, or **integrating** into one of the complementary markets, rather than attempting to create external supply for them. Game console makers typically offer some content themselves to make sure the platform (or its new generation) takes off but also enable outside game developers to sell content on their platform (cf. Nintendo + Super Mario Bros.). The tighter the complementarity between the platform and the add-on service, the more it makes sense for the platform innovator to also offer the complement. However, if a competitive market of complements already exists when the platform enters, it is unlikely to be a lucrative opportunity to also integrate into

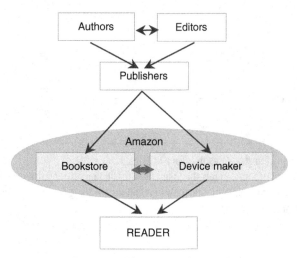

Figure 11.3 The Amazon platform ecosystem in e-books
Note: By offering both the e-bookstore and the reading device, Amazon has built a platform in the e-book market that controls the bottleneck between publishers and readers.

the complement markets. The key goal of the innovator is to control whatever is the bottleneck of the platform market. For example, Amazon created a thriving market for e-books as an extension of its online book business, and it has substantially leveraged this platform that connects readers and publishers (or even authors directly) by creating and supporting the Kindle device that is the key complement to the bookstore (see Figure 11.3). Similarly, Netflix and later Amazon created platforms for movie viewers to stream (license) content from studios. However, a handful of major movie studios exercised strong control of the content market and charged high prices or didn't allow their content to be streamed at all. Both Netflix and Amazon decided to integrate into the content market themselves.[4]

KEY IDEAS

- Digital platforms are powerful commercial structures because they provide many benefits and improvements over simple e-commerce or offline commerce: scale, liquidity, trust, matching, and lower costs of search and transaction.
- Depending on the nature of interactions among participants, platforms may exhibit network effects both within each side (same-side network effects) and across sides (cross-side network effects). It is critical to understand the strength and nature of these interactions in order to effectively promote early adoption of the platform.
- Platforms need to reach critical mass on each side that is essential for the interactions, which is often called the chicken-and-egg problem. It is a complicated

---

[4] For example, Amazon purchased MGM studios in 2021: https://www.cnbc.com/2021/05/26/amazon-to-buy-mgm-studios-for-8point45-billion.html retrieved in August 2022.

strategic challenge to ensure that there is a critical mass of users on each of the positively interacting sides of the platform.

- Platform strategies to populate the sides include pricing and integration, in addition to the network strategies of openness and compatibility.

DEFINITIONS

The **chicken-and-egg** problem describes the difficulty for a newly launched platform of gaining momentum and reaching critical mass on the different "sides."

A **cross-side network effect** makes the platform more valuable to users on one side when there are new users on the other side.

Digital trust is a form of trust that may emerge in digital platforms in interactions among strangers or anonymous users. Digital trust forms when users trust digital technologies as a replacement for interpersonal or organizational trust. Reputation mechanisms are usually central for the formation of digital trust.

Liquidity refers to the probability of a trader finding a counterpart within a reasonable time and for reasonable transaction costs.

Matching is an essential function of a marketplace whereby it allows willing buyers to find willing sellers of the specific traded goods. Matching is particularly challenging in labor markets and in markets for very unique or idiosyncratic goods and services.

A **multisided market** brings together two or more distinct "sides," or types of trading parties, who depend on each other in some important way.

Platform adoption can also be facilitated by **network strategies** related to the openness of interfaces and compatibility with other platforms or systems.

Platform strategies include pricing and integration to facilitate coordinated adoption of the platform by users on different sides.

A **same-side network effect** applies when users interact with other users on the same side of (in the same role on) the platform.

Search costs can reduce the efficiency of a marketplace by making it difficult and costly to find the demanded goods.

Transaction costs include all costs that arise from completing a specific transaction, including the costs of financing, de-risking, exchanging currency, searching, and matching.

DISCUSSION QUESTIONS

1. Consider an airport as a multisided platform. What are the different sides, and how are the network effects structured within and among the sides? How does your analysis inform pricing of access to the airport?

2. Write down the (approximate) game structure for search users and advertisers who participate in Google's search platform (cf. Figure 11.2).

3. Venmo is a peer-to-peer payment application. Describe the sides of this platform and the network effects among them. Why are the direct transfers among individuals free?

4. Many recent car models offer in-vehicle WiFi and driving data transfer based on a wireless telecommunication connection (e.g., 5G). If you were an auto manufacturer like Tesla, would you integrate into communication services and build your own communication platform or connect with an existing platform?

FURTHER READING

Cusumano, M.A., Gawer, A., and Yoffie, D.B. (2019). *The Business of Platforms: Strategy in the Age of Digital Competition, Innovation, and Power*. New York: HarperCollins Publishers.

Kretschmer, T, Leiponen, A, Schilling, M, and Vasudeva, G. (2022). Platform ecosystems as meta-organizations: implications for platform strategies. *Strategic Management Journal* 43 (3): 405–424.

Parker, G.G. and Van Alstyne, M.W. (2005). Two-sided network effects: a theory of information product design. *Management Science* 51 (10): 1449–1592.

Rysman, M. (2009). The economics of two-sided markets. *Journal of Economic Perspectives* 23 (3): 125–143.

CASE 3: EPIC GAMES: UNREAL BATTLE ROYALE

Epic Games, the creator of the hugely popular computer game Fortnite described itself as an "interactive entertainment company and provider of 3D engine technology."[5] Tim Sweeney, while a mechanical engineering student at University of Maryland, founded the company in 1991 under the name Potomac Computer Systems out of his parents' home. He continued as the CEO in 2021. In addition to games, Epic Games also created Unreal Engine, the 3D game creation tool that powered a large array of games and 3D design by film, TV, simulation, architecture, automotive, and manufacturing companies. Furthermore, Epic Online Services facilitated content development for a variety of platforms, including Apple, Xbox, PlayStation, Steam, Nintendo, and Android. Epic Game Store was a distribution channel for Epic's in-house games and those by third-party developers such as Rockstar Games (creator of Grand Theft Auto), Firaxis Games (Civilization franchise), Hangar 13 (Mafia), and Supergiant Games (Hades). Major game categories on the distribution platform included action, adventure, puzzle, racing, role-playing, shooter, strategy, and survival.

---

[5] For the history of Epic Games, see, for example, https://apps.voxmedia.com/at/polygon-a-history-of-epic-games/ and Gebel, M. and Gilbert, B. (2020). The life and rise of Tim Sweeney. Business Insider, August 18, 2020. Retrieved from www.businessinsider.com/fortnite-maker-epic-games-ceo-tim-sweeney-history-timeline-2019-10#tim-sweeney-50-was-born-in-1970-and-raised-in-potomac-maryland-with-two-older-brothers-his-father-was-a-cartographer-for-the-us-government-and-his-mother-took-care-of-sweeney-and-his-brothers-1 in August 2022.

Case 3.1 History

Tim Sweeney copied his first game, ZZT, on discs that his father mailed to customers who sent him checks in return. ZZT's popularity was at least in part because of its high degree of modifiability. Sweeney's father kept mailing these games until 2013.[6] In a few years, the company grew to 25 employees.

Software piracy became a challenge for single-player games in the early 2000s – they would be copied soon after launch – and Epic shifted its offerings toward console games. Over the years, Epic developed games for consoles, PCs, and mobile devices. It developed them both in-house and in collaboration with external parties such as People Can Fly that co-developed Bulletstorm with Epic Games, published by Electronic Arts.

Unreal Engine was first developed and commercialized in a first-person shooter game. It was one of the most advanced 3D creation platforms on the market. It opened for other creators in 2015, making the development tools and technologies freely available for all developers. Only after the developed games launched commercially would Epic Games start collecting 5 percent royalties out of the game revenue.

Next, Epic Games opened the Game Store in 2019. The goal was to compete against other app and game stores with "fair economics" (lower commission) and enable direct connections between creators and players.[7] Epic Games had realized that having its store only offer its in-house games would not be very attractive. The company therefore invited other developers, particularly startup creators, to join in its effort to enter the game store competition.

Finally, Epic's Online Services provided development tools such as matchmaking and P2P connectivity of players, player leaderboards and statistics, and motivational tools such as achievements and ticketing for special resources. Epic was very clear about the benefits of scale and network effects:

> There is no catch. We built many of these services for Fortnite and are now operating at enormous economies of scale, and we also rely on these services for the Epic Games Store. Now, we are happy to offer these services to game developers for free with the goal of encouraging wider adoption of all of Epic's offerings, and of making cross-play, cross-progression, and other open and interconnected, online features more accessible to everyone. Ultimately, when developers choose to use Epic Account Services, Epic and all participating partners benefit by growing a cross-platform account base and social graph available to all.[8]

Epic first revealed Fortnite in 2011 although it wasn't launched until 2017. Epic Games created and maintained six other games: Battle Breakers, Infinity

---

[6] Epic Games timeline. Retrieved from https://populartimelines.com/timeline/Epic-Games in August 2022.

[7] Epic Games company website www.epicgames.com/store/en-US/about retrieved in August 2022.

[8] Epic Games company website: https://dev.epicgames.com/en-US/services retrieved in August 2022.

Blade, Robo Recall, Shadow Complex, Spyjinx, and Unreal Tournament. With the proliferation of broadband and streaming services, the company made a bet that PC gaming and direct digital distribution would be the next major gaming market, bypassing consoles and other walled gardens. *Fortnite*, like many of the new streaming games, was free to play and collected revenue from in-game purchases such as "skins" or character costumes that do not give players a competitive advantage in the game. With 350 million players, by 2020, Epic Games had collected over $4 billion in three years from *Fortnite* virtual goods. *Fortnite* also allowed players to stream game play, with superstars such as Tyler "Ninja" Blevins making millions annually on Twitch or YouTube. In 2012, Tencent validated the new product and platform strategy by buying a 40 percent ownership stake for $330 million, indicating a valuation of $825 million.[9] Fortnite fueled the rapid growth of Epic Games, and, in 2018, the company was valued at $4.5 billion, and after another large funding round in 2020, the valuation had climbed to $17.3 billion.[10]

Case 3.2 Revenue Model

Epic Games collected revenue from game sales, in-game digital good sales, and commissions from the game store and the game engine tools. It took a 12 percent commission from store sales, and a 5 percent royalty from developer revenues from games built on Unreal Engine. In an effort to attract unique content to the game store, the company signed exclusive distribution deals with developers. In 2019, the game store generated $680 million in revenue, and 108 million unique user accounts had purchased or downloaded a game from the game store.[11]

Fornite generated $1.8 billion in 2019, mostly from in-game goods.[12] *Fortnite* revenue tended to spike every time an updated version was released and new virtual goods became available for purchase.[13] To further fine-tune its revenue model, the game introduced Battle Pass, a subscription pass that provided game updates on exclusive features and discounts for game

[9] See https://populartimelines.com/timeline/Epic-Games retrieved in August 2022.

[10] Browne, R. (2020). Fortnite creator Epic Games is now valued at $17.3B after blockbuster funding deal. CNBC, August 6, 2020. Retrieved from www.cnbc.com/2020/08/06/fortnite-creator-epic-games-is-now-valued-at-17point3-billion.html in August 2022.

[11] Perez, M. (2020). Epic Games Store has hit $680 million in revenue, 108 million customers. Forbes, January 14, 2020. Retrieved from www.forbes.com/sites/mattperez/2020/01/14/epic-games-store-has-hit-680-million-in-revenue-108-million-customers/#5e835584b99a in August 2022.

[12] Shanley, P. (2020). Global digital game spending hits record $109 billion in 2019. *Hollywood Reporter*, January 2, 2020. Retrieved from www.hollywoodreporter.com/news/global-digital-game-spending-hits-record-109-billion-mark-2019-1265275 in August 2022.

[13] Russell, J. (2018). Epic Games, the creator of Fortnite, banked a $3 billion profit in 2081. TechCrunch, December 27, 2018. Retrieved from https://techcrunch.com/2018/12/27/epic-fortnite-3-billion-profit/ in August 2022.

accessories, and an in-game currency called V-bucks to incentivize players to purchase items in the game.[14] In total, Epic Games was estimated to generate $5 billion of revenue in 2020.[15]

Case 3.3 Cost Structure

Epic Games had significant up-front fixed costs of game development, but once games were released, the firm could digitally distribute a nearly unlimited volume. Game development primarily depended on talented and hard-working employees.[16] The costs of sales and other services were relatively small. In 2020 the company was estimated to employ 4,468 people, and with a revenue of $5 billion, each employee generated over a million dollars of revenue.[17]

Another cost category for Epic Games was acquiring exclusive rights to third-party games. For example, Epic Games Store exclusively distributed the popular PC game Control from 2019. Its exclusive distribution rights reportedly cost Epic $10.5 million up-front.[18] Epic Games also paid approximately $2.25 million to secure a one-year exclusive of the game Phoenix Point.[19]

Through mobile platforms such as the Apple App Store, Epic Games paid 30 percent of all revenue from micro-transactions to Apple. Fortnite consistently ranked as one of Apple's highest grossing apps on its store. By 2020, Fortnite had generated over $1 billion in micro-transactions from the mobile version of the game, so Epic Games had paid over $300 million in commission to Apple and Google for Fortnite distribution alone.[20]

---

[14] Ganti, A. (2020). How does Fortnite make money? Investopedia, September 10, 2020. Retrieved from www.investopedia.com/tech/how-does-fortnite-make-money/ retrieved in August 2022.

[15] Takahashi, D. (2020). Epic Games unveils $1.78 billion funding round at $17.3 billion valuation. VentureBeat, August 6, 2020. Retrieved from https://venturebeat.com/2020/08/06/epic-games-unveils-1-78-billion-funding-round-at-17-3-billion-valuation/ in June 2021.

[16] Campbell, C. (2019). How Fortnite's success led to months of intense crunch at Epic Games. Polygon, April 23, 2019. Retrieved from www.polygon.com/2019/4/23/18507750/fortnite-work-crunch-epic-games in August 2022.

[17] Epic Games. Craft intelligence portal. Retrieved from https://craft.co/epic-games in August 2022.

[18] Raevenlord (2019). Exclusivity costs: Epic Games Store's Control cost $10.5 million to become PC exclusive. TechPowerUp, September 23, 2019. Retrieved from www.techpowerup.com/259476/exclusivity-costs-epic-games-stores-control-cost-usd-10-5-million-to-become-pc-exclusive in August 2022.

[19] Blake, V. (2019). Phoenix Point's Epic Store exclusivity deal is worth $2.25 million says Fig investor. *PC Gamer*, April 22, 2019. Retrieved from www.pcgamer.com/phoenix-points-epic-store-exclusivity-deal-is-worth-dollar225-million-says-fig-investor/#:~:text=Phoenix%20Point-,-,Phoenix%20Point's%20Epic%20Store%20exclusivity%20deal,%242.25%20million%2C%20says%20Fig in August 2022.

[20] Hume, C. and Deller, W. (2020). Epic Games goes to battle with Apple and Google: The dispute so far. *Lexology*, September 25, 2020. Retrieved from www.lexology.com/library/detail.aspx?g=a0a16d4d-a41e-4a51-8e12-68625af1e47d#:~:text=The%20revenue%20Epic%20makes%20is,Store%20and%20Google%20Play%20Store. in August 2022.

Case 3.4 Competition

Epic's main competitors in game development included companies like Electronic Arts and Activision Blizzard. As of 2019, both Activision Blizzard and Electronic Arts generated more annual revenue than Epic Games, with $6.5 billion and $5.5 billion, respectively.[21] These companies produced high-quality, big-budget games, typically releasing them across all available platforms. There was heavy competition for the limited budget and attention of users.

In game store competition, Steam remained the most formidable. Steam was a pioneering game distributor since 2003, and had amassed a library of content spanning two decades.[22] In 2020, Steam outranked the Epic Store in popularity, due to a much larger library of both independently developed ("indie") games and Triple-A titles (games developed and released by medium-to-large game publishers). Steam's game recommendation tool was highly praised, recommending titles based on previous gaming habits.[23] In turn, the Epic Store featured exclusive titles that could only be purchased through the platform, creating some switching costs. Steam rarely featured exclusive content. Additionally, developers like Ubisoft and Activision Blizzard distributed their own entertainment content and offered exclusive games as well.

Dozens of vendors offered game development tools, including the highly popular distribution platforms Roblox and Steam. Some of the tools like Unity, CryEngine, Lumberyard, and Godot targeted lower-end developers.[24] Each offered services designed for specific types of games (2D or 3D), scripting languages (e.g., C#, Lua, or GDScript), and operating systems (e.g., Windows, macOS, or Linux) and prices ranging from free to a monthly subscription to a 5 percent royalty fee from commercial revenues.[25] Epic's selling points included an intuitive editor, superior graphic quality for 3D games, and a direct pipeline to publish games via the Epic Game Store.

With well-established companies like Steam and Apple already in the game development and distribution platform markets, Epic attempted to differentiate its offerings. First, it charged a lower commission. Compared to a 30 percent cut

---

[21] Epic Games competitors. *Craft intelligence portal.* Retrieved from https://craft.co/epic-games/competitors in August 2022.

[22] Sayer, M. and Wilde, T. (2018). The 15-year evolution of Steam. *PC Gamer*, September 12, 2018. Retrieved from www.pcgamer.com/steam-versions/ in June 2021.

[23] Minor, J. (2020). Steam vs. Epic Games Store: Which PC game store deserves your dollars? *PC Magazine*, August 25, 2020. Retrieved from www.pcmag.com/comparisons/steam-vs-epic-games-store-which-pc-game-store-deserves-your-dollars in August 2022.

[24] Moore, D.M. (2020). 11 tools to get you started making video games. *The Verge*, April 14, 2020. Retrieved from www.theverge.com/2020/4/14/21219609/video-game-tools-editor-developer-make-price-free-programming in August 2022.

[25] Wilson, L. (2019). Godot, Unity, Unreal Engine, CryEngine: which game engine should I choose? *Medium*, November 1, 2019. Retrieved from https://medium.com/@thelukaswils/godot-unity-unreal-engine-cryengine-which-game-engine-should-i-choose-553f8ff7999f in August 2022.

offered by many competitors, Epic Games only took a 12 percent cut from game developers. Second, it attempted to better support game developers. For instance, Epic's CEO explained, "when we're building tools, we respect developers' complete creative freedom."[26] Third, the company paid developers to have their titles exclusively on the Epic platform. For example, Borderlands 3 and Metro Exodus for PC were only available on the Epic Games platform. Additionally, the Epic Store interface design was clean and user-friendly. Meanwhile, deals and discounts were often more attractive on the Steam platform that offered substantial seasonal sales. The Epic Store countered by regularly releasing big-title games free-of-charge.

Epic Games' main challenge was to keep up with its major rivals Activision Blizzard and Electronic Arts. This depended on extending the interest of gamers in long-standing products like Fortnite to maintain its revenue streams. Regular updates to game content were essential.

Another competitive challenge for Epic Games was navigating the relationships with the major game console providers Microsoft (the Xbox), Sony (the PlayStation), and Nintendo (the Switch). These industry giants generally preferred exclusive games. In contrast, Epic Games depended on a large network of users spanning multiple platforms. For a period of time, Sony refused to allow Fortnite players on PlayStation to "cross-play," that is, access their account from multiple consoles such as Microsoft's Xbox and Nintendo's Switch.[27] This severely reduced the size of Fortnite's network, decreasing its value to players. To resolve the issue, Epic Games needed to reassure console providers that its products were an asset to the system and worth giving up some of the console's differentiation.

Gamers' initial reaction to the Epic Game Store was lukewarm. The store launched with technical problems and a limited offering. Furthermore, conspiracy theories surrounding Epic suggested that the major investor, Tencent, controlled the company and that the store distributed spyware stealing consumers' personal data. The company denied all allegations, but the public relations damage was done.[28] Entering the game distribution market was riddled with challenges.

Case 3.5 Epic Platform Strategies

Epic Games made a number of strategic moves to open up its player and developer networks and attract new users. Between 2015 and 2019, Epic made its Unreal Engine open and available to all developers and only charged royalties

[26] Statt, N. (2019). Epic vs. Steam: the console war reimagined on the PC. The Verge, April 16, 2019. Retrieved from www.theverge.com/2019/4/16/18334865/epic-games-store-versus-steam-valve-pc-gaming-console-war-reimagined in August 2022.

[27] Warren, T. (2018). Sony enabling Fortnite cross play for PS4 against Xbox and Switch. The Verge, September 26, 2018. Retrieved from www.theverge.com/2018/9/26/17905146/sony-fortnite-ps4-cross-play-support in August 2022.

[28] Hall (2019). The fury over the Epic Games Store, explained. Polygon, April 5, 2019. Retrieved from www.polygon.com/2019/4/5/18295833/epic-games-store-controversy-explained in August 2022.

if they developed a commercial game. This made Unreal Engine more attractive for first-time developers, compared to competing engines such as Unity and GameMaker.[29] It also provided free online services with a variety of development tools and resources. Further, Epic invested in video game start-ups such as Manticore Games, which fundraised $15 million with Epic Games' support.[30]

By lowering entry barriers for video game creators it diversified its game selection at a lower cost than by in-house game development. With the concurrent rise of popular "indie" games such as Undertale (with over 3.5 million individual sales on Steam), Papers, Please (over 2.8 million sales), and Stardew Valley (over 5 million sales), there was a large profit to be made from small-time developers with few resources.[31] The free distribution of Epic's development tools allowed developers to create multiplayer experiences that mirrored those of Epic Game's in-house games. Gamers could connect with each other using accounts across games developed with this system. This services kit included many key multiplayer features for game developers, including cross-platform support and multiplayer lobbies. Epic Games was using the free tools and online services as a means to create a gaming ecosystem that end users could recognize and feel a part of.

Beyond gaming, Epic Games began to partner with automotive manufacturers to use its Unreal Engine to develop in-car software, which Epic Games described as its "human–machine interface" initiative.[32] The partnership with General Motors was a potential pathway into the development of autonomous vehicles. Epic hoped to position the Unreal Engine as the basis for features and functions for these vehicles.

Case 3.6 Litigation

By 2020, Epic Games' Fortnite boasted 350 million players, and iOS users could only download it through Apple's App Store. Although Google allowed "side-loading" of apps for Android phones, it was also available on the Play Store where most of the Android downloads took place. As such, Epic had agreed

---

[29] Su, Jake (2020). Epic Games unveil Unreal Engine 5 with breathtaking PS5 demo. Geek Culture, May 14, 2020. Retrieved from https://geekculture.co/epic-games-unveil-unreal-engine-5-with-breathtaking-ps5-demo/ in August 2022.

[30] Manticore (2020). Epic Games leads $15M investment in Manticore Games. Press Release, September 22, 2020. Retrieved from https://apnews.com/press-release/business-wire/corporate-news-north-america-software-industry-investment-management-financial-services-c6b2db4276e4476c878e1bc1763d8c46 in August 2022.

[31] Orland, K. (2018). Valve leaks Steam game player counts; we have the numbers. Ars Technica, July 6, 2018. Retrieved from https://arstechnica.com/gaming/2018/07/steam-data-leak-reveals-precise-player-count-for-thousands-of-games/ in August 2022.

[32] Statt, Nick (2020). GMC's all-electric Hummer will be the first car with software built using Epic's Unreal Engine. The Verge, October 7, 2020. Retrieved from www.theverge.com/2020/10/7/21506572/epic-games-unreal-engine-general-motors-gmc-hummer-ev-human-machine-interface in August 2022.

to the 30 percent commission arrangements on both platforms. Nevertheless, it worked to bypass the mobile platforms by offering players a 20 percent discount on in-app purchases if they paid directly to Epic Games, rather than through Apple or Google payment systems.[33] As a result, both Apple and Google removed the game from their stores for violating the platform rules. Epic then sued Apple and Google for anti-competitive practices related to app distribution and payments. Epic claimed that the platforms had excessive market power that allowed them to impose unreasonable restraints.[34] Epic requested that the companies repeal their monopolistic practices. It also sought "injunctive relief that would deliver Google's broken promise: an open, competitive Android ecosystem for all users and industry participants."[35] Epic wanted to open up the mobile ecosystems so that Epic and other companies could create competing app stores on iOS and Android devices, and offer users and developers more innovation and more choice, including in payment processing. Thus, Epic attacked Apple's and Google's fundamental business models in seeking access to app distribution on their devices.

Outside the courtroom, Epic Games joined forces with Spotify, Match Group, and other prominent app developers to form the nonprofit alliance Coalition for App Fairness to push for changes in the app market.[36] Epic Games also launched the #FREEFORTNITE campaign, intended to turn millions of Fortnite fans against the tech behemoths. To underscore the irony of just how powerful Apple had become, Epic Games published "Nineteen-eighty-fortnite," a parody video of the tech titan's iconic 1984 Super Bowl commercial.[37] A chilling call to action, the video asserts, "Epic Games has defied the App Store Monopoly. In retaliation, Apple is blocking Fortnite from a billion devices. Join the fight to stop 2020 from becoming 1984."

The court's decision in this case could prove consequential to the antitrust rules applicable to the ever-evolving tech industry. The case had the potential to permanently disrupt the status quo – potentially prying control of the mobile platform markets, the foundation of their profitability, from Apple and Google. Considering that public opinion appeared to be siding with Epic Games, the tech giants could lose user goodwill if they were unable to alter public perception. On the other side, losing the case could prove costly to Epic Games.

---

[33] BBC (2020a). Fortnite: Epic Games sues Google and Apple over app store bans. BBC News, August 14, 2020. Retrieved from www.bbc.com/news/technology-53777379 in August 2022.

[34] D'Anastasio (2020). Epic Games' lawsuits fire a shot at Apple and Google's app store 'monopolies.' Wired, August 13, 2020. Retrieved from www.wired.com/story/epic-games-sues-apple-fortnite-app-store/ in August 2022.

[35] Sherr, I. and Van Boom, D. (2021). Apple scores legal win over Epic in Fortnite lawsuit: what you need to know. C/NET, September 13, 2021. Retrieved from www.cnet.com/news/epic-suing-apple-and-google-over-fortnite-bans-everything-you-need-to-know/ in August 2022.

[36] Griffith, E. (2020). Apple and Epic Games spar over returning Fortnite to the app store. The New York Times, September 29, 2020. Retrieved from www.nytimes.com/2020/09/28/technology/apple-epic-app-court.html in August 2022.

[37] Fortnite (2020). Nineteen Eighty-Fortnite – #FreeFortnite, August 13, 2020. Retrieved from www.youtube.com/watch?v=euiSHuaw6Q4 in August 2022.

DISCUSSION QUESTIONS

1. Where are there network effects in Epic's gaming system? Are they direct or indirect?
2. Why do you think Epic Games made online services freely available? Do you think that was a good strategic choice?
3. How can Epic Games Store compete against more established game stores such as Steam or mobile app stores?
4. Based on the case reading about the litigation between Epic Games and Apple, what are the main arguments for Epic Games, and what are the main arguments for Apple?

PART IV
Organizing Digital Innovations

· ·

Equipped with an understanding of the technological and market dynamics of digital innovations, we will now shift gears to investigate organizational approaches to commercialize such innovations. This is not a trivial issue, because digital technologies can enable radically novel products and services, and it can take time and effort to discover how to organize entirely new types of resources and activities.

We begin the organizational exploration by noting what business organizations try to achieve and how digital organizations may deliver the key tasks differently. In particular, by "inverting" the organization using digital technologies, some tasks may be completed more efficiently by engaging an external "crowd" or a market rather than having employees assigned to them. Inverted organizations depend on technology-enabled coordination and communication, and there can be benefits and costs to relying on technological rather than hierarchical solutions.

The broader goal of a digital innovator is to create economic value, and, at a minimum, that value should exceed the costs of creating it. We compare the overall configurations of value creation to notice that, in contrast to traditional value chains, digital services are often better characterized as value shops or value networks. The overall logic of the business then shifts from producing something efficiently to solving unique problems or facilitating efficient exchange. The configuration points to the key strategic issues that must be addressed for the innovation to succeed and become economically viable.

Next we drill down to a set of very practical choices of value propositions, revenue mechanisms, and activity and resource systems. These elements of business model design implement the value configuration and support the overall logic of value creation. The selected business model design must be functional in the ecosystem context for the digital innovation. We finish this part of the book by delving into the business model of Uber to investigate how the inverted organization enhances its value configuration, and how the elements of Uber's business model interact with the ecosystem in which it is embedded.

12 | The Inverted Firm

How does digitization change the internal organization of firms? Gig economy platforms and freelancing agencies are rapidly taking over market share changing our very definition of a "firm," whereas those who still work for traditional firms increasingly rely on virtual tools and external digital platforms to coordinate and communicate. For example, instead of using an internal company mail system, employees may use cloud-based email servers, and instead of visiting the company cafeteria for lunch, they may order food from online food delivery services. Similarly, many others of the firm's production activities may be "outsourced" to external providers, including inputs, manufacturing, assembly, logistics, marketing, and even R&D. What is then a "firm" if other organizations carry out much of its activities?

To explore how digitization transforms firms, we first need to clarify what we mean by firms. While we tend to take this concept for granted, it is useful to try to articulate a definition in order to have a benchmark for the changes induced by digitization. The *Cambridge English Dictionary*, for example, defines a firm as "a group of people who work or perform together." Indeed, although an individual can operate a firm in the form of a sole proprietorship, we usually think of a firm involving a group of people cooperating and coordinating their productive actions. Initially, a start-up consisting of a small number of founders does not have much structure, but as it grows and begins to hire employees, most firms begin to create a hierarchical structure to manage, coordinate, and monitor the activities carried out. **Hierarchy** has been the dominant form of organizing groups of people working together since the Industrial Revolution.

12.1 Hierarchical Firms versus Market Contracts

A classical question in economics is why we need firms in the first place. Why can't we conduct all economic activities using **market contracts**? For example, if someone wants to build a house, they can hire a construction firm or contract separately for the different services involved in building a house. According to the National Association of Builders, people who decide to build the house themselves, on average, hire 22 subcontractors. If we can build a house this way, can we also build a car or a software package?

To answer this question, let's assess what functions hierarchical firms provide to get the work done and why such functions are not easily performed through independent contracting. For example, to build a car, an automotive firm needs to hire engineers, assembly line workers, inventory managers, marketing specialists, salespeople, and many others. First, the firm needs to make sure that there is an alignment of incentives so that everybody works toward a common goal, building a functioning car. Properly aligned incentives should prevent an assembly line worker from holding up the production line and a salesperson from running a promotion that boosts their quarterly sales numbers at the expense of their firm's profitability. Second, the firm must ensure that the activities are coordinated. For example, coordination is needed to ensure that, when the car design is finalized, manufacturing workers are there and ready to start the production, supported by inventory managers who ordered correct parts meeting the assembly requirement needs. Third, a car is a complex product requiring the integration of diverse knowledge to come up with innovative solutions to emerging problems. Producing a car will rely on employees' ability to address expected and unexpected problems through the integration of expertise across diverse disciplines and professions.

A traditional firm achieves the alignment of incentives, coordination of activities, and integration of expertise (ACE for short) by relying on well-known principles of administration based on managerial **authority** and **employment contracts**. Authority fundamentally stems from the ownership of productive assets by the investors, and their ability to exclude employees from the productive activities. Owners allocate this authority to a trusted manager who they can incentivize to pursue profitable activities. For example, if two employees fail to cooperate and each acts just to maximize their own interests, a manager can step in and address the conflict in a way that benefits the overall enterprise. If the employees refuse to do what the manager instructs (within the open-ended employment contract), they can be fired. To achieve coordination, managers can draft project plans, assign tasks to individuals, monitor task completion, and create mechanisms to communicate and hand over tasks. Finally, managers can integrate diverse sets of expertise by creating cross-functional teams for creative projects and by supporting the creation of an organizational culture that allows experts to develop a shared understanding of tasks and goals necessary to communicate their knowledge and jointly produce an innovative solution (see Figure 12.1).

Thus, a managerial hierarchy can get the work done, but can alignment of incentives, coordination of activities, and integration of expertise also be accomplished through market contracts rather than administrative oversight? People who decide to build a house by subcontracting all the work separately rather than hiring a construction firm must believe that market contracts can accomplish a complex project. Similarly, movie production companies may contract for many or most of the individual roles and activities. The benefit of the contractual approach seems obvious: It allows saving on the overhead costs. Overhead costs are the costs of the managerial hierarchy. What are the downsides of contracting for services?

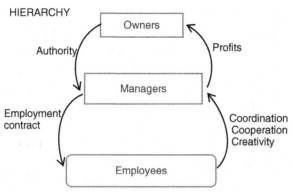

HIERARCHY

Figure 12.1 Traditional hierarchy
Note: In a hierarchical organization, owners delegate their power to managers allowing them to exercise authority over the resources and activities of the firm. Managers hire employees under open-ended and often long-term employment contracts that motivate employees to cooperate, coordinate, and do creative tasks in exchange for continued employment. Such actions enable collective productive activities that generate profits for the owners.

12.2   Digitization Makes Market Contracts More Attractive

The primary mechanism through which market contracts operate is paying a guaranteed price for pre-specified work. Suppose all of the work of building a house or making a car could be fully decomposed into well-specified tasks ahead of time and did not require any adjustments. In that case, we could write a series of market contracts with specific deadlines and achieve incentive alignment. The problem is that it is very hard, if not impossible, to foresee all the tasks that might arise during the project, so writing such complete contracts would be challenging. Additionally, if there are any unexpected circumstances such as inclement weather or breakage of machinery, all contracts need to be adjusted, potentially leading to extra costs. It is also difficult for the work contracts to mandate expertise integration. Integration of expertise involves cooperative innovation that is a creative activity. It is difficult to write a contract about producing something completely novel. Some contractors may be willing to engage in joint problem solving, but without shared goals and culture, it may be hard for them to arrive at creative solutions to problems. Thus, when tasks to be completed are complex and evolving with unexpected needs, and when individuals need to coordinate, communicate, or innovate, hierarchical organizations provide advantages that are difficult to replicate through short-term contractual relationships.

It thus seems that monitoring, coordination, communication, and collective creativity are activities that hierarchies may achieve better than market contracts. However, digital tools can significantly alleviate the costs of achieving these. First, imagine building a house with 22 contractors without a telephone, email, a credit card, spreadsheet application, or electronic order management systems. One might think twice about such an undertaking and be more willing to pay the "managerial overhead" to a construction firm.

Next, consider digital marketplaces for independent contractors like Upwork for online professional work, TaskRabbit and Angi for home-related tasks, and Rover for pet care. They may achieve incentive alignment by providing clients with tools for tracking the contractors' reputations, paying via escrow accounts, and monitoring the completion of work. For example, Upwork enables people looking for software developers to find qualified developers, get a price for the project based on the proposals that work providers submit, and monitor the work in real time through a desktop monitoring tool. It also provides a variety of quality signals to the potential client, including certifications that a provider obtained on the platform, the provider's work portfolio and educational background, and the reputation earned on the platform through the volume and ratings of their prior work.

Even more prominent is the ability of digital tools to facilitate the coordination of activities. Through electronic calendars, fast and cheap communication tools, and shared document repositories, digitization has had a big impact on our ability to coordinate complex work over great distances. For example, in the past, a new pet owner who had not yet established a neighborhood network of pet helpers was in a bind if they needed urgent help and could not leave their pet at home alone. Now, they can use the Rover or Wag! platforms to hire reputable pet caregivers to watch their pet for any increment of time. Pet caregivers' digital availability calendars and digital maps allow for easy and quick service scheduling – a coordination task that would have taken quite a bit of time to accomplish before digitization. Even when plans change, users can rely on location devices and digital maps to coordinate an unanticipated meeting location and time.

Perhaps the most challenging function a manager performs in an organization, especially when it comes to knowledge work, is enabling creative teamwork. This managerial function facilitates innovation in organizations as diverse experts combine their know-how to create new products and services. Managers often accomplish this by building a creative culture. Apple is a prominent company that has been able to produce a series of innovative products and services by building its unique innovation culture. It is also famous for its history of closely controlling its products and designing much of its technology internally. Yet even Apple "opened up" its organization for digital enhancements. For example, it learned to collaborate with manufacturing suppliers by using Corning Corporation's innovative Gorilla Glass for the original iPhone screen and Toshiba's' large capacity and small-size hard drive for the original iPod. It also embraced the power of Open-Source Software development communities, even for its operating systems software Max OS X – a crown jewel of Apple's original control strategy. These communities do not rely on managerial hierarchies or even contracts to get the work done. Instead, they use digital resources like GitHub with its code management repositories, discussion forums, and mailing lists to create innovative technologies "without a corporate boss."

12.3   Why Do Some Hierarchical Firms Still Prosper in the Digital Age?

One might be skeptical about hierarchical firms going away simply because technology makes contracting easier. After all, hierarchical firms are made up of people who are used to this form of work. Moreover, some form of supervisor–subordinate relationship has existed for many thousands of years of human history. Organized religious institutions such as the Catholic Church have developed and maintained hierarchical management structures for almost two thousand years, persevering through several technological revolutions. Moreover, if there is no managerial oversight, what would motivate people to contribute their full effort and talents? Going against tradition, today's professionals are increasingly choosing to work as independent contractors. Some knowledge workers go as far as to become digital nomads – traveling around the world with their laptops, setting their own hours, preferring to be judged based on the quality of their work rather than on the number of hours they put in.

The hierarchical firm is under attack from all sides: It is losing its advantage over market contracting as an organizing structure, and it is losing its attractiveness culturally because young people are not interested in joining the highly bureaucratic structures of traditional firms. Nevertheless, even the giants of the digital era, such as Amazon, Microsoft, Apple, Google, and Facebook, organize some of their activities through managerial hierarchies rather than market contracts, but, like Apple, they also engage with or even orchestrate digital markets for select inputs and activities. Compared to IBM, a traditional computer company with 345,000 employees generating $78 billion of revenue in 2020, Google's ad markets and associated digital properties employ "only" 140,000 people but generated $182 billion in that same year. Even Microsoft as a software platform company generated more revenue per employee than IBM ($44 billion with 163,000 employees in 2020). Another traditional firm, General Electric, generated $99 billion with 313,000 employees in 2017, and has been restructuring ever since. A traditional hierarchy, thus, tends to generate a lower labor productivity than digital platforms that benefit from vast scale economies and the efficient use of digital markets for key inputs. However, Amazon is an interesting exception to this observation. Despite being a platform company, Amazon employs over a million people, because many of the warehouse activities continue to be highly labor intensive. These employees generated $113 billion in revenue in 2020. Meanwhile, Amazon was busy trying to develop robots for its warehouse operations.[1]

It thus seems that the future of organization is moving toward a greater degree of market contracting, but even digital platforms will always continue to carry

---

[1] Feiner, L. (2021). Amazon details new warehouse robots, "Ernie" and "Bert." CNBC, June 14, 2021. Retrieved from www.cnbc.com/2021/06/13/amazon-details-new-warehouse-robots-ernie-and-bert.html in August, 2022.

out many tasks and activities in-house. While market contracts are becoming more effective due to digitization, there are still many situations where managerial hierarchies have an advantage in coordinating and innovating. Furthermore, the hierarchical firm can also adopt digital technologies to implement the ACE and gain some of the same efficiencies that such technologies offer in market contracting. Managers organizing work within the firm can use digital technologies to achieve better alignment of incentives through more precise work monitoring and performance evaluation systems. They can achieve better coordination of activities through shared work repositories, project management systems, and communication tools, and they can improve expertise integration through digital collaboration tools and enterprise social media platforms. So, the question of whether to organize work through hierarchical firms or market contracts in light of digitization turns into a question of how efficient firms can become at using technology to augment their organizational structures. Can firms use technology so efficiently as to justify the overhead associated with providing managerial oversight when market contracts in the digital age accomplish ACE with greater ease?

Part of this efficiency would come from relying on market contracting and tapping into external resources when the cost of hierarchy is not justified. The other part would come from achieving higher levels of performance on one or more of the ACE dimensions by integrating technology and management. Both Walmart and Amazon have become famous for creating and managing integrated digital supply chains and robot-augmented warehouses. It is hard for small individual shops to compete with these giants even if they could access the same technology resources. In fact, they can access these resources because Amazon makes its technology available to small businesses through platform partnerships. It is hard to compete with these giants because the control over supply chains and warehouses that they have built allows them to adjust to unexpected contingencies and new market needs by using their management hierarchy. For example, during the early days of the COVID-19 pandemic, Amazon made managerial decisions on how to ration some of the high-demand items (e.g., favoring healthcare institutions) and prioritize delivery requests (e.g., delivering household necessities in shorter time frames). Even though Amazon did not manufacture these goods, it could implement these decisions due to its enormous degree of control over the global supply chain.

Hierarchical firms that are good at using digital technology to organize their ACE can survive and prosper in the digital age. Moreover, these firms are often the ones building the digital technology that enables market contracting. As a result, those firms that create and oversee markets in ways that can successfully match buyers and sellers will be able to collect the modern version of market fees – digital subscription and transaction fees. To entice users not only to find a match on the platform but to also stay on it for getting the work done, digital platforms often expand their capabilities beyond matching and strive to enable some or all of ACE functions for their users.

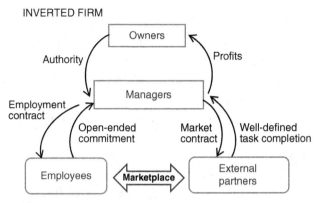

Figure 12.2 Inverted firm

Note: An inverted firm operates a marketplace in parallel with a hierarchy. Employees continue to provide ACE activities through a relatively open-ended and flexible commitment to the organization, whereas external partners complete well-defined and specifically contracted tasks through the marketplace.

Let's consider Upwork – a platform that enables subcontracting professional work such as software development, graphic design, and editing. It built a variety of digital tools to support each of the ACE functions. Not only does it provide extensive seller profiles to allow for a good market match (an equivalent of accessible market stalls), but also it further supports incentive alignment by providing templates for digital contracting, enabling work monitoring through a shared desktop function, verifying payment methods, setting up escrow accounts, and building a nuanced reputation system. Similarly, Upwork supports coordination of activities and expertise integration through its extensive project management and communication tools and shared digital workspaces. The better Upwork supports ACE functions, the more likely the buyer and seller are to stay on the platform and tell their friends about it. Moreover, the longer both parties use Upwork, the better they become at it. Not only do they build reputations that allow them to collect premium fees, but they also build tacit knowledge about what it takes to be good at "Upworking." This stickiness helps Upwork collect its transaction fees which, in turn, lets it build new technology and grow the market. Moreover, Upwork regularly taps into the marketplace it has created to get its own work done. It hires in-house employees to do work that is strategic for Upwork, but much of the commoditized services such as basic programming and design tasks are subcontracted.

Upwork is an **Inverted Firm** (see Figure 12.2). It operates a technology-augmented hierarchical organization. It chooses which ACE functions can be implemented more effectively inside the firm and orchestrates external resources (subcontractors and partners) where markets are more efficient than internal employees. Moreover, it makes money by developing and monetizing digital technology that enables a marketplace, which provides Upwork with subscription and transaction fees. To remain competitive, it needs to run this marketplace in a way that offers the best match between buyers and sellers as well as supports ACE functions, enabling users to get their work done on the platform.

KEY IDEAS

- Any form of organizing should provide three fundamental functions:
  Alignment of incentives
  Coordination of activities and information exchange
  Expertise integration for problem solving and innovation.
- Hierarchies often perform these functions better than markets, but they are costly to run.
- Digitization helps markets become more efficient in performing ACE functions
- Digitization makes market contracting more attractive
- Hierarchies that prosper in the digital age are inverted firms that can:
  - use external resources via market contracts (by default) where hierarchical management does not provide an economic advantage
  - augment their managerial structures with digital technologies allowing them to achieve ACE in a way that makes them more efficient than markets
  - build technologies and networks that enable digital markets.

DEFINITIONS

Managerial **authority** gives a manager the power to make unilateral decisions concerning the activities or resources of the organization.

An **employment contract** is typically an open-ended agreement that specifies some of the job expectations and tasks in exchange for a monthly salary. It may include bonus payments for high performance but most of the tasks are expected to be completed within the job description without specific individual payments.

Hierarchy is an organization where the top manager oversees middle managers who each manage business units, for example, product divisions or functional departments that employ individual workers – employees. There can be many more layers of operations in large firms.

Inverted firm brings markets inside the hierarchy. Even though digital platform companies such as Google and Uber operate various markets for external participants (e.g., search and advertising markets, ride markets), they also contain (traditional) hierarchical units such as technology development and marketing departments.

A **market contract** describes specific tasks, results, or products exchanged usually against a monetary compensation. A spot market contract is a short-term contract that defines one single exchange or transaction. A market contract can also be long term, but it does not bring the worker inside the client firm as an employee under the legal framework of employment.

DISCUSSION QUESTIONS

1. What is the impact of digitization on ACE?
2. What does digitization mean for doing work within firms as opposed to market contracts?

3. Think of your favorite digital platform (e.g., TikTok, Netflix, eBay). Which firms were providing the services before the digital age that are now provided by these platforms? How well are these "old" firms doing today? How are ACE functions performed on your platform of choice? If an "old-economy" firm is still competing with your chosen platform, how does it use technology to compete?

4. Compare two digital platforms, eBay and Wikipedia. While both platforms strive to excel at all components of ACE on the platform, their goals and priorities are not the same. Which of the three ACE functions are more important for eBay and which for Wikipedia? Would eBay benefit from investing equally in all three ACE functions versus focusing on one or two?

FURTHER READING

Van Alstyne M.M., Parker G.G., and Choudary S.P. (2016). Pipelines, platforms and the new rules of strategy. Harvard Business Review April. HBR Reprint R1604C.

Williamson O.E. (1975). *Markets and Hierarchies: Analysis and Antitrust Implications.* New York: Free Press.

13 | Digital Business Models

13.1 Assessing Value Configurations and Envisioning a Business Model

A business model is a framework for creating value by organizing available resources and activities to address a user need. As such, each product or service requires a business model in order to be commercialized. A business model can be embedded in a hierarchical or inverted firm. We start analyzing business models by exploring value configurations. A **Value configuration** is an overall model of the value creation logic of the firm.[1] Once an innovating firm has settled on a value configuration, it needs a feasible business model. A **business model** is a more detailed description of the structure of activities and transactions that enables the firm to deliver its products and services. It includes the description of the value created in the form of a **value proposition**, whom the firm targets to offer the value – the target market – and how it creates value – the implementation of the delivery in terms of key assets, activities, and partnerships. The value proposition and the target market together inform the company's **revenue mechanism** that defines who is willing to pay for what aspects of the service under the current or expected competitive conditions. The key assets, activities, and partnerships inform the company's **cost structure**, and, in particular, how much it costs to deliver the value proposition to the target market. Finally, these analyses allow the firm to assess whether and how to scale the business.

13.2 A Configuration for Creating Exceptional Value

Traditional analyses of firms tend to focus on sequential activities that source and transform physical inputs into tangible products to be distributed, marketed, and ultimately serviced. However, much of the digital economy consists of services. Two other configurations more accurately reflect the value creation logic of digital services: Value shop and value network.[2] The key distinction concerns whether the

---

[1] Thompson, J.D. (1967). *Organizations in Action.* New York: McGraw-Hill.
[2] Stabell, C.B. and Fjeldstad, O.D. (1998). Configuring value for competitive advantage: on chains, shops, and networks. *Strategic Management Journal* 19(5): 413–437.

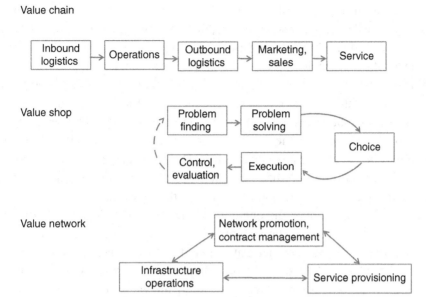

Value chain

Value shop

Value network

Figure 13.1 Value configurations for digital innovations
Note: Value configurations pinpoint the essential activities that contribute the most to value creation in the organization. A value chain is a linear sequence of productive activities. A value shop is a cycle of activities oriented toward problem solving. A value network consists of concurrent activities that facilitate connections and exchange among the network participants.
Adapted from Stabell, C.B. and Fjeldstad, O.D. (1998). Configuring value for competitive advantage: on chains, shops, and networks. *Strategic Management Journal* 19(5): 413–437.

primary purpose of the organization is to create new information (value shop) or to connect parties in a network (value network). Figure 13.1 describes the main activities of each value configuration.

Value shops create value by developing unique solutions to customers' problems. They solicit important problems from customers, apply their proprietary methodology to solve the problems, and often facilitate choosing between feasible solutions, executing the solution, and, finally, quality control and evaluation of the outcomes. Here, the transformation process manipulates a system of activities through a service intervention rather than the physical state of inputs. While there are sequential aspects to this process, there is likely to be constant iteration and feedback loops to the problem definition and subsequent stages. In fact, the object of transformation (individual, organization) might participate in the service process by contributing information inputs, as many services are co-created. However, because each problem is unique, so is each solution, and its quality is difficult to contract for. Nevertheless, firms compete on solution quality. Therefore, this type of a business operation relies on a strong reputation for high quality, and, in many cases, professional associations or certification agencies that monitor and certify quality standards. In the offline realm, typical value shop businesses include professional services (e.g., medical, engineering, legal, and consulting services). In the digital realm, value shop businesses include technology-mediated expert services (e.g., digital health, education, advisory) and, increasingly, artificial intelligence-based solutions and recommendations (content recommendations, complex optimization, search, navigation).

Value networks are structures that primarily connect participants in the system. A digital value network enables communication, transactions, or other forms of exchange, and naturally encompass any kind of a market or communication system. As the value is in the facilitated connections, per Metcalfe's Law, value networks require a large scale to be effective. Their critical activities involve bringing participants into the network through promotion and contracting, facilitating interactions among the participants already in the network, and maintaining the infrastructure underpinning the operations. These activities happen continuously and concurrently. However, the network operates differently in the initial launch phase, where there are few participants and critical mass hasn't been reached, and in the mature phase, where the network is large and supported by network effects. Scale is an important driver of value creation for value networks, and distinct strategies may be required to grow beyond critical mass to a fully efficient scale. As such, firms with value network configurations tend to be inverted firms.

Firms may implement pure value configurations or mixed configurations. Many digital companies provide some unique data- and analytics-based solutions and develop some community or networked activities to accelerate growth and enhance the value proposition. For example, the cloud storage innovator Dropbox started out by providing an improved software-based solution for the storage problem (value shop) and grew virally by allowing users to securely share access to the stored information (value network).

Value configurations are important to analyze because they highlight the key activities, resources, and structures that maximize value creation and differentiation, and thus lead to maximal value capture from the innovation. In a value chain, competitive advantage may originate from a cost-efficient manufacturing process or a product technology that is difficult to copy. A value shop competes on differentiated solution quality, requiring unique sources of information and proprietary analytical methods or processes. Finally, the competitive advantage of a value network depends on liquidity arising from the scale of connections and the quality of matching.

The value configuration thus informs whether innovation strategy should emphasize product innovation and process efficiency (value chain), learning and knowledge/information/data accumulation (value shop), or scale and connectivity (value network). For example, Snapchat, the social network that offers opportunities to share fleeting moments with friends, is a value network. It also offers to advertisers and media companies (publishers) opportunities to connect with the user network of young adults, enabling two-sided network effects. Its primary competitive goal is to grow large and offer well-targeted connections among the social network users, and between the individuals and the commercial entities seeking to advertise and attract attention to their content. However, as with any social network, the behavioral data about users can be very valuable. Snapchat could analyze the data and sell solutions to commercial entities, for example, in the form of predictions about purchase behavior. This data analytic consulting business would be a value shop that seeks to create additional value from the information accumulated during the network operation. However, the return on investment is likely higher for Snapchat in activities that grow the social network relative to activities that enhance the data analytics, at least initially.

13.3 Value Proposition: Does the Innovation Enhance Demand or Reduce the Cost of Operations?

Once an overall value configuration has been identified, the innovator needs to design a more specific business model that implements the plan to create value. A useful starting point is the value proposition to pinpoint how and for whom the value configuration generates new value. Any innovation needs a unique and defensible value proposition. To convince potential buyers and users, the innovation must either substantially enhance the user experience, if it targets external customers, or make internal operations significantly more efficient. A value proposition articulates what sets the innovation apart from other products and services available in the ecosystem. When the innovation enhances user experience beyond state-of-the-art in the market, it will attract customers who will be willing to pay extra for the product or service. When the innovation enhances internal efficiency of operations, production costs decrease or the quality of the service improves, ultimately increasing business profitability. However, to sustain the innovation benefits, the innovation needs to be both unique, that is different from competitors' offerings, and defensible, that is the innovator can make it difficult and costly for rivals to imitate the innovation. For example, Snapchat's value proposition to its individual users includes unique creative tools and "lenses" and, perhaps counterintuitively, the commitment to destroy the content after a set amount of time.

A digital innovation may address a need in business-to-consumer markets (B2C) or business-to-business markets (B2B). Digital consumer markets tend to be fickle, and the reception of value propositions may depend on fast-moving social interactions and trends. B2B markets typically focus on efficiency and performance, and hence value propositions usually deliver business benefits. Nevertheless, in both markets, a thoughtful design can enhance the value proposition and make for an easy-to-use, smooth, and pleasant user experience.

While the user experience is the key factor driving user engagement, digital innovators often need to consider multiple different types of user groups and develop unique value propositions for each. For example, Snapchat's paying customers include advertisers and content providers. Advertisers are interested in access to the social network participants, and hence the more users and the more information is available about them the better the advertisement targeting. Snap, the parent company of Snapchat, also forms licensing relationships with content providers who can make news content available on the platform or pay

Table 13.1 Competitor grid example: a (fictional) new electronic device

Benefits	Your innovation	Competitor 1	Competitor 2	Competitor 3
Portability	++	+	–	++
Battery life	+	+	++	–
Weight	++	++	+	+
Backlit screen	+	++	+	++

Note: The competitor grid helps innovators pinpoint the key benefits and features of the product or service that differentiate its value proposition.
Key: ++ = exceptional
+ = functional
– = lacking at this time

for sponsored tools such as branded lenses. Thus, the company needs to maintain three value propositions because the service maintains a multisided platform where the different sides are interested in accessing content and opportunities provided by the others. The individual users are B2C customers who appreciate the service features and connections to friends. The advertisers and media companies are B2B clients who must be convinced with performance metrics such as detailed targeting, reach, and click-through rates.

The value proposition should articulate the following aspects of the innovation:

- the key benefits to the different customer groups
- what makes these benefits valuable
- a specific customer need and how the key benefits address that need
- how the key benefits exceed the benefits that competitors provide.

It is often helpful to describe and evaluate the value proposition by using a competitor grid that specifies the key product features and benefits and compares the innovation against the products of the main competitors. The table below illustrates the competitor grid for a new electronic device. We will use it later in the Fashion AR business example. The comparison suggests that the innovation is exceptional in terms of portability and weight, and functional with respect to battery life and the backlighting of the screen. Competitor 1 is clearly at least functional in all the product features whereas competitors 2 and 3 are deficient with respect to at least one key feature. Competitor 1 thus appears to be the main rival, and the innovator could initially launch in market niches where users particularly value portability and low weight (see Table 13.1).

13.4   Digital Service Revenue Mechanisms

The revenue mechanism is the financial architecture of a business. While we are used to thinking that the user of a product or service pays for it, and that the price is at or slightly above marginal cost of production, in the digital economy things are rarely that simple. Physical products produced in value chains are often priced individually per unit, but users of information-based services from value shops often pay subscription fees for access, depending on the structure of the service. However, there may also be good reasons to give individual users free services and collect revenues elsewhere. This is particularly common in value network configurations such as Snapchat, where the firm attempts to maximize the number of users to achieve critical mass and sponsor network effects. The revenue mechanism depends on the willingness of each complementary party to join the platform and, at least some of them, to pay for services. Furthermore, the service provider might try to discriminate prices to capture a part of the consumer surplus. This requires charging different prices to different types of customers and offering different access or feature bundles to allow customers to self-select into high-value or low-value offerings. Thus, depending on the drivers of competitive advantage for the main value configuration, an innovating firm can choose the revenue mechanism to provide ideal incentives for the right set of customers to maximize usage and revenue.

Fee-for-service: one-time payment for a unique experience. The simplest service revenue mechanism is fee-for-service, where the price of access to digital content or network depends on the volume or time of usage. Nevertheless, the service provider can enhance their revenues by experimenting with the willingness to pay of their users. For example, prices to access to a live 5G-based entertainment event could be tiered based on what service features are included. The marginal cost of offering a digital service to the audience may be exactly same for all features – once they have been developed at a high fixed cost, the marginal cost of digital goods is often close to zero. Then, individuals choosing the high-end bundle reveal themselves as high willingness-to-pay types and can be charged substantially more than those selecting a basic service bundle. Fee-for-service works with a value chain or value shop configuration that does not depend on repeated interaction.

Subscription model: ongoing service relationship. Many digital applications involve ongoing service relationships where users repeatedly access the service such as a movie streaming service. Repeated service relationships typically entail subscription pricing. Subscription also makes it easy to provide different "versions" of the service without having to even package and separately transact to sell the versions. Customers do it themselves by picking and choosing the content or services in which they are interested. Per our pricing models in Chapter 5, a subscription price will probably be set approximately at the amount of consumer surplus for the low-end customers. This is the highest price that the low-end consumers are willing to pay to participate. High-end customers will then get much more value (consumer surplus) because they are willing to pay more but they actually pay the same price as the low-end customers. However, the innovator can do even better by excluding select highly valuable services from the basic subscription bundle and asking high-WTP customers to pay extra for these items. This is how streaming services such as Amazon's Prime video-on-demand (VOD) service work. Customers pay a low monthly subscription fee to access the basic content, and more for newer movies, usually around $4–$7 per viewing. However, the most recent and highly popular feature films may cost $15 per viewing, limiting that market to the highest willingness-to-pay customers – until the movie gets a bit older and is offered first for the regular VOD price and ultimately as part of the basic package. A subscription revenue model usually works well with a value shop configuration.

Consumer platform: free service + advertising. The advertising model requires very large traffic and sophisticated ad technologies, because ad markets have become very concentrated due to Google's and Facebook's dominance. For example, Snapchat, with 186 million users in 2019, was able to collect a CPM (cost per 1000 ad impressions) of about $3 from open ad auctions as opposed to Facebook's CPM of $5, or CPM of $4 on Instagram. This is despite the fact that Snapchat has invested millions in developing an automated self-serve ad auction platform. At the time, the company's increasingly sophisticated ad technology platform generated a quarterly ARPU (Average Revenue per User) of about $2. Facebook's quarterly ARPU was in the order of $7 worldwide, and over $30 in the US. The advertising revenue model thus works best with a highly-scalable value network configuration.

Harvesting data to leverage in adjacent markets. Digital businesses can also choose to offer a free service to collect user data for market insights or for sale. An interesting version of this is a coffee shop that offers free coffee in exchange for data.[3] However, it is difficult to accurately assess the value of user data in analytics markets because such transactions are very sensitive and secretive. According to one estimate, the data that Facebook holds of its users is worth about $50 per user per year.[4] Valuations as high as $100 per year have been presented,[5] and one individual sold his data for $2,733 on Kickstarter. However, limited behavioral data from a smaller digital service might be worth much less than these examples. Data harvesting tends to be viable only in very large value network configurations (see Table 13.2).

A different way to harvest users' behavior is to engage in affiliations with other services. For example, the streaming service Hulu has an affiliate program with websites that can show a Hulu ad and a link to click through, and if the visitor does sign up with Hulu, the website gains $6.[6]

[3] Shaffel, C. (2018). No cash needed at this café: Students pay the tab with their personal data. *NPR*, September 29, 2018. Retrieved from www.npr.org/sections/thesalt/2018/09/29/643386327/no-cash-needed-at-this-cafe-students-pay-the-tab-with-their-personal-data in August 2022.

[4] Wibson (2018). How much is your data worth? At least $240 per year. Likely much more. *Medium*, January 19, 2018. Retrieved from https://medium.com/wibson/how-much-is-your-data-worth-at-least-240-per-year-likely-much-more-984e250c2ffa in August 2022.

[5] Lengen, S. (2019). How much is your data worth to tech companies? Lawmakers want to tell you but it's not that easy to calculate. The Conversation, July 11, 2019. Retrieved from http://theconversation.com/how-much-is-your-data-worth-to-tech-companies-lawmakers-want-to-tell-you-but-its-not-that-easy-to-calculate-119716 in August 2022.

[6] King, M. (2021). How to become a Hulu affiliate. Retrieved from Chron.com https://smallbusiness.chron.com/become-hulu-plus-affiliate-48992.html in August 2022.

Table 13.2 Revenue mechanisms for digital consumer services

Mechanism	Revenue source	Benefits	Challenges
Fee-for-service	One-time consumer payment for a specific service	• Simplest revenue model • Works well when the experience value is high but not consumed regularly • Can be turned into a tiered or bundled offering to leverage the WTP of some customers	– Creates an upfront cost for the consumer, which can seem high if the service benefits are not very obvious
Subscription service	Recurring payments from consumers for access to a service	• Consumers choose their content • Consistent revenue stream • Works best when the service is used repeatedly • Use when the marginal cost of delivery is low and set price at the low end of the consumers' WTP to maximize market size • Consider a tiered system to capture the WTP of higher-end consumers	– Creates an upfront cost and an ongoing commitment for the consumer – If unfamiliar with the service, consumers may be wary of committing to a repeated payment
Free service with advertisements	Payments from advertisers placing ads to be viewed by users	• No direct cost to the consumers • Works well with a large number of potential users and a low WTP	– Digital advertising is an evolving market highly concentrated to large platforms – For innovations that are not easily scalable, ad revenue per user is low
Free service with data harvesting	Payments from third parties to access user data	• No direct financial cost to the consumer • Works well with a large number of potential users and low WTP • Can be combined with advertising	– Requires a very large number of users and detailed information to make the data commercially valuable – Consumer privacy and protection laws are changing which makes this a risky model

Note: These are common revenue mechanisms used in digital business-to-consumer (B2C) service business models. The different revenue structures create different incentives for consumers. A digital innovator needs to align the consumer incentives with the business goals.

13.5   Hardware and System Revenue Mechanisms

Product sales. There are a few common revenue mechanisms for hardware products, including for devices, components, and intelligent equipment such as sensors and instruments (see Table 13.3). In addition to phones or computers, there may be a number of other hardware innovation opportunities within the digital ecosystem, such as, VR or AR headsets, instruments ranging from RFID tags to larger electronic sensors, or industrial mobile devices to detect and monitor various activities, including medical devices. There are also adjacent component markets associated with many of these devices, such as those for chipsets, modems, antennae, and memory products. Physical products are often offered in exchange for a simple unit fee. In addition to a specific price per product unit, products are frequently bundled or sold with volume discounts to mitigate the preference dispersion of potential buyers. As such, these product businesses rely on a value chain configuration.

Anything-as-a-service. However, products don't necessarily need to be priced based on units or even bundling. In the digital economy, innovators can offer anything as a service. For example, users of industrial heavy machinery often rent rather than purchase the equipment for ownership, but one can also imagine whole sensor networks being sold as a service by the sensor manufacturer who also connects the instruments to a software system that collects and analyzes the data. This model transforms a product business to a service business, and unit pricing to a subscription model. It also transforms a value chain business to a value shop – solving the customer's problems and forming a longer-term relationship.

System integrator. Service business models culminate in the system integrator model, where one party offers to coordinate and integrate all the devices, components, and software needed to run a communication system. This can be a high-margin business but it may also be highly labor intensive, and the profitability of the model depends greatly on the context. Like the anything-as-a-service model, this corresponds to a value shop configuration.

Software platform provider. Finally, software solution providers might aspire to become communication platform providers. For example, an industrial IoT system that collects, manages, and shares data among a group of companies would require a central intermediary, or a platform, that manages the access and modification of the data. Once such a platform software system has been developed, it would be very advantageous for the platform provider to replicate it in many other similar industrial IoT groups. As a result, the software platform provider might seek to launch an industry platform for data sharing and transaction management in a broader ecosystem. Such an industry platform could allow the firm to transition from a value shop to a value network and leverage greater economies of scale and network effects.

Table 13.3 Revenue mechanisms for hardware products and systems

Mechanism	Revenue source	Benefits	Challenges
Fee-for-product	Price per unit or bundle sales	• Traditional, clear and simple	– For large networks, equipment, or infrastructure, the up-front pricing can be financially prohibitive
Anything-as-a-service	Recurring payments via a rental or leasing agreement	• Consistent revenue stream • Can be tiered to segment low-end and high-end customers	– The innovator must finance the asset – No transfer of ownership means the innovator carries the risk
System integrator	A large up-front payment in exchange for a coordinated installation of devices, components, and software to run a communication network or a system	• Clarity about service expectations and payments • Easy to adopt complex products and services	– Up-front commitment can be large and prohibitive – Innovator bears the risk of delays or failure
Platform provider	Access fee, membership fee, or revenue commission	• Easy and cheap to join the platform • Clear and standardized terms and conditions	– Revenue commissions may add up – Participants may worry about the platform provider's market power

Note: Revenue mechanisms for hardware may focus on product sales or service provision, depending on the value configuration of the firm. Price per unit involves a spot market transaction whereas a service contract sets up an ongoing relationship with commitments, continuous revenue streams, and additional service innovation opportunities.

KEY IDEAS

- A digital innovation has to create new value for users and stakeholders in order to succeed.
- A value configuration articulates the primary mode of value creation of the innovation. The innovation may facilitate linear transformation of inputs (value chain), solve customer's problems (value shop), or facilitate exchange (value network).
- The critical drivers of success differ for each value configuration. A value chain requires efficiency; a value shop depends on quality; and a value network depends on connectivity.
- A value proposition and a revenue mechanism are the key elements of a business model.
- A value proposition articulates how the innovation creates new value for a specific user or a user group. Businesses with multiple user groups will need multiple value propositions.
- Each value proposition should connect with a revenue mechanism that takes into account the user's willingness to pay for the product or service.
- The success drivers associated with the value configuration inform the choice of a revenue mechanism. Some revenue mechanisms are appropriate for highly-differentiated services or products, and others are appropriate for reaching scale quickly.
- A digital innovator will need to coordinate the designs of the value configuration, value propositions, and revenue mechanisms in order for them to become mutually reinforcing.
- The value proposition and the revenue mechanism ensure that the business model is scalable and incentive-compatible for users, and allow the firm to discover users' willingness to pay.

DEFINITIONS

A **business model** is a detailed description of the structure of activities and transactions that enables the firm to deliver its products and services. It includes the description of the value created, the target market, and the implementation in terms of key assets, activities, and partnerships.

The **cost structure** of the firm characterizes the financial commitments arising from the key assets, activities, and partnerships needed to deliver the value proposition to the target market.

A **revenue mechanism** describes the structure of financial exchange associated with the innovation. It will need to align users' preferences, behavior, and their willingness to pay.

A **value chain** configuration sets up a sequence of physical transformation activities that create products from raw materials and ultimately deliver them to customers.

A **value configuration** is an overall model of the value creation logic of the firm. The main configurations include a value chain, a value shop, and a value network.

A **value network** is a configuration where the primary activity entails connecting exchange participants.

A **value proposition** pinpoints how and for whom the innovation generates new value

A **value shop configuration identifies and solves clients' problems, and facilitates the execution and evaluation of the solutions.**

DISCUSSION QUESTIONS

1. You're a manufacturer of cars. Describe what kind of a business model you would have if you chose a value chain configuration. What would the business model be like if you chose or a value shop configuration? What about a value network?
2. What revenue mechanism would you select for each of the value configurations in Question 1?
3. Could you improve the revenue mechanism by implementing a nonlinear pricing structure, such as a two-part tariff? Why or why not?
4. Discuss the benefits and challenges of selling the car as a hardware product vs. selling timed access to the car as a service.

FURTHER READING

Casadesus-Masanell R. and Ricart J.E. (2011). How to Design a Winning Business Model. Harvard Business Review Reprint R1101G.

Stabell, C.B. and Fjeldstad, O.D. (1998). Configuring value for competitive advantage: on chains, shops, and networks. *Strategic Management Journal* 19(5): 413–437.

Tidhar, R. and Eisenhardt, K. (2018). Get rich or die trying: finding revenue model fit using machine learning and multiple cases. *Strategic Management Journal* 41: 1245–1273.

14 Business Model Framework

14.1 From Value Proposition to Implementation

Once the value configuration, a distinct value proposition, and an initial plan for the revenue mechanism or the internal benefits of the innovation are clear, it is time to scope the business potential of the innovation. This involves thinking through the resources and activities needed to implement and deliver the innovation and assessing how to organize them and how much they would cost to offer or access. The innovator now needs to identify the resource base needed for the value configuration designed in the first stage. We start by analyzing how the value configuration relates to the broader **business ecosystem**.

A digital innovation may consist of hardware and software components, IT services, communication network services, human cooperation, communication, or judgment, and distribution channels. Its delivery may depend on access to a marketplace, and legal institutions and governmental regulation may affect its consumption. An innovator needs to decide which of the needed resources and activities will be offered in-house and which ones will be outsourced. Such decisions are inherently long term and strategic in nature and depend on whether the resources or services are competitively provided in the ecosystem, or whether the innovator has to develop and manufacture the resource itself. Considerations also include whether the innovator can use the resource or activity to differentiate itself from competitors and protect its share of the created value, or whether it is too challenging for the innovator to develop the resource because there are already more efficient providers with proprietary (and protected) technologies in the ecosystem. Figure 14.1 illustrates a generic digital innovation ecosystem.

For example, Snapchat is a software-based application that requires computing and storage systems, advertising technologies and processes, and marketplaces for distributing the app to consumers. In 2020, Snap Inc., the company behind Snapchat, decided to focus its investments in continued technological innovation, spending over a billion US dollars on software R&D (primarily highly-educated software engineers).[1] It outsourced computing and storage systems to cloud providers, committing to long-term and multi-billion dollar license agreements with Google Cloud Platform and Amazon Web Services under the assumption that these

---

[1] Yahoo! Financials (2022). Snap financials 2020. Retrieved from https://finance.yahoo.com/quote/SNAP/financials/ in August 2022.

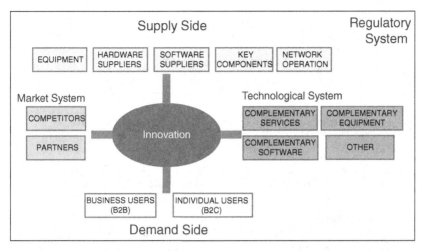

Figure 14.1 Digital innovation ecosystem
Note: An innovation ecosystem consists of the market, technological, and regulatory systems enabling and constraining the digital innovation. It also includes suppliers of inputs and services and users of the innovation.

companies were in a much better position than Snap to provide efficient computing resources. Similarly, it distributed the app via mobile app stores instead of building its own application market or sales channel. Thus, to deliver its value proposition to consumers, its ecosystem included Amazon, Google, Apple, and other smartphone manufacturers and wireless service providers.

However, the Snapchat platform also needed to implement the value proposition for the paying customers, including advertisers, content creators such as news sites, and event organizers such as major sports leagues. Snapchat needed to create systems for these platform partners to supply their content and distribute it efficiently to consumers, and payment systems to monetize these B2B services. A substantial part of the software development effort in fact concerned media distribution and advertising technologies. The business services also needed to be sold and delivered to the platform partners, which necessitated employing a large number of sales and advertising specialists. Indeed, in 2020, selling, general and administrative costs amounted to over one billion US dollars, of which selling and marketing was over half. Advertising sales and platform marketing thus generated heavy expenditures and highly labor-intensive activities that the firm carried out in-house, with highly skilled employees as the key resource.

Thus, considering Snapchat's value propositions to consumers, advertisers, content creators, and event partners, Snapchat created value by developing technologies to connect these participants to each other – a value network configuration. It chose to offer network promotion, contract management, and service provisioning in-house, and outsource infrastructure operations. The value this configuration created was divided between Snap and its service providers (primarily cloud), complementors (mobile app stores, device vendors, and network providers), and platform partners and users. Additionally, competitors attempted to capture some of Snapchat's value by developing similar social network, content publishing, and advertising services. For example, Instagram (then owned by Facebook, now Meta)

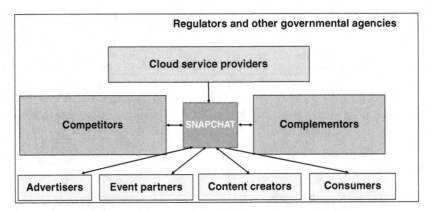

Figure 14.2 Snapchat ecosystem

Note: The innovation ecosystem of Snapchat, a digital social network, includes the cloud computing service providers Google and Amazon Web Services; competitors such as digital social networks Twitter, Facebook, TikTok, and Kakao; and complementors such as Google's Android operating system and Apple with its iOS system. Advertisers include branded consumer products such as those of Adidas, Samsung, and P&G; event partners include various sports leagues such as the NBA and the NHL; content creators are typically digital media companies; and individuals participate as creators and consumers of content. Regulatory agencies have influenced the company, for example, with respect to personal data practices.

developed the Stories product as a direct copy of Snapchat and thereby averted losing business to the latter.[2] Snapchat, in turn, competed against other social networks by investing in proprietary technologies and knowhow embodied in the software-based technologies (some of which were patented or kept secret for extra protection), relationships with users, service providers, and partners, and the data generated by the dense interactions among users and partners (that was also kept secret). These resources allowed Snapchat to differentiate from its competitors and to maintain its distinct position in the ecosystem (see Figure 14.2).

14.2   Business Model Framework

We finish this chapter by putting the various aspects of the business model into a framework that allows a digital innovator to carry out an initial assessment of the innovation. This framework organizes the analysis to determine whether the innovation is commercially viable. To develop a business model, there are many assumptions about revenue and cost parameters that innovators will need to test. They need to explore the revenue mechanism and customers' WTP; estimate the resources and activities required to deliver the service; calculate the potential cost structure and the price–cost margin; examine how scaling will affect the

---

[2] Kantrowitz, A. (2020). Snapchat was an "existential threat" to Facebook. Until an 18-year-old developer convinced Mark Zuckerberg to invest in Instagram Stories. *Business Insider*, April 7, 2020. Retrieved from www.businessinsider.com/how-developer-mark-zuckerberg-invented-instagram-stories-copied-snapchat-2020-4 in August 2022.

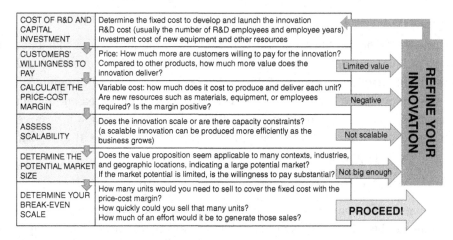

Figure 14.3 Initial Business Model Assessment
Note: This assessment framework allows digital innovators to generate a rough estimate of the commercial potential of the innovation. In addition to the key elements of the business model, this framework considers the development cost, scalability, and break-even potential of the innovation.

business operations; and scope the potential market size. Once these are estimated, it is possible to determine the expected break-even scale of the business idea and whether the innovation appears to be commercially promising. Initially, comparable numbers from existing businesses and industries will be sufficient, and the assumptions can be refined as the innovation is developed and parameters become better known. The initial objective is to develop a rough estimate of all the activities needed to implement the innovation and the resulting sources of revenues and costs to understand if the potential revenue streams can ever be sufficient to cover all the fixed and variable costs to deliver the service.

If the rough estimate that emerges seems promising, the innovator can proceed to more detailed and careful analyses of the data underlying the assumptions. If those more elaborate analyses suggest the innovation is promising, the innovator may pursue internal or external funding for prototype development and market experiments, as well as an analysis of the potential long-term competitive advantage of the innovation (see Figure 14.3).

The following estimates are critical for the initial business model assessment:

1. *The cost of R&D and capital investment.* The fixed cost of operationalizing the innovation.

How much would it cost to develop and launch the innovation? How much is the R&D cost (usually how many R&D employees and how many employee-years it would take) and the investment cost of new equipment or other resources? This amounts to the fixed cost of innovation.

2. *The customers' willingness-to-pay* for equivalent/analogous services.

Would the innovation increase customers' willingness-to-pay for the product or service? By how much? Comparing against competing products, how much more value does the innovation deliver to the users/customers?

3. *The price–cost margin.* Variable cost of product or service delivery.

The **price–cost margin** highlights the expected operating profit. How much does it cost to produce and deliver each product/service? Are marginal costs close to zero or are there extra steps involved? For example, if new materials, equipment, or expert employees are needed to deliver each product, those increased production costs must be factored into the price–cost margin. Is the margin still positive? If it is not positive, the innovation may not be realistic at this time. If it is positive, the analysis may proceed.

4. *Scalability.* Does the innovation scale infinitely or are there capacity constraints?

If the number of employees must be doubled when the production quantity or sales are doubled, the innovation is not **scalable**. For example, some digital companies like Groupon get so little repeat business that they continuously need to attract new buyers, thus the sales effort grows linearly with the sales. Consulting companies and law firms usually have to add new consultants/lawyers as they sell more services. This is not a scalable business. Scalability (or economies of scale) means that the innovation can be delivered more and more efficiently when the business grows. Physical production systems eventually run into capacity constraints, but digital systems can often expand practically without limits, although complexity can sometimes hinder scaling of software-based systems.

5. *Nature and size of the market.* How many and how wealthy are the potential buyers? How diverse are their preferences?

If you have a positive price–cost margin and the innovation scales well, you can consider how large the potential market, the **Total Addressable Market**, might be. If the value proposition seems applicable to a large number of contexts, industries, and geographic locations, the market may be very large. However, if the value proposition is only meaningful to a specific industry and situation, the ultimate market potential may be limited. Nevertheless, if the customers' willingness to pay is substantial, solving this narrow problem for a small number of clients may still be highly profitable. A careful analysis of the targeted user groups is essential to understand the potential market.

6. *Determine your break-even scale.* Q = fixed cost/profit margin

Knowing the fixed cost, pricing, and variable cost of production, you can calculate a rough estimate of the **break-even scale**, that is, how many units you would need to sell in order to cover the fixed cost. Profit equals price*quantity – variable cost*quantity – fixed cost. If we want to break even, profit has to exceed zero. As a result quantity has to exceed fixed costs divided by the price-cost (profit) margin. If the fixed cost is large, the break-even scale will also be large. How quickly could you possibly sell that many units? How much of an effort would it be to generate those sales?

If the outcome of the final analysis suggests that the positive price–cost margin scales and covers the fixed costs in a reasonable amount of time that can realistically be financed from internal or external sources, the business model can proceed to the next stage; that includes a strategic analysis (Chapter 16) and business model launch (Chapter 15).

14.3 Business Model Example: AR Fashion Network

To apply the initial business model assessment framework, let's consider a fictional innovation idea that proposes a social network with an augmented reality (AR) application for fashion enthusiasts. The innovation would generate a 3D rendering of the user's body that would enable trying on clothing using AR. The user would stand in front of a full-body mirror at a certain distance and capture their body dimensions using the phone camera. Similarly, fashion vendors would render their apparel in 3D so they could be displayed on the 3D body rendering, or simply by pointing a phone camera at a mirror. Once the body and the clothing are captured and the images merged, users could share their findings and ideas with like-minded friends using the social network feature.

This innovation combines features of a value shop and a value network configuration. The value shop aspect helps users explore and choose fashion items, and it helps vendors reach users in a new way. However, the value network is probably the more critical aspect of the configuration: it allows users to engage with each other and with fashion vendors, creating social interaction and advertising opportunities that would help grow the market. Clearly there are potential network externalities and, hence, the innovation will need to reach a critical mass of users and vendors in order to succeed.

The ecosystem for this platform would primarily include the two sides of the market: users and fashion vendors. AR Fashion Network might also depend on external parties for some technologies such as patented AR features that would need to be licensed from other innovators. A key issue for this business is to figure out which tasks must be done internally and which ones the ecosystem partners are able to complete. For example, it is uncertain whether fashion vendors are capable of digitizing their goods and using the application to make their 3D renderings available for the system, or whether AR Fashion Network would need to take on that task that would add a large expenditure to their cost structure.

Value Proposition
The value proposition of AR Fashion Network addresses two types of customers: (1) individual users who would join the network to discover and share ideas related to fashion and apparel, and (2) apparel vendors who can advertise their fashion items and engage consumers in new ways. The innovation provides several benefits:

- The AR rendering allows customers to more easily determine whether a clothing item will fit or look good on them, improving customer satisfaction and reducing the number of returns.
- The service provides automated suggestions for additional clothing items, which enables customers to more easily find items they might like.

Table 14.1 AR Fashion competitor grid				
Benefits	AR Fashion	Stitch Fix	Mode-Relier	ShopStyle
Suggestions for new purchases	++	++	–	–
Upload 3D sizing data	++	–	–	–
AR viewing	++	–	–	–
Social network	++	–	–	–
Styling with existing clothes	+	–	++	++
Regularly receive new clothes	–	++	–	–

Note: This competitor grid analysis for the fictional venture AR Fashion Network highlights that the innovation would be the most differentiated by offering AR viewing, uploading of 3D sizing data, and creating a social network. It would not focus on styling with existing clothes or regular shipments of new items.
Key: ++ = exceptional
+ = functional
– = lacking at this time

- The network provides a highly effective form of advertising based on real customer experiences, and it can help customers find vendors or items they might not have identified on their own.
- The break-through technology is easier to use than any similar product on the market.

As illustrated in the competitor grid in Table 14.1, when the proposed value proposition is compared against those of the closest competitors in the market, it seems to offer multiple new types of benefits. In particular, none of the existing rivals have built a significant social network around their offering.

Next, let's work through the assessment framework to evaluate the economic potential of the innovation.

1. *Cost of R&D and capital investment.*

Based on views of knowledgeable experts in software development, the fixed costs needed to develop and launch the innovation include:

- app development for an AR-based 3D rendering technology: 12 months of work for eight software engineers: 8*$150,000 = $1.2 million
- 10 high-end computers, software, and other equipment: $200,000.

2. *Revenue mechanism and customers' willingness to pay.*

This innovation will require multiple revenue mechanisms to address both sides of the platform. We envision a mechanism with freemium, advertising, and referral features. Because we need to build a network, the innovation would be free for users to adopt, but we will offer some premium features for high-end (the most enthusiastic) customers. As it is equally important to build the vendor side of the platform, the network would also be free for vendors to join. However, if vendors wanted to be featured on the platform, they would need to engage in an advertising and referral agreement and pay for the promotion and for any click-through sales. Thus the potential streams of revenue include:

- Advertising: apparel partners pay to have their garments featured in the network. Assume a CPM rate (cost per 1,000 ad impressions) of $4 and that each user checks the app three times a day, resulting in an annual revenue of about $4 per user.
- Referrals: 5 percent commission from clothing sales directly resulting from being featured in the system. Assume an average garment price of $50 and three purchases per user, per year, resulting in $7.50 revenue per user, per year.
- Premium subscription features: 10 percent of users pay $30 per year, resulting in $3 average revenue per user.

These revenue streams add up to an estimated $14.50 per user, per year.

3. *The price–cost margin.*

Although cloud computing services are usually bought on an annual basis, they will grow with the number of users in the system and we will view them as variable costs here. The 3D content exchanged in the system will take up significant computing and storage resources. Based on comparable business cases, we estimate a computing cost of $5 per user and per year. As a result, we anticipate a per-user profit margin of $14.50 – $5 = $9.50 per year.

This business model will require significant human resources in sales, general, and administration (SGA). We anticipate a team of 10 in the first year to grow to 100 by Year 5. We assume an average salary cost of $100,000 per person, resulting in an initial annual fixed cost of $1 million, growing to $10 million per year by year 5.

We also anticipate a substantial cost of digitizing apparel, but this is borne by our fashion partners using our software application (note that the digitization process creates a switching cost for fashion vendors to join our network).

There are also additional costs such as office space rental and financing, but we ignore these for now.

4. *Scalability.*

The innovation has a high initial development cost and a high annual fixed cost of selling and maintaining relationships with users and fashion partners. However, per-user variable costs are very low and constant, even declining with size. It is a business with strong economies of scale, or scalability.

5. *Potential market size.*

There is no market for AR-enhanced fashion networks yet; it would need to be created. The main challenge is to connect fashion vendors with buyers/users on the platform. We anticipate that the potential market is initially younger adults and clothing sellers in the US. Young adults are more likely to engage with new technologies such as AR and value the social network aspect of the innovation. Snapchat is a social network geared toward young adults and has 100 million US users, which is probably the extent of the reachable user market in the US. The US fashion e-commerce sales were $75 billion in 2018, so it's potentially a very large and growing addressable market, but the willingness of fashion retailers to engage with new technologies is unknown at this time.

6. *Break-even scale.*

Here we want to calculate how many users we need to cover the initial development cost and the annual fixed and variable costs with the per-user profit margin of $9.50. To simplify the analysis for now, we ignore depreciation and the cost of capital.

Summing up the initial development cost and the annual fixed cost through Years 1–5 amounts approximately to $23 million. To cover that amount with the $9.50 per-user/per-year profit margin, we need about 2.4 million user-years over the five-year period. If we grow the service volume linearly from 0 to 2.4 million user-years, we would need about 1.2 million users by the end of Year 5.

Conclusion

This analysis suggests that if the technology works and apparel vendors are supportive, the innovation might attract enough users over a reasonable amount of time to break even. The cost structure and market size suggest strong scalability, and it seems worth exploring whether individuals would actually be interested in engaging in this type of fashion network and whether retailers have the capabilities to take advantage of digitizing their apparel for 3D rendering and to engage in e-commerce. In other words, the rough analysis is supportive of moving forward and testing the many assumptions and parameters with potential users and partners. The primary value configuration of AR Fashion is a value network, and the critical issue is reaching a critical mass of users. Beyond technology development, network building is thus the foremost strategic challenge for this innovation.

KEY IDEAS

- An ecosystem is the broader market context that defines external parties that contribute to value creation and compete for value capture.
- A business model must define which resources and activities are provided by the innovator and which ones are provided by ecosystem partners.
- The initial assessment framework for the business model provides a method to determine whether the innovation is commercially promising.
- The revenue potential, cost structure, characteristics of the target market, and scalability determine whether the innovation idea is worth developing further.

DEFINITIONS

Break-even scale is the quantity at which the firm's total cost (up until that point) equals the total revenues. While annual profitability (annual revenues exceeding annual fixed and variable costs) is a useful benchmark for many innovative startups, it is also important to consider in what time frame the company might be able to cover the cost of development and start generating returns for the investors.

The **business ecosystem** illustrates how the innovating firm relates to the external environment. It determines which resources and activities are provided in-house and which ones are sourced from the external environment, the ecosystem, and on what terms. These decisions determine the cost and revenue streams of the innovating firm.

The **price–cost margin** is the difference between unit price and variable cost (unit cost of services). If price is greater than variable cost, the margin is positive and it may be possible to cover the fixed costs and reach profitability in the future.

A **scalable** business becomes more profitable as it grows. Most digital business that have a high fixed cost and low variable costs are highly scalable.

Total Addressable Market (TAM) is the size of the market segment that might conceivably purchase the innovation. This is the total value of sales in this market segment, for example, the total value of online apparel sales might be a relevant benchmark for AR Fashion Network.

DISCUSSION QUESTIONS

1. How does the initial development cost influence the commercial viability of the innovation?
2. How does it matter for scalability whether the innovation involves a high fixed cost or a high variable cost?
3. What data would you ideally like to have about the target market and how would you collect that data?
4. Why do we need to explore the ecosystem to develop a business model for our internally-developed innovation?

FURTHER READING

Johnson, M.W, Christensen C.M., and Kagermann H. (2008). Reinventing your business model. Harvard Business Review (December).

Tidhar, R., Hallen, B.L., and Eisenhardt, K. (2021). Measure twice, cut once: Achieving exceptional growth in nascent online fashion markets. Unpublished manuscript. Stanford University, Department of Management Science and Engineering.

Various authors (2019). On business model innovation. Harvard Business Publishing. Product # 10235E-KND-ENG. Cambridge MA.

CASE 4: UBER AND THE INNOVATION OF SHARED MOBILITY

Uber was founded by Garrett Camp and Travis Kalanick as "UberCab" in 2009. The original idea was focused on a phone app that would allow booking a timeshare limo service. Kalanick and Camp were both serial entrepreneurs, and UberCab was the third company Kalanick had founded since dropping out of UCLA in 1998. The app launched in San Francisco in June 2010, and the same year, the company received its initial venture capital.[3] In 2011 it changed its name to Uber Technologies to highlight the digital platform as opposed to the facilitated taxi services. Uber launched in New York City in 2011 where it started to receive strong pushback from the taxi industry, while at the same time beginning international expansion, first to Europe and soon to India and Africa. By 2013, the company was valued in excess of $1 billion. At the same time, the long-standing controversy about the employment status of Uber drivers began to surface.

Uber was leveraging the "sharing-economy" trend with companies like Airbnb, Stashbee, and Hubble. This "crowd-based capitalism" associated with inverted firms was shifting consumers away from traditional industries by creating technologies to connect people so that underutilized assets could be accessed and shared. Consumer behavior changed and people started to get used to not owning expensive and infrequently used items like cars, tools, clothes, and remote accommodation.

Uber characterized itself as a technology platform that used operational excellence, product expertise, and a massive network to power mobility.[4] By 2021, Uber was a multisided platform whose main services included rides (Mobility), food delivery (Eats), and freight logistics (Freight). Accordingly, Riders, Eaters, Merchants, Delivery People, Mobility Drivers, Shippers, and Carriers constituted the sides of the platform. Its distinct capabilities included marketplace, routing, and payment technologies. In particular, the marketplace embedded proprietary demand prediction, matching, dispatching, and pricing technologies. In 2019, before the global pandemic, Uber facilitated almost 7 billion trips for 111 million monthly active platform consumers (Riders and Eaters), generating $65 billion in gross bookings and $13 billion in company revenue from trip commissions. Despite significant revenue growth, the company posted a net loss of $8.5 billion. By 2021, Uber had not yet had a year where its revenue exceeded its cost of operations.

Case 4.1 Value Creation through Ride Sharing

Uber was not in the taxi business as it owned no cabs and employed no cab drivers. It was a matchmaker, linking independent drivers with consumers in need of rides and taking a share of that revenue. Its primary value propositions to Riders and Mobility Drivers arose from its capability to screen passengers and drivers to ensure safety, its revenue mechanism that offered different levels of service with varying pricing options, and convenience as users could easily track and pay for the service from their mobile devices, and drivers could easily

---

[3] Hartmans, A. and Leskin, P. (2019). The history of how Uber went from the most feared startup in the world to its massive IPO. Business Insider. May 18, 2019. Retrieved from www.businessinsider.com/ubers-history#may-2011-uber-launches-in-new-york-city-which-is-today-one-of-its-biggest-markets-but-which-also-presents-some-of-the-strongest-pushback-from-the-taxi-industry-10 in August 2022.

[4] Uber Annual Report 2021 retrieved from https://s23.q4cdn.com/407969754/files/doc_financials/2021/ar/FINAL-Typeset-Annual-Report.pdf in August 2022.

enter the business and work flexible hours. Uber's organization structure was inverted, which allowed for lower costs and thus, lower prices. Compared to taxi services, the firm had no inventory and did not need to pay regulatory fees, as it was not classified as a taxi service operator in most locales, although there was regulatory pressure to change this. Uber also offered delivery services with Uber Eats and Uber Freight, and it experimented with driverless cars and a program called Uber Elevate that could make daily air travel a reality.

Depending on availability and location, Uber offered different levels of service for Riders. The lowest cost option was Express Pool, which did not provide door-to-door service. Instead the user was often required to walk to their pick-up and from their drop-off location. Additionally, the ride could be shared with up to three other Riders along the way. The Pool option provided door-to-door service with up to three other Riders. These services were provided with a number of cars, but typically non-luxury vehicles. The lowest-cost private option, UberX, typically offered rides in regular cars like Toyota Prius. Uber Black was the company's original "affordable limo" service, costing a bit more but offering high-end town cars with professional drivers. Uber SUV charged a premium for a larger vehicle, and Uber LUX was the top-of-the-line option, operating with luxury cars such as Porsche and BMW. The variety of service levels allowed Riders to choose the most appealing ride for their situation. For example, the prices for Uber Express Pool were usually extremely low, particularly in metropolitan areas and near universities, appealing to young adults and students.

Uber allowed riders to rate their drivers and drivers to rate their riders out of 5 stars. Riders could leave a reason for their rating such as good conversation, clean car, and other options. Drivers could also leave a reason for their rating such as wait time, courtesy, and safety. Individual ratings were anonymous, but the average rating was public and visible to both sides of the market. If a driver had a very low average rating, their account was deactivated. If a rider had a very low average rating, they could be blocked from the app permanently or temporarily. This encouraged users to be timely and courteous, which increased the value of every ride. Furthermore, Uber added the 'quiet mode' option that allowed users to choose a silent ride to catch up on work or make phone calls. This allowed riders to politely avoid unwanted conversation, facilitating service personalization.

Other benefits of the platform included the ability of riders to book using the app on their smartphones and see the availability and location of drivers in the area, as well as the price and suggested routing of the ride before booking it. Drivers could also see the rating of the rider before accepting the ride and communicate with the rider using the app to facilitate pick-up. Additional benefits included inexpensive car rental and support services.

Case 4.2 The Uber Experience

Uber set out to recreate the entire taxi ride experience. Its initial audience was the tech-savvy young urbanites in San Francisco for whom it was easy to adopt the app, but over time it reached mainstream audiences. Uber targeted areas that have many restaurants and a lot of nightlife; holiday celebrations and events; weather events during which people prefer rides to public transport; and sporting events. For example, Uber saw rapid growth in Chicago, where there is a lot of nightlife, inclement weather, and a lively sporting scene.[5] In New York City, Uber made a name for itself by serving the outer boroughs that traditional cabs sometimes refused to serve.[6] Uber's innovative use of smartphone technology to conveniently summon a ride on the go enabled this disruptive growth. In other cities, Uber's tech-centric business model allowed it to serve the underserved while growing into a mainstream force over time.

In the US, 8 percent of online adults were reported to have used Uber at least once a month; young adults were the most enthusiastic users, making up about two-thirds of the US user base. Urban residents used Uber more heavily than suburban or rural residents, and more than a quarter of users were in the top income quartile.

By 2017, Uber had launched in almost all major US cities and covered around 70 percent of the US. That year, the company completed 35 million trips, or about 100,000 rides per day. It continued to expand into global markets across 63 countries.

Many of the Drivers relied on Uber as a source of additional income.[7] Drivers often had fluctuating incomes in their primary jobs; "smoothing out" one's income was a frequently cited reason for joining Uber. Uber also offered drivers flexibility. Additionally, there was greater diversity in terms of age, race, and gender among Uber drivers than among taxicab drivers nationally, more closely resembling the demographics of the national workforce and suggesting that Uber provided opportunities to drivers who might otherwise not be able to enter the market. However, many of the Uber drivers said this work wasn't enough to supplement their income. They would have preferred extra hours at their primary job, because the revenue and timing of rides were difficult to predict.

To attract and incentivize drivers, Uber provided extra benefits for new or high-performing drivers. In 2018 it announced a new rewards program for top drivers. The Uber Pro pilot program was launched in eight cities across the US. Drivers had to maintain a high rating to qualify, and they earned points based on their ratings, cancellation rates, and numbers of completed rides.

Uber Eats restaurant food delivery had evolved from an experimental service to serving much of the US and major cities worldwide. The management believed that its rapid expansion had shown them the path to further growth and profitability. In 2018, about 50 percent of first-time Uber Eats customers

---

[5] Ellis, S. and La Com, E. (2021). Uber – what's fueling Uber's growth engine? Retrieved from https://community.growthhackers.com/posts/uber-whats-fueling-ubers-growth-engine in August 2022.

[6] Bialik, C. (2015). Uber is serving New York's outer boroughs more than taxis are. *FiveThirtyEight*. Retrieved from http://fivethirtyeight.com/features/uber-is-serving-new-yorks-outer-boroughs-more-than-taxis-are/ in August 2022.

[7] Hall, Jonathan V. and Krueger, Alan B. (2018). An analysis of the labor market for Uber's driver-partners in the United States. *ILR Review* 71(3): 705–732.

were new to Uber's platform. The company believed that speed of delivery was the major factor consumers cared about. However, food delivery was a highly competitive field. Caviar, Postmates, and DoorDash all focused on quick and inexpensive restaurant food delivery.

Uber Freight entered the $700 billion trucking industry in the United States by leveraging the product knowledge, technical expertise, and operational experience to reshape the business logistics market into an on-demand market. In 2019, Uber Freight expanded to the $600 billion market in Europe. Uber Freight offered a diversification strategy to generate profits by applying their platform connectivity model to services where wider margins might be available.

Case 4.3 Competition Closing In

Although Lyft was a smaller ride-sharing service, it presented tough competition for Uber. In particular, the anti-tipping policy of Uber made many drivers prefer Lyft, and many more "multihomed" by driving for both companies. Uber also faced competition from the traditional taxi industry. However, the US taxi industry utilized technology poorly, struggled to incorporate customer feedback, might not agree to drive to certain (far away) neighborhoods, and required that customers "flag down" rides. However, the traditional taxi industry benefited from strong regulations in many cities and countries. Uber had been banned in several major markets due to regulations that protected the taxi industry. In Denmark, Uber drivers were hit with fines for noncompliance and tax avoidance. Uber had also been banned in many other European countries and cities.

In Asia, companies like Ola in India, Didi Chuxing in China, and GrabTaxi in Singapore were strong rivals. Collectively these firms had raised billions of dollars in VC funding. In the Southeast Asia region, Uber had to sell its business to Grab, the parent company of GrabTaxi. This was the third time that Uber had either sold or merged one of its businesses outside the US; the company previously sold its China business to Didi Chuxing and merged its operations in Russia and neighboring countries with local tech company Yandex. However, it continued to hold equity in both companies, although the investors of Didi Chuxing also invested in Lyft.

Although Lyft was struggling to keep up with Uber, it was favored by some drivers because of its organizational culture. Lyft framed the ride as a social experience to celebrate humanity and enjoy meeting people. Lyft created opportunities for riders to socialize and meet new people on a shared ride. This attitude transcended the companies' mission statements and extended into the appearances of the Uber and Lyft cars on the roads. While Uber encouraged drivers to dress professionally, open doors for riders, and stroll around in black cars, Lyft encouraged uniqueness in cars and drivers. For example, drivers who were artists or musicians created concepts such as the "Disco Lyft" and "Karaoke Lyft" that billed the Lyft ride as more of an experience. Lyft's encouragement for drivers to express themselves more freely may have been appealing to drivers, whereas some riders may have preferred Uber's sleek and professional demeanor.

Some US drivers saw Uber as the less appealing platform. There had been disputes about ride fares and drivers had been paid more per ride with Lyft. In response, Uber launched the "180 Days of Change" campaign in 2017 to build stronger relationships with drivers. This included new features for drivers such as tipping, 24/7 customer service support, long trip notifications, and two-minute cancellation times. Uber also launched an "Early Tester Program" so that drivers were able to test new features before they became available to everyone. Uber Pro was a driver reward program to further promote driver commitment through benefits and higher fares.

Uber faced stiff competition in the meal delivery market as well. Although it was a fast-growing industry, experiencing a 77 percent growth since 2013, delivery platforms such as GrubHub, DoorDash, Deliveroo, Swiggy, Postmates, Zomato, Delivery Hero, Just Eat, Takeaway.com, and Amazon were presenting competitive challenges.

In the shipping industry Uber Freight competed with global and North American freight brokers to connect shipping and carrying services on a single platform. The American Trucking Association reported that of the $700 billion that US businesses spent on trucking in 2017, about $72 billion was spent on brokerage. This segment of the market had grown at a compound annual growth rate of over 11 percent between 1995 and 2017, and with outdated business logistics models advancing towards on-demand technology that Uber had already perfected in the personal mobility and meal delivery markets, the company was in a prime position to compete for a larger share of this expected future growth. Uber Freight's main competition came from freight brokers such as C.H. Robinson, Total Quality Logistics, XPO Logistics, Convoy, Echo Global Logistics, Coyote, Transfix, DHL, and NEXT Trucking. Gross bookings of $359 million for 2018 suggested that Uber had penetrated less than 0.5 percent of the freight brokerage market. Its main advantages included the platform technology and on-demand booking capacity within the US while simultaneously expanding into the highly fragmented trucking industry of Europe, where it encountered smaller competitors.

Case 4.4 Inside Uber

Uber connected riders with drivers using a mobile app that was easy to use and allowed following the arrival of the ride or the delivery. To ensure passenger safety, Uber ran background checks, driver record checks, and credit report checks on aspiring drivers. Once approved, the driver had access to the driver app. At the end of the trip, the company would process the transaction, charge the passenger's card, and send the receipt to the passenger directly from the platform. The driver would receive their revenue share at the end of the week.

Ride matching required a complex system of algorithms to process supply and demand data in real time. Uber analyzed a large volume of data that was constantly changing (e.g., time of day, location, weather, and traffic patterns) as well as streams of data that changed slowly (e.g., driver rating, rider rating, rider behaviors) and data points that were static (e.g., vehicle type). Furthermore, these algorithms had to work consistently across various markets. If Uber was to enter a new city, their computing stack had to function immediately and adjust rapidly to the specifics of the new location. The company needed to accurately predict customer demand and mobilize drivers accordingly. Uber protected its technologies with dozens of patents, including patents for driver routing, push notifications, and surge pricing.

Uber's mobile payment methods were a core feature in the competition against traditional taxi companies. To develop the system, Uber partnered with Braintree, a leading mobile payment provider and a subsidiary of PayPal. Braintree facilitated the design of a mobile payment system that used client-side encryption to increase speed and security. Braintree's tools were essential for international payments, with support for over 130 currencies around the world. Additionally, Uber used the services of Card.io to scan a new credit card to a person's account using the phone's camera. These features contributed to Uber's hallmarks of speed and simplicity.

Case 4.5 Prospects for Profitability?

Uber set the ride fares and split them 80 percent–20 percent between the driver and the company. Surge pricing allowed charging premium fares during peak hours. Uber drivers were classified as independent contractors and were responsible for their own costs. These costs included the car, gas, maintenance, insurance, etc.

Uber also experimented with subscription-based models such as Uber Plus, where riders paid a monthly fee in exchange for 20 or 40 trips and different flat rates for UberPool and UberX. The Rider Pass charged customers a monthly fee of $14 for discounted rates for UberX, UberPool and Uber Express Pool.

By 2020, Uber's financials did not demonstrate a clear path to profitability based on scale economies (see Table C4.1). The cost of revenue, operations, sales and marketing, and general and administrative held steady shares of revenue showing no signs of decrease. During the IPO year of 2019, costs increased in part because of stock-based compensation to different employee groups. Nevertheless, continuing charges such as driver incentives, discounts, loyalty expenses, and promotions suggested that the company still needed to compete very hard for drivers and riders in all the markets.

Uber initially received a seed round investment in 2009. Additional venture capital financing came from angel investors and venture capital funding rounds from investors such as First Round, Benchmark, Menlo Ventures, Google Ventures, and Fidelity. Uber also received private equity funding from Baidu,

Table C4.1 Uber's financial results (in $ millions)

Year ended December 31	2018	2019	2020	2021
Revenue	10,433	13,000	11,139	17,455
Costs and expenses				
Cost of revenue	4,786	6,061	5,154	9,351
Operations and support	1,516	2,302	1,819	1,877
Sales and marketing	3,151	4,626	3,583	4,789
Research and development	1,505	4,836	2,205	2,054
General and administrative	2,082	3,299	2,666	2,316
Depreciation and amortization	426	472	575	902
Total costs and expenses	13,466	21,596	16,002	21,289
Loss from operations	(3,033)	(8,596)	(4,863)	(3,834)

Note: Uber's financials showed strong revenue growth but even faster growth of costs. It was particularly concerning that the cost of revenue grew faster than the revenues, suggesting that the incentives for platform participants continued to take a heavy toll.
Source: Uber Annual Report 10K filing. Retrieved from https://s23.q4cdn.com/407969754/files/doc_financials/2021/ar/FINAL-Typeset-Annual-Report.pdf in August 2022 and from https://investor.uber.com/news-events/news/press-release-details/2022/Uber-Announces-Results-for-Fourth-Quarter-and-Full-Year-2021/default.aspx in August 2022.

and debt financing from Goldman Sachs in 2015. In total, Uber received over $25 billion of venture financing from 116 investors.[8]

The company officially went public on May 10th, 2019, at an Initial Public Offering (IPO) price of $45 per share. The performance of Uber's stock on its opening day was very poor – a disappointment considering that it was the biggest US technology IPO since Facebook. Weak stock performance indicated investor concerns about Uber's unproven business model. Lyft also experienced a disappointing IPO earlier in the same year, suggesting general skepticism about ride-sharing platforms and about the value of network effects in delivery businesses where all sides of the market were easily able to multihome.

Case 4.6 Regulatory Challenges and Resistance

Government agencies are often slow to update their regulations as technology advances and business models evolve. Uber was constantly at odds with local governments and regulating bodies over its practices. Uber's drivers were not classified as employees, but contractors. This allowed Uber to avoid providing employee benefits such as health insurance and expense coverage. Uber's model also allowed the company to skirt around regulations that traditional taxi companies were forced to follow such as licensing fees, price controls, and

---

[8] Crunchbase Company Financials. Retrieved from www.crunchbase.com/organization/uber/company_financials in November 2022.

location limits. However, the advantage was a fragile one. Uber faced widespread opposition from local governments and countless lawsuits. For example, Spain suspended the company's operation and Uber lost a major case surrounding the legality of its employment practices in the state of California.

In a groundbreaking statement, the State of Oregon's Labor Commissioner wrote in 2015 that Uber drivers are employees, not contractors, despite their use of personal vehicles and ability to decide their working schedule. A similar ruling was made in California, where a former driver was declared to be eligible for unemployment benefits, and in May, a similar decision was made in Florida. Nevertheless, labor boards in nine states had declared that Uber drivers are contractors.

Uber had particularly thorny regulatory challenges in New York City. In the spring of 2015, Melrose Credit Union, the city's biggest financier of taxi licenses, wrote a letter to Mayor Bill de Blasio threatening the city with a multi-billion-dollar lawsuit if Uber didn't begin to comply with the local taxi regulations. Taxi medallion (license) prices had fallen significantly as Uber was gaining market share. Critics of Uber argued that as taxi drivers had invested in their medallions and complied with a variety of regulations, it was unfair for Uber drivers to take fares without complying. In August 2018, the New York City Council voted to approve a proposal to freeze new vehicle licenses for car services such as Uber for a year to study the effects of ride-sharing services on congestion. In the summer of 2018, Mayor de Blasio signed into law new for-hire vehicle legislation that halted the issuance of for-hire licenses in New York. For-hire licenses were required for all Uber drivers in the state of New York. Additionally, the legislation forced the local Taxi and Limousine Commission to raise for-hire vehicle driver take-home pay by nearly 20 percent. This cut into Uber's revenues and raised the floor on payments to their drivers.

In 2019, Uber drivers in Manhattan filed a lawsuit alleging Uber violated its own agreements regarding service fees. The plaintiffs argued that Uber had not paid taxes it took out of their drivers' wages for almost four years. More generally, Uber drivers' rights were often unclear. Uber ultimately formally recognized the Drivers Guild, a group advocating for the interests of drivers. The Guild focused on issues such as higher pay and restrictions on new drivers.

The legislative change in New York City inspired drivers in other cities to pursue similar changes. Taxi and ride-share drivers demanded new legislation from the city of Chicago. Typically taxi and ride-share drivers are competitors, but they were uniting to fight for limits on the number of drivers. With opposition from all sides, Uber was looking for new ways to expand.

In 2016, Uber had to address a consumer fraud lawsuit as the city of Chicago sued the company for an alleged year-long silence about a personal data breach affecting more than 57 million drivers and riders. Uber had also been caught bending regulatory rules on transporting customers. The UberPOP business that Uber had been using in France allowed uncertified and unlicensed drivers to conduct business, offering drastically reduced rates even compared to normal

Uber transportation services. The reduced-price service decreased demand for conventional taxi services. The resulting taxi driver riots and public outrage in Paris and Marseille caused the French government to ban the UberPOP business, forcing Uber to suspend its services. France also decreed a fine of up to €300,000 and two years in prison for allowing drivers to operate without proper licenses and registrations.

In 2017, the European Court of Justice ruled that Uber was to be categorized as a transportation service and, as a result, be governed and regulated as such; a decision that could not be appealed. Now Uber had to assume liability for accidents during Uber rides and give its drivers benefits and livable wages.

Personal risks to drivers and riders were always a concern for sharing economy companies. There had been many reports of deaths, robberies, and fights involving Uber drivers and riders. For example, in India, an Uber driver sexually assaulted a passenger. The legal proceedings led to a period when Uber was banned in India due to inadequate background checks. Uber's position was that as a software company offering an app as a service, the most it could do was to create transparency and safety through its screening process. Nevertheless, the company had been sued multiple times regarding allegations of unsafe conditions and operations. Additionally, Uber came under fire regarding its autonomous vehicles. The first incident of death regarding autonomous vehicles came from an Uber vehicle in 2018. Uber divested the autonomous driving unit in 2020.

DISCUSSION QUESTIONS

1. Discuss Uber's value configuration and how the configuration relates to Uber's revenue mechanisms. Can you suggest any potential improvements to the revenue mechanisms?
2. Map Uber's ecosystem (cf. Figure 14.1) to describe the parties that contribute to and compete for the value the platform creates. What ecosystem challenges do you identify that influence the performance of the current business model?
3. Does Uber scale? Examine the evolution of Uber's fixed and variable costs presented in Table C4.1 in the context of the case and explore which parts of the business appear to scale well or poorly, and why that might be the case.
4. By 2022, Uber had accumulated losses of about $27 billion in 13 years of existence.[9] Do you think the company will find a way to ultimately become consistently profitable and justify its existence by covering these losses? How might they achieve this?

---

[9] Funk, J. (2021). Today's unicorns have bigger cumulative losses than Amazon, lost money far longer than Amazon, still no turnaround. Wolf Street, July 5, 2021. Retrieved from https:// wolfstreet.com/2021/07/05/todays-unicorns-have-bigger-cumulative-losses-than-amazon-had-lost-money-far-longer-than-amazon-still-dont-show-a-turnaround/ in August 2022.

PART V
Gaining Ecosystem Momentum

....

It is easy to design innovations and make plans for fabulous success, but it is difficult to actually make new things happen. The process of launching and building economically and socially sustainable businesses is tedious and hard, and can take several years or even more. Most of the famous digital platform companies took a decade or longer to become reliably profitable, and most of the less famous ones failed well before reaching that stage. It is crucial to have a thoughtful strategy for gaining momentum with all the important stakeholders of the innovation: customers, suppliers, complementors, regulators, and other relevant societal partners. Momentum means that the stakeholders find the innovation increasingly compelling, useful, and worth exploring and supporting. Customers find it valuable for themselves and recommend it to their peers. Suppliers and complementors find it promising and are willing to commit some precious resources to providing inputs or systems necessary to commercialize and deliver the innovation. Regulators and various social communities find that the innovation is not too risky, harmful, or outright illegal.

A compelling innovation is thus legitimate from the perspective of all the relevant ecosystem parties that the innovator needs to support the process of commercialization. To reach legitimacy, the innovation must be technologically, economically, and commercially viable. Reaching this level of legitimacy and viability is an iterative process of communication, experimentation, development, prototyping, and demonstration.

This section starts from the process of market experimentation and customer acquisition, and then explores the ecosystem strategies that ensure differentiation and value capture potential on the supply side of the business. It concludes with a discussion of the legal and regulatory issues in the digital marketplace, particularly focusing on the intellectual property regime that shapes innovation.

15 Launching a New Digital Business Model

The design of a new digital business model is typically based on shaky assumptions and rough estimates. As the innovator further develops the proposed product or service, they need to carefully collect user feedback and market data to refine the assumptions and generate more precise estimates. Some of the trickiest challenges in launching a digital innovation include customer acquisition, business model validation, and gaining network momentum. We first discuss how to address the challenges of customer acquisition in digital markets. We then describe an experimental method for validating the features of the business model. This chapter finishes with tools for kindling network effects and fomenting the growth of the platform ecosystem.

15.1 Acquire Customers: "If You Build It, They Might NOT Come"

For any new business or product, attracting the first paying customers is a big test of legitimacy. For a digital innovation, the challenges are even more accentuated. When the product is intangible, usually software-based, how does one get the word out that it even exists? How to convince users that the product works as suggested and provides the promised benefits? How to get users to change their habits of consumption and communication and adopt the new service? Although some of the same hurdles afflict innovators of physical products or traditional services, it is much more difficult to get a consumer to adopt a new network for social communication than it is to get them to buy a new pair of shoes, even though the shoes are probably much more expensive. The benefits of a new social network are opaque and difficult to imagine, not to mention appreciate, before the network is fully formed, and it requires changing patterns of behavior within a social group which depends on multiple individuals coordinating their actions. In contrast, it is easy to imagine the benefits of new shoes, and physical shoe stores can locate themselves in busy shopping streets or malls and show the shoes to lots of daily passers-by.

Traditional product launches often rely on advertising and sales promotion campaigns. For example, the maker of a new kind of cereal might run a TV ad, include the cereal in a discount campaign with a supermarket chain, and negotiate to place the cereal in a prime location such as the end of the aisle within the supermarket. For a new digital application, things are more complicated. Advertising to reach online users tends to be very expensive. For example, the potential users of a new computer game are unlikely to watch much TV. The game developer could certainly advertise using ad auctions, but the effectiveness of that type of advertising might be limited compared to the expense. The developer could attempt to form partnerships with powerful distribution platforms, but considering there are thousands of game developers and very few platforms, the deal might not be highly beneficial: most game developers have limited bargaining power with respect to gaming platforms. On the other hand, just placing the new game on a distribution platform and hoping for the best might not work well, either. One of the major lessons from the first internet boom was that "If you build it, they will come" is almost always incorrect.[1]

A digital innovator needs a more surgical approach to developing the initial user base that then propagates the innovation to their networks and adjacent market segments. Usually, the key tactics include reaching out directly to early adopters and market leaders, utilizing specific channels to create groups of knowledgeable and compelling beta users. Most successful digital companies also rely on social networks and other digital network structures to spread the innovation "virally." This requires that the innovator understand the potential user groups (market segments) and, in particular, what aspects of the value proposition are the most appreciated by each type of user.

The key aspects of digital market segmentation include demographics, education, geography, income, and individual or organizational needs. For example, Pew Research Center reported in 2021 that social media adoption varies significantly by age, gender, income, education, and geography (rural vs. urban) but not much by race.[2] Pew also found that the dependence on a smartphone for internet access (as opposed to a fixed broadband internet) among US adults varies by race, age, income, and education, but not by gender or geography.[3] These types of market data can inform the digital innovator, for example, that it might be challenging to reach young, lower-income individuals with an application that requires fixed-line broadband internet to function well. Before planning the market launch (also called **go-to-market strategy**, or GTM), it is therefore valuable to investigate the prevalence and behavior of the targeted market segments, and the degree to which existing competitors already cover the same segments. The market segment grid can be a helpful tool. This analysis reveals the unique user groups of the proposed innovation and pinpoints how to design the market launch to identify and reach the targeted users (see Table 15.1).

---

[1] Mullen, S. (2021). Startup fallacies: If you build it they will come. Retrieved from https://samuelmullen.com/articles/startup-fallacies-if-you-build-it-they-will-come in August 2022.

[2] Pew Research Center (2021). Social Media Fact Sheet, April 7, 2021. Retrieved from www.pewresearch.org/internet/fact-sheet/social-media/?menuItem=45b45364-d5e4-4f53-bf01-b77106560d4c in August 2022.

[3] Pew Research Center (2021). Mobile Fact Sheet, April 7, 2021. Retrieved from www.pewresearch.org/internet/fact-sheet/mobile/?menuItem=d40cde3f-c455-4f0e-9be0-0aefcdaeee00 in August 2022.

Table 15.1 Target market segment grid for individual users

User characteristics	My Innovation	Competitor 1	Competitor 2	...	Competitor N
Age					
Gender					
Education/tech skills					
Income					
Geographic market					
Ethnicity/race					
Pain point/need					

Note: The target market segment analysis helps an innovator identify user segments where their unique features are particularly valued. This informs the go-to-market, or launch strategy to approach the users who most appreciate the product.

Table 15.2 Target market segment grid for organizational (business) users

User characteristics	My Innovation	Competitor 1	Competitor 2	...	Competitor N
Organization size (number of employees)					
Organization type (e.g., for-profit, non-profit, public sector)					
Industry					
Availability of tech skills					
Revenues					
Geographic market					
Pain point/need					

Note: Business users should be analyzed along a different set of characteristics compared with individual users. However, the prevalence of technological skills, user needs, and users' income levels influence the adoption decisions of both organizations and individuals.

Similarly, in the B2B market, segmentation can tremendously facilitate market launch by efficiently focusing marketing and communication efforts (see Table 15.2). Among potential business users, characteristics such as the number of employees, revenue base, profit orientation, technological capabilities, and specific business needs can influence the willingness and ability to adopt and pay for new digital services. For example, large corporations are likely to have financial and technological resources that enable them to absorb even complex new technologies, but their procurement processes can be slow and cumbersome for untested innovations. Small and medium-sized enterprises (SMEs), in contrast, have typically limited funds available but their decision making can be much more nimble. Non-profit and public-sector organizations, on the other hand, tend to have both very limited funding and few technical skills available, but their digital needs may be very acute.

In the case of multisided platforms, as with value propositions, market segmentation and launch strategies need to be thought through for all sides of the platform. For example, as we saw in Chapter 14, Snapchat must maintain attractive value propositions for individual users, advertisers, and publishers of digital content. Similarly, they need to analyze the market segments for each of the platform user groups, and tailor their market launch based on how to find each group and attract their attention with the least marketing expenditure and time.

Dropbox is famous for its successful product development and launch strategy.[4] The company was founded in 2007, the product launched in 2008, and by 2011, the company had 25 million registered users (although 96 percent of the users were paying nothing).[5] According to the founder Drew Houston's conference presentation in 2010, the initial product announcement was done in 2007 on a website for computing enthusiasts called Hacker News. At this time, the product wasn't even finished, so there was no live demonstration, just a short video with some screenshots explaining how the service would work.[6] However, this was enough to attract interest and high-quality feedback from a very knowledgeable crowd of "hackers." A year later, the product was nearly finished, and the company posted a full-featured video on another website, the news aggregator Digg. The goal of this second post was to both advertise and recruit **beta users** to get more technical feedback. Beta users are usually selected from among the high-skilled and informed or experienced users who find it relatively easy to use the product and can provide thoughtful feedback. They tend to be early adopters of advanced technologies. This second video posting was also extremely impactful, and the waitlist to become a beta user grew from 5,000 to 75,000 in just one day.

Dropbox also tried traditional marketing techniques. It hired a skilled marketing expert who set up web marketing through search-engine optimization (SEO) and Google's AdWords. After multiple campaigns, the company noticed that this approach was very costly and almost useless. Out of a campaign that cost about $1,200, they generated 650,000 ad impressions (indicating a CPM of about $1.84), of which 0.11 percent (700 individuals) clicked through to the Dropbox landing page. Seventy-four new users registered, leading to four new paying customers. As a result, Dropbox found that each new paying user cost about $300 to acquire. With an annual subscription price of $99, this was not

[4] Houston, D. (2010). Dropbox: Startup lessons learned. Slideshare presentation. Retrieved from www.slideshare.net/gueste94e4c/dropbox-startup-lessons-learned-3836587 in August 2022.

[5] Statista Research Department (2016). Number of registered Dropbox users. Statista, March 7, 2016. Retrieved from www.statista.com/statistics/261820/number-of-registered-dropbox-users/ in August 2022.

[6] Houston, D. (2007). My YC App: Throw away your USB drive. Hacker News Apr 5, 2007. Retrieved from https://news.ycombinator.com/item?id=8863 in August 2022.

a sensible approach. After a few trials, the advertising strategy was abandoned. Drew Houston explained that SEO was primarily a way to harvest demand, not create it. For a truly novel digital business, search optimization and ad auction markets are not likely to generate many valuable leads, because "nobody wakes up in the morning wishing they didn't have to carry a USB drive." In other words, when the product is novel, potential users don't even know they might need it. For a new service like Dropbox, it was much more likely that a new user heard about the service from a friend or a colleague, tried it even though they did not realize they needed it, was delighted that it actually worked, and told other friends about it. This is **viral marketing**, where the product essentially sells itself through word-of-mouth.

To trigger word-of-mouth marketing, the product obviously has to have a compelling value proposition. It also helps to have built-in network effects. Here, file sharing was one critical aspect of Dropbox's success. Many of the users joined because someone shared a larger file with them that was not practical to share via email. This was even more common among co-workers within or across companies. It was easier to share files in a joint project via Dropbox. In this manner, one user might bring in several others to work on shared files. Dropbox further accelerated this viral spread by providing incentives to both sides of a referral. Between late 2008 and early 2010, 4 million new users registered, mostly from word-of-mouth dissemination. Thirty-five percent of the new registrations originated directly from the referral program, and another 20 percent from shared folders. Sharing folders with co-workers within a company acted as a "Trojan Horse" by stealthily spreading the application inside the organization, until its IT noticed and perhaps switched everyone to an enterprise subscription. This allowed Dropbox to avoid the complications of the B2B sales process.

Another famous customer-acquisition case is Airbnb.[7] The origins of Airbnb can be traced back to the founders' idea to generate a little extra income from renting their own apartment to attendees of a professional conference in San Francisco in 2007. They set up a website called Airbed and Breakfast and hosted a few individuals during the event, and a few more during a subsequent political convention. Although they received some requests from around the world to set up similar websites in different cities, the website on its own got limited traction in growing the customer base.

Airbnb quickly realized the importance of growing both sides of the platform, hosts and their listings on one side, and guests on the other side. The first brilliant "growth hack" was an integration with Craigslist. Craigslist was already a major platform for short-term rentals. Airbnb exploited this by allowing hosts who listed a rental on Airbnb to choose to automatically also list on Craigslist to gain sufficient visibility when there were relatively few users on the guest side.

---

[7] Brown, M. (2021). Airbnb: the growth story you didn't know. GrowthHackers, June 9, 2021. Retrieved from https://community.growthhackers.com/posts/airbnb-the-growth-story-you-didnt-know in August 2022.

Essentially this enabled growing Airbnb's host network by "borrowing" Craigslist's tenant user base. Airbnb did this by developing a bot that would visit Craigslist, copy a unique listing URL, input the accommodation details, and send the URL to the host. Airbnb also set up automated emails to all renters on Craigslist from "an excited Airbnb user" encouraging the host to visit the Airbnb website.

On the guest side, the company leveraged users' pre-existing Facebook connections through a feature called Social Connections which tapped into Facebook Connect. If hosts and guests had mutual contacts through either their Facebook or Airbnb networks, they had greater mutual trust. Like Dropbox, Airbnb also created a referral program. Interestingly, referrals gained a lot of momentum after the company changed the program from receiving benefits ("refer a friend and get $25 toward your next booking!") to giving gifts ("refer a friend and give them $25 off of their booking!").

Our final example is an Ithaca-based start-up company in the philanthropy space called GiveGab. GiveGab was building a platform for donors to support nonprofit organizations' fundraising efforts. Philanthropic fundraising used to be a complicated and inefficient market, with many nonprofits struggling to find donors but also so poorly resourced as to not be able to market themselves effectively. A digital platform could make a huge difference in enabling coordination and communication within this fragmented market, but with over a million very small and cash-constrained organizations in the US, GiveGab's sales effort to sign up these organizations was going to be a nightmare.

GiveGab's co-founder and CEO Charlie Mulligan developed the idea of a marketplace for charitable giving based on the concept of "Giving Days." GiveGab Giving Day is typically a day of fundraising focused on a single geographic market, such as Ithaca, NY ("Giving is Gorges" campaign) or Hudson Valley, NY. A Giving Day could also be focused on a multi-unit organization like the YMCA that raised funds for all its New York-based units afflicted by the COVID-19 pandemic with its "Open for Good" campaign. GiveGab would set up a website and a dedicated platform for the targeted nonprofits within the specific giving market to sign up and inform their stakeholders about the campaign. The giving platform generated advertising and communication materials and provided training and resources to the participating nonprofits. The joint effort of the Giving Day kept costs for each organization low while maximizing the attention and engagement of the local donor community. Via Giving Days, GiveGab could cost-effectively bring larger numbers of nonprofit organizations and donors together than would have been possible by trying to engage the two sides of the platform individually. The one-day campaign duration also created a sense of urgency for donors to act.

While Giving Days tended to take place just once a year within a local market, after participating in one event, the nonprofits and local donors were registered and enrolled on GiveGab's platform. Nonprofits could run their own campaigns easily using the platform. This was a part of GiveGab's conversion plan to acquire and retain clients and address all their ongoing fundraising needs, not only the Giving Day event.

Charlie Mulligan explained:

> GiveGab giving days create a marketplace where donors can choose from almost every nonprofit in their local area, drastically upping their options. This has a huge, positive impact on the nonprofits because the donors they gain on a giving day chose them, meaning they have a far stronger connection to the actual mission to the nonprofit and are thus far more likely to come back and donate again throughout the year. So giving days are an amazing way to bring on nonprofits and donors at the same time, building a critical mass on a local level of both supply and demand (nonprofits and donors), benefitting the nonprofits, the donors, and GiveGab too.[8]

What is common among the three examples above is that each digital innovator first identified the key user groups that benefited from interacting with each other on the platform. They then utilized an existing online or offline network structure among the users to speed up network formation within the innovative service. When the market is highly fragmented, building off an existing community (a hacker discussion board, Craigslist, or a geographic locale) can significantly lower the cost of identifying and onboarding the early user groups. Moreover, if the innovation has social network features, bringing individual users into the system will be ineffective as they have no existing "friends" to interact with. The innovator has to bring onboard whole communities, such as co-workers in an organization, students on a college campus, or nonprofits or renters in a local area.

15.2 Validating the Business Model through Experimentation

Digital innovation is to a significant degree a process of experimentation. With great uncertainty about user behavior and preferences – even users themselves may be unclear about their preferences – innovators need to create opportunities for preference discovery. While investigating the potential user groups and market segments is helpful, those users are not necessarily very informative regarding whether they would actually buy the product, what they like or dislike about it, or how much they would pay for it. These more specific preferences may not be formed yet, because the product may require learning by the users to see how it fits within their daily lives and coordination by users to adopt it together with their social group and interact. The social process of figuring out how a digital product influences a user's everyday habits and practices, and how the product is interpreted and used by a social group, is called **social construction**.

Because of this preference uncertainty, digital innovators may benefit from experimental research to assess user preferences. It is often very easy and inexpensive to run experiments in digital service environments. As a result,

---

[8] Personal communication, June 14, 2021.

companies such as Uber[9] and Facebook constantly run hundreds of experiments on user behavior while we use their products and services. Experimental product development requires seeking user feedback on features and **affordances**, or properties of the product that suggest how it can be used, as early as possible. The company can then use the feedback to guide further product development, iterating between feedback and development until the feedback is positive enough to support market launch. This approach corresponds to the concept of **lean** in manufacturing and entrepreneurship: avoiding waste by expending effort only based on need. In manufacturing, lean principles enable avoiding unnecessary inventory of supplies or finished products; in innovation and entrepreneurship lean principles enable avoiding unnecessary effort or time spent on developing features that users do not desire.

The iterative process of user feedback and product development should primarily be structured to accelerate learning and discovering user preferences. "Time is money," and most innovators have a finite timeline and budget to prove the project before they run out of support. With limited time and a great urgency to understand user reactions to the new product, the best approach is to demonstrate the features and explore how users interact with them. Product developers can study and facilitate the acceptance of the innovation by offering an early prototype to exploratory (beta) users – or even just screenshots as the Dropbox example suggested. The lean innovation process also engages the principles of **design thinking** by creating opportunities to observe and learn how users interact with the innovative product.

Design thinking is a critical ingredient in digital innovation. In addition to the iterative process of ideation, rapid prototyping, and testing outlined above, the design thinking approach highlights empathy. According to Lockwood (2009),[10] design thinking is a "human-centered innovation process that emphasizes observation, collaboration, fast learning, visualization of ideas, rapid prototyping, and concurrent business analysis." This approach works best when behavioral uncertainty and solution ambiguity are high (Liedtka et al., 2013). The product designer thus needs to approach the users and the design with empathy related to their incomplete knowledge and limited experience of the design context. The designer's task is to meet the users where they are and try to understand the skills, knowledge, and resources needed to adopt and benefit from the innovation. If the designer doesn't adequately empathize with and understand the users' skills and needs, the product design may become overly complicated and frustrating or even harmful by causing users to lose time, digital resources, or efficiency. According to Eisenmann et al. (2014), early in its product development, Dropbox hired regular (unskilled) potential users from Craigslist to try to install and use the product, only

---

[9] Deb, A. et al. (2018). Under the hood of Uber's experimentation platform. Uber Engineering, August 28, 2018. Retrieved from https://eng.uber.com/xp/ in August 2022.

[10] Lockwood, T. (ed.). 2009. *Design Thinking: Integrating Innovation, Customer Experience, and Brand Value* (3rd ed.). New York: Allworth Press.

to realize that the product was way too complicated for non-expert users. This illustrates how highly-skilled engineers might have a very different view of the product's usability than users in the mass market. Engineers tend to enjoy and be fascinated by advanced technology and features, whereas regular people tend to prefer ease-of-use and features that make their lives simpler.

While Airbnb has been a marvelous success story, many early observers doubted its potential. One key concern was that people will not want to stay in strangers' homes. Although the service started out as a "couchsurfing" business, it quickly evolved, based on customer feedback, to a more traditional short-term rental business where almost all rentals involve a whole apartment or a house, not shared accommodation with the owner or other guests.

Another concern, particularly by potential investors such as the founder of Y-Combinator, was that two of the three founders were designers by vocation. Traditionally, internet start-ups were founded and dominated by IT specialists who could quickly evolve the technological platform. However, in the case of this hospitality start-up, it turned out that the founders' capacity to apply design thinking was actually an asset, not a liability.

Airbnb's product development focused on user experience. First, the goal was to make the website's user interface and the process of posting a new listing very easy to use. Joe Gebbia, the co-founder in charge of customer service, explained that the site was developed primarily on the basis of observed user behavior and explicit user feedback.[11] According to the CEO Brian Chesky, the company set out to discover the "perfect" user experience and then work backward to deliver it.[12]

In practice, figuring out the perfect user experience was often a lot of work. For example, during summer 2009, Chesky himself stayed in listed accommodations to understand how customer service could be improved. In 2010 the company was not gaining traction in New York City. The three founders went to visit and noticed that the photographs that hosts took of their accommodations were often of poor quality. They decided to send and pay for a professional photographer to take attractive photos. This photo service was made available for all hosts and became standard practice. Although not cheap, it substantially improved rentals, and by 2012 Airbnb retained more than 2,000 freelance photographers on six continents.[13]

Regarding service design, trust and security were always big challenges for Airbnb. The company instituted fraud prevention processes within the payment system and made it easy to keep all communication on the website to be able to track security issues. Despite the precautions, in 2011, the company experienced a

---

[11] Allentrepreneur (2011). Travel like a human with Joe Gebbia, co-founder of Airbnb. August 26, 2009. Retrieved from https://allentrepreneur.wordpress.com/2009/08/26/travel-like-a-human-with-joe-gebbia-co-founder-of-airbnb/ in August 2022.

[12] Carr, A. (2012). 19_Airbnb for turning spare rooms into the world's hottest hotel chain. Fast Company Feb 7, 2012. Retrieved from www.fastcompany.com/3017358/19airbnb in August 2022.

[13] Brown, M. (2021). Airbnb: the growth story you didn't know. GrowthHackers, June 9, 2021. Retrieved from https://community.growthhackers.com/posts/airbnb-the-growth-story-you-didnt-know in August 2022.

major disaster when a host's apartment was ransacked by a visitor. In response, the company introduced a substantial liability guarantee, voice and video verification systems, and a customer support hotline that was always available.[14]

In summary, Airbnb's service development approach was characterized by a painstaking effort to understand the users' perspective and design the service to provide the best possible experience. Similarly, GiveGab emphasized "customer love" as their leading light. While this may not be the most cost-effective strategy, it is possibly the most conducive to growth in the end. And we know that, with digital platforms, gaining early growth momentum is key.

The power of experimental innovation arises from the ability to pinpoint causal effects of product design. The scientific method is based on the idea of providing randomly distributed treatments to a subset of the sample, while others receive a placebo treatment. If the treatments are truly randomized, the innovator simply needs to compare the statistical means of the outcomes of the two subsamples. The idea of A/B testing is essentially the same. A random group of users receive treatment A and another random group receive the placebo B. After a period of observation, the innovator can compare the feedback or actions of users from the two groups.

In order to identify the causal effect, the assignment of the treatment can't be correlated with the user types or preferences. Sometimes it can be difficult to randomize treatment, and then the effect estimates can be biased. For example, the current user base might not be representative of the market, as in the case of Dropbox's beta users that were much more skilled and experienced than the rest of the market. Running user experiments in a population of skilled beta users to decide between alternative features thus might not inform the innovator about the true preferences in the mainstream market for these features.

To develop an experiment, the innovator needs a hypothesis, or a justified statement about the impact of the treatment on the outcome. Hypotheses should be developed based on either empirical or conceptual evidence justifying the expected effect. This could concern changes in users' needs or willingness to pay, or even observations of people using the product in new or unexpected ways. A useful starting point to develop a hypothesis about user behavior is the value proposition. If the value proposition is accurate and properly articulates how the product benefits users, it should give clues as to how the innovator could further improve the product to provide more value for the same cost structure. The idea needs to be defined in terms of testable implications, and the resulting hypothesis must be **refutable**, in other words, there must be a way to determine whether the experimental treatment sufficiently improved the desired outcome.

An important consideration is the **statistical power** of the experiment. Sufficient power means that the test is likely to detect an effect, if the effect truly exists. A

[14] Carr, A. (2012). 19_Airbnb for turning spare rooms into the world's hottest hotel chain. Fast Company, February 7, 2012. Retrieved from www.fastcompany.com/3017358/19airbnb in August 2022.

power of P = 0.9 means that 90 percent of the time the test would reveal a significant difference between the treatment and the control groups. Power analysis defines how many observations are needed to generate a reliable estimate of the treatment effect. Power depends on the desired precision range and confidence level of the prediction, and the expected dispersion (standard deviation of the treatment characteristic) of the targeted population. For a simple mean statistic, the required number of observations N is the following:

$$N = (Z)^2 * (SD)^2 / (R)^2$$

Where Z is the desired Z-statistic (often Z = 1.96 reflecting a 95 percent confidence level in a two-sided test of a larger sample); SD is the assumed standard deviation of the test statistic in the population; and R is the range within which the experimenter wants to know the statistic. For example, for a Z = 1.96 and SD = 5.0, the needed sample size is 96 subjects if the experimenter wants to know the test statistic within a precision range of 1.0. For example, these numbers could reflect the average consumption of Easter eggs by a population of college students. Thus, the larger the standard deviation tends to be (some students really love to eat lots of Easter eggs, and some students don't eat any), the larger the sample has to be to obtain a precise estimate of egg consumption. However, before the experiment, the researcher might not know the actual standard deviation in the population. They would need to "guesstimate" it from related previous studies, for example studies of consumption of different types of sweets.

Let's work through a specific fictional product development experiment. In 2011, Dropbox had a freemium revenue model whereby 97 percent of users used less than 2GB of storage for free, and 3 percent of users paid $9.90 per month for up to 50GB of storage space. There was also an option of paying $19.99 per month for up to 100GB of storage. However, the company's revenues suffered because few users switched from freemium to become a paying customer. One idea to address this problem is to experiment on how this "conversion" from free to paying can be made easier for users.

Your product development team might come up with the option of offering 10GB of storage for $5 per month, offering a lower monthly subscription fee but moving some users into the paying category and getting them used to being a subscriber. How would you test whether this solution is feasible and profitable?

Hypothesis: offering up to 10GB of storage for $5 per month will increase switching from free to paid use by more than 20 percent (and in doing so cover the cost of creating and handling this price point).

Treatment group: randomly select a sample of free users and extend the offer when they log in within the subsequent 2 weeks.

Control group: randomly select a sample of other free users and extend the pre-existing offer to them when they next log in (50GB for $9.99 per month) within the subsequent 2 weeks.

Statistical power: in other similar conversion samples, your product development team has noticed that the standard deviation of the decision to switch from freemium to paying is approximately 0.15. At the 95 percent confidence level of a two-tailed test, the Z-statistic would be 1.96. You would like to know the effect within a range of 1% = 0.01. In this case, the number of observations $N = (Z)^2 * (SD)^2 / (D)^2 = (1.96)^2 * (0.15)^2 / (0.01)^2 = 864$.

You might thus target a population of, say, 1,000 users, and hope to observe at least 864 individuals within the study period.

Observation: Collect data about both user groups' switching behavior: how many free users become paying users within the study period?

Data:

2.1 percent of free users in the treatment group switched to the $5 for 10GB subscription (standard deviation 0.14)

0.6 percent of free users in the treatment group switched to the pre-existing package of $9.99 for 50GB (standard deviation 0.07)

Total new paying users in the treatment group: 2.7 percent. $\mu_1 = 0.027$ ($SD_1 = 0.16$). In the control group, 1.1 percent took the pre-existing offer $\mu_2 = 0.011$ ($SD_2 = 0.10$).

Analysis:

The null hypothesis is that the difference between the means is less than 20 percent of the baseline frequency of switching d = 20%*0.011 = 0.0022:

$$H_0: \mu_1 - \mu_2 < d \quad (0.027 - 0.011 < 0.0022)$$

The main hypothesis is that the difference between the means is greater than 20 percent of the baseline:

$$H_a: \mu_1 - \mu_2 > d \quad (0.027 - 0.011 > 0.0022)$$

Difference in means test:

$$\text{T-statistic} = (\mu_1 - \mu_2 - d) / \sqrt{\left\{\left(SD_1^2 / N_1\right)^2 + \left(SD_2^2 / N_2\right)^2\right\}}$$
$$= 0.014 / 0.0061 = 2.3$$

$$\text{P-value} = 0.011 \ (\text{d.f. } 1705)$$

Thus, the test supports our main hypothesis that 20 percent more users switch from free to paid use when we offer an intermediate subscription option of $5 per month.

15.3   Gain Platform Momentum and Develop the Ecosystem

For digital innovations with a communication network or community features, it is critical to both develop the product experience and the network at the same time. For Airbnb, it does not matter how amazing the photos or security features are on the website if there are no listings in the city where a user would like to visit. On the other hand, hosts will not bother to post listings if there are few guests in the community. Thus finding ways to coordinate the adoption process and to bring a large number of users on each side of the platform and in each role of the ecosystem is a key strategic challenge for any digital innovator. As we saw in the examples of Airbnb "poaching" Craigslist's user base or GiveGab bringing whole local communities on the platform in one Giving Day, the innovator needs to find mechanisms and appropriate pre-existing communities that can be engaged with a reasonable amount of time and effort.

Furthermore, in many social network services, the user communities must be acquainted "IRL," or in real life. While a dating site such as Match.com is based on creating new connections among strangers (but in fairly close physical proximity), most social platforms such as Snapchat are based on offline friends sharing their experiences online. To make that a worthwhile value proposition, Snapchat has to bring whole groups of friends on the platform. No surprise, then, that many social networks are focused on young adults and are launched on college campuses. Snapchat, Facebook, and, for better or for worse, Yik Yak, were all created by college students who launched the apps for their student peers to connect. While not all innovators can be college students, college campuses or other offline communities of young adults such as sports or youth organizations can nevertheless be fertile grounds for achieving viral adoption of networked social applications.

While scouting for potential communities to approach for coordinated adoption, a digital innovator needs to design the most convenient adoption process possible. How can new users quickly and easily access the service based on a friend's recommendation or sharing, leave a short-form registration, and hopefully return later for a full registration, and ultimately sign up for an ongoing subscription or paying relationship? For Dropbox, that process consisted of accepting to receive access to a friend's file. This would leave the new user's email with Dropbox. Next, the service could ask the user to set up a password to continue to access the file. Next, there may be an offer to set up their own free user account and download the application on the local computer for fast access to the files. Finally, once the user is saving more and larger files in their Dropbox, for example, photos or videos, they would quickly use up the free storage and be offered to purchase a cheap subscription package and become a paying customer. This is the **adoption and conversion "funnel"** that should be as intuitive and smooth as possible to support rapid customer acquisition.

KEY IDEAS

- Customer acquisition is a challenging process for digital innovators because users' discovery of intangible products can be difficult to facilitate.
- Identifying and understanding the needs and preferences of target market segments will help focus customer acquisition efforts.
- In digital markets, any amount of market research can't replace experimentation. Randomized controlled experiments can pinpoint features that cause or prevent product adoption. Experimental strategies can be used to validate the value proposition and other aspects of the business model such as the revenue mechanism.

- Design thinking principles help an innovator to empathize with users and develop the best possible user experience.
- A platform takes off if the innovator is able to facilitate coordinated adoption by the interdependent user groups. Therefore, it is critical that the innovator understands the pre-existing social networks and interaction preferences of the users.

DEFINITIONS

The **adoption and conversion funnel** facilitates users learning about the product, adopting it, and, ultimately, becoming paying customers.

An **affordance** is a property of the product that suggests how it can be used. For example, an affordance of a mobile phone is to enable long-distance voice conversations.

Beta user is a user willing to try out a prototype or an unfinished product. Usually beta users are highly skilled and enthusiastic about new technologies.

Design thinking is a human-centered innovation process that emphasizes observation, collaboration, fast learning, visualization of ideas, rapid prototyping, and concurrent business analysis to develop products that are easy to adopt and use and that address actual user needs.

Go-To-Market strategy is the plan of action that an innovator will pursue to find a significant customer base.

Lean principles in production or innovation focus on avoiding wasteful actions.

Market segment is the group of customers who have relatively more similar preferences and behaviors compared with other customer groups. The segmented customers are thus more similar to each other than to the rest of the market.

A **refutable hypothesis** allows the innovator to determine whether the experimental treatment such as a novel product feature sufficiently improved the desired outcome.

Social construction is the social process of figuring out how a digital product influences users' everyday habits and practices, and how the product is interpreted and used by a social group.

Statistical power means that the statistical test is likely to detect an effect, if the effect truly exists.

Viral marketing strategies attempt to set in motion networked communication that disseminates the product or information about it without the innovator having to design and pay for it.

DISCUSSION QUESTIONS

Imagine that you are developing a digital mental health service platform for providers of services such as counseling and therapy. You want to develop a telehealth application for remote access to these services.

1. Using the target market segment grids (one for individual patients, the other for care providers), what would be your target market segments and why?
2. Discuss with five individuals what would be their preferences and concerns regarding such an application.

3. How would you apply design thinking in the development of the telehealth application?
4. How would you coordinate the adoption process of individual users (patients) and care providers on the platform?
5. Map the ecosystem of your telehealth platform (the ecosystem participants and their interactions). What strategies would help expand the ecosystem and improve your position in it?

FURTHER READING

Autio, E. (2022) Orchestrating ecosystems: a multi-layered framework. *Innovation: Organization and Management* 24(1): 96–109.

Eisenmann, Thomas R., Pao, Michael, and Barley, L. (2011). "Dropbox: 'It Just Works'." Harvard Business School Case 811-065, January 2011. (Revised October 2014.)

Kerr, W. R., Nanda, R., and Rhodes-Kropf, M. 2014. Entrepreneurship as experimentation. *Journal of Economic Perspectives* 28 (3): 25–48.

Kohavi, R., Longbotham, R., Sommerfield, D., and Henne, R.M. 2009. Controlled experiments on the web: survey and practical guide. *Data Mining and Knowledge Discovery* 18: 140–181.

Liedtka, J., King, A., and Bennett, K. 2013. *Solving Problems with Design Thinking: Ten Stories of What Works*. New York: Columbia University Press.

Lockwood, T. (ed.). 2009. *Design thinking: Integrating Innovation, Customer Experience, and Brand Value* (3rd ed.). New York: Allworth Press.

Symeonidou, N., Leiponen, A., Autio, E., and Bruneel, J. (2022). The origins of capabilities: resource allocation strategies, capability development, and the performance of new firms. *Journal of Business Venturing* 37(4): 106–208.

16 | Sources of Competitive Advantage in Digital Ecosystems

16.1 Profiting from a Digital Innovation: Deriving Value from an Ecosystem

There are many factors that influence the profitability of an innovation. In addition to industry or market-level factors, macroeconomic conditions influence aggregate demand and the cost of capital, and societal trends such as cultural norms and regulatory changes may affect the desirability of products and the costs of operation. Within innovation strategy we focus primarily on factors that the innovating firm itself can influence. These include the relationships with other parties in the ecosystem and some aspects of the regulatory environment.

Economic models of competition focus on the strategic interactions among rivals in a narrowly defined market. Generally, the more firms in a market, and the more similar their products, the more intense the competitive rivalry. However, firms also compete for profits in their other relationships such as those with customers and suppliers. Bargaining power in a supply or customer relationship depends on how many alternatives there are on each side, and how unique their products or needs are. In digital systems, innovators also need to work with many providers of **complementary products, technologies, or services**. External partners may provide critical materials, information, components, technologies, physical assets, distribution channels, communication systems, and other major inputs that facilitate the commercialization of digital innovations. For example, if a mobile game needs to be distributed via an app store, then the app store is an essential complement. Similarly, electric cars need a network of charging stations. While an electric car is a major innovation, its market will remain limited until the charging infrastructure becomes available. The electric car manufacturer could create the charging infrastructure in-house, but it might be more practical to rely on external partners who are already in the service business, such as gas stations, to do that. This creates an external dependence for a critical resource that needs to be strategically managed. However, developing and offering complementary products in-house may be too difficult and expensive.

Innovation strategy often involves managing trade-offs, such as the benefits and costs of sourcing complements and inputs externally vs. internally. In considering all such arrangements, the innovator's ability to differentiate in a way that enhances the customers' willingness to pay tends to increase its profitability. Although the innovator may depend on outside partners for complements and inputs, the partners may depend on a highly differentiated innovator even more, creating a better bargaining position for sharing the returns. In other words, an innovator should seek to develop a position where it can create significant value for customers and also remain distinct from ecosystem partners and rivals to ensure its profitability. This should be the guiding principle to decide which complementary products and services are created in-house vs. outsourced: Internalize activities where the value-creating differentiation is the greatest and the most durable.

Differentiation depends on the inherent technical characteristics of the innovation as well as the firm's strategic actions. Technology areas vary with respect to the ease of imitation of innovations. For example, personal services can be easy to copy unless the provider has unusual skills or talent. It's easy to set up a restaurant but difficult to provide, or build a reputation for, an outstanding culinary experience. Mechanical innovations like new tools can also be easy to copy unless they are patented, and even then, they can often be invented around by building on similar but not exactly the same ideas. Chemical inventions, including pharmaceuticals, also need to be patented to prevent imitation, but such patents tend to be quite strong because they protect a specific chemical compound that is difficult to design around. Patenting is thus an important strategy of enhancing differentiation but it doesn't help in all areas of technology.

In the digital economy, electronics hardware (computers and devices) often consists of many, even hundreds of, components that can be separately patent-protected. For example, a typical smartphone contains hundreds of patented hardware components and designs, some of which are made by the phone manufacturer (e.g., Samsung, Apple), while many others are made by other companies.[1] Without patenting, these inventions may be easily imitated, although some components such as semiconductors may require very sophisticated expertise and know-how to manufacture. A smartphone also contains very complex software elements, including an operating system and embedded software. Complexity of the technological design can in itself make it difficult to copy. For example, copying elements of the Windows operating system with its 50 million lines of code[2] is very difficult, because the software system contains many interdependencies among the elements, so copying and tweaking some elements is not likely to lead to a functioning product. Some software innovations can also be patented, although software-based innovations such as e-commerce business methods can be rather easy to invent around. For example, Barnes & Noble was able to circumvent Amazon's "one-click ordering" patent by adding a second click of the computer mouse to essentially the

---

[1] Engstrom, E. (2017). So how many patents are in a smartphone? Engine, January 19, 2017. Retrieved from www.engine.is/news/category/so-how-many-patents-are-in-a-smartphone in August 2022.

[2] Metz, C. (2015). Google is 2 billion lines of code and it's all in one place. Wired, September 16, 2015. Retrieved from www.wired.com/2015/09/google-2-billion-lines-codeand-one-place/ in August 2022.

same process. It is also noteworthy that the European Patent Office rejected this patent application because it was assessed to be obvious.[3] Such disputes and challenges are commonplace in the area of software patenting.

Organizational strategies can also be used to prevent or reduce imitation. Secrecy is powerful as long as it lasts. Internal innovations that enhance the efficiency or quality of operations should almost always be kept secret. Secrecy can last for decades and does not require any disclosure. However, it can end quickly after products or services are launched in the market if they can be reverse engineered.

Firms can also attempt to enter the market more quickly than competitors or attempt to lock in customers and partners via contractual, network-related, or reputational switching costs. Speed-related advantages tend to be effective in very rapidly moving markets where new innovations are constantly coming out and where imitators may rather quickly catch up with the original innovator. Then the innovating firm doesn't need to bother with other strategies intended to prevent copying. In contrast, if there are few innovation opportunities and imitators can easily copy the innovation, the innovating firm will quickly lose its distinction.

Table 16.1 summarizes the benefits and challenges of the strategies to enhance differentiation.

Differentiation and negotiation for complements are the key challenges of digital innovation strategy. Ideally, an innovator can easily maintain differentiation and has abundant access to all the necessary complements. With a unique high-tech product, it may be sufficient to just patent and sell the product! Unfortunately this is a rare case. More often an innovator has to work hard to keep imitators at bay and negotiate with powerful providers of complements. There may be a few critical complementary products or services that are necessary in order to launch the innovation. An innovator may thus need to cooperate and negotiate with multiple ecosystem partners.

Figure 16.1 illustrates the archetypal strategic positions of digital innovations with respect to providers of complementary products and services. When imitability of the innovation is high and there are no significant complements, it is difficult to make a profit (quadrant I). An example of this type of a market is digital information services such as a news aggregator or weather updates. Information can be copied easily and if the words are slightly changed then they are not covered by copyright. Digital news aggregators such as HuffPost could publish at least partly machine-created and search-engine optimized news summaries based on information from original news outlets and timed for optimal trending online (Voigt et al. 2016[4]). However, it appears that by 2014 the SEO

---

[3] Kirk, J. (2011). Europe rejects one-click-to-buy Amazon patent application. PCWorld, July 7, 2011. Retrieved from www.pcworld.com/article/235190/article.html retrieved in August 2022.

[4] Voigt, K.I., Buliga, O., and Michl, K. (2017). Journalism 2.0: the case of the Huffington Post. Business Model Pioneers pp. 95–111. Springer, Cham. Retrieved from https://link.springer.com/chapter/10.1007/978-3-319-38845-8_9 in August 2022.

Table 16.1 Strategies to enhance differentiation of digital innovations

Strategy	Benefits	Challenges
Patent	A strong form of protection for innovative ideas	Costly to acquire and enforce; not helpful with services or content; requires disclosure of the invention
Copyright	Long-lasting protection against exact copying of original expression	Does not cover technological ideas or similar but not exactly the same expression
Trademark	Helps to enhance brand identity and reputation	Does not protect innovations themselves
Trade secrecy	A strong form of protection for process innovations	Difficult to maintain, especially for product innovations; can't prevent independent innovation
Communication standards	Potentially long lasting for hardware, especially if combined with patents	Costly to achieve and maintain
Talent, expertise, know-how	Very difficult to directly imitate	Difficult to control employee mobility
Complexity of technology, design	Works well for some areas of software, process innovations	Can be costly to maintain
First/early mover advantages	Powerful if first-to-market or first-to-scale enables locking in users or resources	Typically costly and highly uncertain
Switching costs	Powerful entry barrier	May reduce customer's willingness to buy in the first place

Note: Differentiation can be reinforced with strategies that extend the time during which the innovator can exclude others from using the innovation, and with strategies that increase the cost of imitation.

news market had changed because Google changed how its search terms worked (and also started its own news services), and the news market started to return to subscription-based original reporting.[5] In other words, digital news still worked within the highly imitable top half of the matrix in Figure 16.1, but demand shifted right toward valuing the complements of reputation and credibility that established high-quality news outlets such as *The New York Times* or *The Wall Street Journal* were able to exploit.

If a highly imitable innovation must be combined with rare and valuable complements, as in quadrant II of the matrix, then the owner of the complements tends to profit. The infamous online grocery start-up Webvan is in this category. Webvan founders, including Louis Borders who was also the founder of the Borders

---

[5] Waterson, J. (2019). As HuffPost and BuzzFeed shed staff, has the digital content bubble burst? *The Guardian*, 24 January 2019. Retrieved from www.theguardian.com/media/2019/jan/24/as-huffpost-and-buzzfeed-shed-staff-has-the-digital-content-bubble-burst in August 2022.

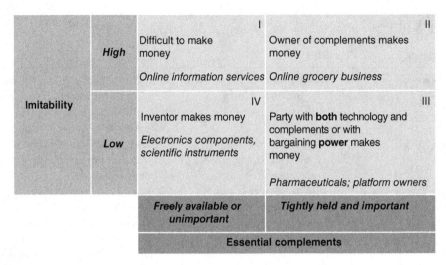

Figure 16.1 Innovation strategy framework
Note: The key aspects of innovation strategy concern the threat of imitation and the access to critical complements and inputs. The innovator should attempt to reduce its own imitation and improve access to complements, and enhance rivals' imitation and raise their cost of access to complements.
Adapted from Afuah, A. and Tucci, C. (2001). *Internet Business Models and Strategies: Text and Cases*. New York: McGraw-Hill, and Teece, D.J. (1986). Profiting from technological innovation: Implications for integration, collaboration, licensing, and policy. *Research Policy* 15(6): 285–305.

bookstore, realized that the fulfillment centers and distribution systems were a critical complement that would erect significant entry barriers into the online grocery market. Webvan therefore set out to commercialize the innovation (online supermarket) by building the complementary distribution assets in-house. Unfortunately, the distribution and fulfillment systems turned out to be very expensive, and investors lost faith in Webvan during the first internet crash because consumers were slow to switch to online grocery shopping.

Peapod was another pioneer of the online grocery market. It decided not to build the fulfillment and distribution system itself. It formed an alliance first with Jewel-Osco and then with Royal Ahold that owned the grocery chains Tops and Stop & Shop. Being able to access the supply chain complementary assets through this alliance, Peapod was able to focus on developing the online interface and delivery.[6] Peapod went public in 1996 but struggled to reach profitability until it was fully acquired by Royal Ahold in 2001.[7] Thus, even though the cooperative strategy of entering the industry by allying with complementary asset providers helped Peapod survive, it was difficult to negotiate lucrative deals when those asset holders had significant market power.

[6] Sachdev, A. (2000). Peapod to sever connection with Jewel. *Chicago Tribune*, 28 December 2000. Retrieved from www.chicagotribune.com/news/ct-xpm-2000-12-28-0012280092-story.html in August 2022.
[7] PYMNTS (2017). Peapod and Alexa deliver greater grocery ordering convenience. Pymnts.com 13 July, 2017. Retrieved from www.pymnts.com/news/retail/2017/peapod-and-alexa-deliver-greater-grocery-ordering-convenience/ in August 2022.

One of the early challenges in the online grocery market was to convince consumers to change their shopping habits and trust a service provider to pick their produce. Consequently, demand grew slowly in the first decade. In the United Kingdom, Ocado essentially followed Webvan's strategy but had a slightly different timing. The company was founded in 2000 and built its first major customer fulfillment center in 2002.[8] During the first decade of the 2000s, the share of households that were online and connected to broadband grew rapidly, and by 2010 Ocado delivered 100,000 orders each week and was listed on the London Stock Exchange. As of 2021, Ocado was still operating, albeit with thin profit margins. It also provided technological consulting services in grocery fulfillment to firms like Kroger operating in other geographic markets. It is difficult for an innovator to survive if it doesn't have control over the relevant complements. However, investment in those assets can be risky and costly.

Profit margins tend to be higher in quadrants III and IV where imitability is lower. The simplest strategies can be pursued by firms in quadrant IV, where no significant complementarities encumber the innovator's relationships with external parties. Here, it is typical that the innovator first invests in significant R&D and then develops strong patents or other forms of protection. If the innovations are difficult to invent around, as is often the case in electronic components and devices, then there are likely to be few competitors and high profits. An example is Qualcomm, a highly innovative developer of chipsets and wireless technologies for telecommunications. It invested about 25 percent of its sales revenue in R&D and its net profits were typically around 20 percent of sales. In 2018, Apple legally challenged the validity of some of its key patents and royalty demands. Qualcomm's technologies were generally very difficult to imitate or invent around, but when another very powerful company challenged its differentiation strategy, it ran into major difficulties. However, after extensive negotiations, the two companies announced a new six-year licensing agreement that included both intellectual property licensing and chipset supply agreement in 2019.[9] Overall, it is certainly not easy to innovate technologies as unique and valuable as those of Qualcomm, whereas its differentiation strategy was relatively more straightforward. Qualcomm did not just rely on its patents, it also worked to embed the patented technologies in standards and to increase switching costs of its customers through contractual agreements.[10]

---

[8] Ocado (2022). Company website. Retrieved from www.ocadogroup.com/about-us/our-history in August 2022.

[9] Apple (2019). Qualcomm and Apple agree to drop all litigation. Press release, 16 April, 2019. Retrieved from www.apple.com/newsroom/2019/04/qualcomm-and-apple-agree-to-drop-all-litigation/ in August 2022.

[10] Gervase, R.G., Miller, J.M., Renaud, M.T., and Song, T.T. (2020). Ninth Circuit reverses FTC win in FTC v. Qualcomm finding no antitrust violations from Qualcomm's licensing of its standard-essential patents. Mintz Insights, 13 August, 2020. Retrieved from www.mintz.com/insights-center/viewpoints/2231/2020-08-13-ninth-circuit-reverses-ftc-win-ftc-v-qualcomm-finding-no retrieved in August 2022.

Profits can also be high in quadrant III where imitation is difficult but commercialization requires complements. Here, the innovator must negotiate with external parties for access or develop the complements internally. If they choose to build the assets internally, like the game developer Nintendo that also offers a gaming system, or Epic Games that offers both games and a game store, they will reap the returns on both investments. However, the up-front costs are high and there are significant risks that the complementary platform fails to attract enough users. In contrast, mobile game developers such as SuperCell are dependent on app markets and mobile operating systems controlled by other parties (Apple and Google). As demonstrated by the large platform fees (typically 30 percent of revenues), it is very costly to depend on a complement provider who has a lot of market power. On the other hand, if the complementor generates a steady stream of innovation like Intel has done over the decades with its microchips for personal computers, then being associated with that partner can still be worthwhile, as Intel's technological improvements in microprocessors have powered innovation in all areas of computing.

In summary, when complementary products or services are essential for the commercialization of a digital innovation, the innovator has to either invest and develop the complements internally or negotiate for access with an external provider. The innovator should consider the financial and technological risks of the investment, the expected development time and the time to market, and its own bargaining power in relation to the potential external providers or the complement, when deciding whether to invest in or outsource the complementary products.

When no critical complements are necessary, the innovator should seek to enhance and maintain its differentiation by any practical means. This might take the form of establishing intellectual property rights or maintaining secrecy, or it might require constant innovation to stay ahead of rivals. In the latter case, the sustainable differentiating factor is not the innovative service itself, but the creative capability to consistently generate novelty. While the service or product may be easy to copy, the capability to repeatedly come up with valuable improvements can be very difficult to copy.

16.2   Architectural Strategies

Architectural strategies include actions that influence the broader constellation of the ecosystem of suppliers of inputs, users of services, and horizontal complementors and competitors. As we saw in Chapters 10 and 11, standardization and platform strategies can define who has access to the technological innovation and on what terms. For example, platform strategies that provide boundary resources for other innovators to connect and complement the core innovation can create a more vibrant and more valuable ecosystem of services. Making available Application Programming Interfaces (APIs), developer toolkits, and clear and benevolent terms and conditions for developers can speed up the innovation process on the platform. While the core innovator may have limited tools to control the direction of innovation in the ecosystem, they can still provide oversight of quality and security features of the connected innovations and cut off any complementor who is not enhancing the value proposition of the whole ecosystem.

When seeking to grow the platform and the ecosystem, more liberal policies regarding open standards can be desirable. For example, when telecommunication technology vendors started to create the 5G wireless system, they agreed to make the system open and standardized to make sure there will be global innovation and subsequently global adoption, creating a large ecosystem – and large markets for each innovation. The companies involved had seen how overly restrictive platform strategies can kill telecommunication systems, despite clear technical advantages, as happened in the case of the 3G system CDMA2000 developed by Qualcomm.

Beyond boundary resources (such as standards, APIs, and toolkits) for complementary innovators to grow off of the ecosystem, the innovator can incentivize innovation through strategic investments in complementary technologies. Many larger companies have corporate venture capital units that invest in technology start-up companies based on their strategic vision of how the ecosystem should evolve. For example, the early investors of the battery start-up company A123 Systems included Qualcomm and Motorola. These companies cooperated to facilitate the entry of a new innovation in the area of lithium ion batteries which were a key component for mobile devices. The consortium supporting this venture also included Chrysler, Ford, and General Motors that were major auto manufacturers. Battery technologies were also critical for electric vehicles. The consortium thus made it easier for each of these companies to support battery innovation that was a complement to each of their core products. They also structured the consortium to prevent any one of the companies from blocking others from using the resulting innovation, thus making sure this adjacent market for complementary products remained open and competitive.

In digital industries where technologies continue to evolve rapidly, the ecosystem structure, or architecture, is rarely fixed for an extended time. One approach to developing an effective ecosystem strategy is to influence the architecture of differentiation and complements within the ecosystem. Specifically, a company should try to enhance the differentiation of its own innovations by reducing their imitability and by reducing the differentiation of others' innovations. It should also try to orchestrate the ownership and availability of complements such that those that are external are abundantly offered in competitive markets while those that are internal are unique and in high demand.

The overall architecture of an ecosystem can be visualized in diagrams such as Figure 16.2. While we mapped ecosystems of core innovations in earlier chapters, we abstracted away from parties with whom the innovator is not directly connected. Here, we attempt to depict all parties, directly or indirectly connected, who can influence the profits of the innovating firm. In this simple example, upstream suppliers A1, A2 and A3 supply their components and materials to

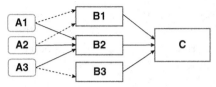

Figure 16.2 Supply ecosystem with competitive supply of inputs and monopsony of the end user
Note: When there are multiple similar suppliers of any input, the upstream markets are competitive and none of the suppliers hold significant bargaining power. When there are very few users, they hold monopsony power and can bargain hard for low input prices.

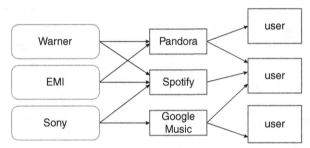

Figure 16.3 Digital music ecosystem
Note: The digital music ecosystem has many providers and users in all market layers.

producers B1, B2, and B3. All producers B can sell to the final customer C. In this case, all suppliers A sell comparable and rival products to the Bs, and similarly, all Bs compete in the market to sell to C. A and B are thus competitive markets, whereas C is the sole customer and in a monopsony position. It is likely that C is quite profitable whereas As and Bs are less so. The strategic goal is to build a market position that entails few rivals and many suppliers, buyers, and complementors. This ensures that the innovator is in a strong bargaining position with respect to its ecosystem partners.

The digital music ecosystem architecture illustrated in Figure 16.3 is quite competitive in all layers. Music rights holders (labels) license their content to streaming services which then provide content access to users.

However, for a long time, the music industry attempted to kill streaming services such as Pandora and Spotify because they were worried about their unfamiliar mode of operation – music labels were used to selling packaged content rather than licensing bits. Hence, major labels attempted to create the ecosystem architecture described in Figure 16.4, instead. While this architecture preserved the price-setting control of the labels and the business logic of selling content to consumers, they appeared to be oblivious to the fact that an Apple iTunes monopoly would not be a lucrative arrangement in the long term.

While certain innovations are inherently easier to imitate than others, there are opportunities for firms to improve their relative positions in the ecosystem in this respect. For example, lobbying for legislative changes has been quite fruitful for music rights holders both in the US and in the UK. The various copyright extensions have enhanced the value of sound recordings over the past decades, making it more

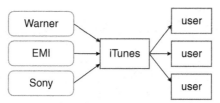

Figure 16.4 Alternative digital music ecosystem with Apple's iTunes controlling distribution
Note: A monopoly of distribution is disadvantageous to both upstream suppliers and downstream users.

difficult for imitators to enter. On the other hand, it may sometimes be easier to make ecosystem partners less differentiated through "property pre-empting" strategies (Pisano and Teece, 2007). Major companies can invite competition into their suppliers' or complementors' markets by placing inventions or software in the public domain in that market. For example, IBM and Intel have been strong supporters of Open-Source Software development by contributing development efforts and software patents to OSS projects in complementary markets. This brings in competition and undermines powerful software suppliers such as Microsoft. They can also incubate new entrants through corporate venture capital investments to start-ups that would potentially challenge their ecosystem partners in the future.

Alternatively, firms can influence the architecture of complementary assets in the digital ecosystem. Decisions related to the openness of interfaces, including APIs and compatibility standards influence access to complementary assets. Open interface and open standard strategies facilitate entry and create markets and competition. Thus, an innovator might invest in the creation of open systems particularly in adjacent markets such as supplier markets and complementor markets. For instance, if a mobile device company is very good at product design and manufacturing, like Nokia in 1995, but doesn't have very original technological inputs into wireless networks, then it is likely to benefit from open standards in the network technology market. This made the market for Nokia's complements more open and competitive. In contrast, Qualcomm at the time controlled some of those network technologies so it tried to build proprietary networks so as to continue to dominate that market and remain a unique provider of complements to device makers and telecom operators. However, Qualcomm wasn't powerful enough to convince the whole global ecosystem of technology vendors and network operators to join its networks, so it had to open up those complements and ultimately became a very successful component provider (see Table 16.2).

In software-based markets, most innovations take the form of applications for specific forms of entertainment (e.g., a newspaper app) or productivity-enhancing activities (e.g., a navigation system). However, most applications require an operating system or a platform that connects the application to a broader digital system in which information is exchanged. The platform or operating system thus often complements software innovations. If the platform is relatively unique, it can charge high fees for access. The strategies regarding openness and

Table 16.2 Ecosystem strategies		
Architectural strategy	How to implement	Example
Enhance own differentiation	Use "blocking strategies" such as intellectual property rights, standards. Lobby for stronger protection.	Patents Copyright extensions
Reduce partners' differentiation	"Unblock" partner's technologies by making resources available.	Contribute to Open-Source Software Publish open data
Reduce competition in internal complements	Build a proprietary platform or a processing facility.	Use APIs (compatibility) to open up interfaces for others
Enhance competition in external complements	Foster competition in partners' markets.	Invest in start-ups to create competition in complements

Note: Ecosystem strategies concern differentiation of own innovations vs. rivals innovations and competition in own vs. adjacent (complementary) markets.

compatibility of the platform determine the interactions of the ecosystem. For example, considering mobile gaming is now a multibillion-dollar industry, and all mobile games pay 30 percent access fees to mobile platform owners Apple and Google, it would make a lot of sense for an innovator to start a web-based gaming platform to compete with the incumbent app stores and offer cheaper market access for mobile game innovators.

KEY IDEAS

- Innovation strategy focuses on the imitability of the innovation and the control of complements to the innovation.
- Imitability of an innovation depends on strategies such as intellectual property rights, secrecy, innovation capability development, and contractual arrangements.
- Access to critical complements can determine the prospects for profitability for an innovation.
- A digital ecosystem arises from positive interactions among the participants. A digital innovator can foment these interactions with architectural strategies that improve and accelerate the adoption process.
- The purpose of architectural strategies is to influence the ecosystem resources and thereby increase the imitability of rival products and enhance the availability of external complements.
- Architectural strategies may involve investments or resources that are made available to or withheld from certain ecosystem participants. These may include compatibility standards, APIs, software development toolkits (SDKs), or financial investments in complementary technologies.

DEFINITIONS

Architectural strategies seek to influence the structure of the ecosystem in terms of the imitability of available products and the availability of complements for them.

Complements are the critical assets, products, or services that are necessary for successful commercialization of an innovation. Hardware is often complementary with software, and services are complementary with distribution channels.

Imitability is the ease with which an innovation can be imitated by rivals. Innovators will almost always try to reduce imitability of their products.

Strategic investments attempt to develop new technologies or other types of assets that facilitate architectural strategies. Strategic investments have implications for the long-term profitability of ecosystem participants.

DISCUSSION QUESTIONS

1. Is a computer game highly imitable or difficult to imitate? Discuss which design choices of a game make it more or less imitable.
2. How can a game developer reduce the imitability of a new game?
3. Describe the ecosystem in which a game can be commercialized. What are the critical complements, and should the game developer create the complements internally or seek to gain access to the complements externally?
4. What architectural strategies could the game innovator pursue to enhance its prospects for profitability?

FURTHER READING

Adner, R. and Kapoor, R. (2010). Value creation in innovation ecosystems: how the structure of technological interdependence affects firm performance in new technology generations. *Strategic Management Journal* 31(3): 306–333.

Autio, E. (2021). Orchestrating ecosystems: a multilayered framework. *Innovation: Organization and Management* 24(1): 96–109.

Jacobides, M.G., Cennamo, C., and Gawer, A. (2018). Towards a theory of ecosystems. *Strategic Management Journal* 39(8): 2255–2276.

Pisano, G. and Teece D.J. (2007). How to Capture Value From Innovation: Shaping Intellectual Property And Industry Architecture. *California Management Review* 50(1): 278–296.

17 Intellectual Property Rights and Digital Technologies

Profitability of digital innovations depends on the ability of the innovator to prevent imitation and control a bottleneck in the ecosystem. As we have seen in previous chapters, the main drivers of value in the markets for information and communication include the perceived inherent value of the information product or service itself (V_i) and the size and structure of the network (N). This chapter will focus on how to protect and enhance the value of information, V_i.

Information and knowledge are peculiar economic goods because they cannot be owned. Intellectual property rights such as patents, copyrights and trademarks provide specific rights to exclude others rather than actual ownership rights. Patents and copyrights are also limited in duration, and, after their expiration, the intellectual property in question enters the public domain. Information can also be kept secret and protected under trade secrecy laws. Contracts can be used to reinforce the legal definition and implications of secrecy. Secrets can last much longer than intellectual property rights. For example, the original recipe for Coca Cola has remained a commercially valuable secret for over 100 years.[1]

Intellectual property rights can protect different aspects of knowledge and information. Patents can cover a useful idea, whereas a copyright can protect original expression but not abstract ideas. Trademarks and designs, in contrast, protect a distinctive identity such as the physical shape and configuration of a product or a non-physical badge of identity such as a logo, sound, or shape. The main goal of trademarks and designs is for consumers to be able to distinguish one product from another. The main goal of patents and copyrights is to reward valuable creativity in society by giving creators a period of time during which they have a right to exclude others from using exact copies of the creations. Indeed, this was formalized in the original United States Constitution from 1789 (Article 1, Section 8): "The Congress shall have power to promote the progress of science and useful arts, by securing for limited times to authors and inventors the exclusive right to their respective writings and discoveries."

---

[1] Coca-Cola (2022). Coca-Cola's formula is at the world of Coca-Cola. Company website. Retrieved from www.coca-colacompany.com/about-us/history/coca-cola-formula-is-at-the-world-of-coca-cola in August 2022.

Pourciaux, A. (2018). The mystery of Coca-Cola's secret formula. The Vintage News, August 20, 2018. Retrieved from www.thevintagenews.com/2018/08/10/coca-cola-formula/ in August 2022.

While patents and copyrights have always been imperfect tools to exclude and reward creators, in the age of digital technologies, the boundaries of intellectual property have been fraught with challenges. Patents are very imprecise (even "probabilistic"[2]) mechanisms of protection for digital technologies, particularly software-based technologies. Communication technologies, on the other hand, have largely demolished the ability of copyright holders to control and enforce their rights. We will first explore the nature and evolution of copyright and then focus on software patents.

17.1 Copyright in the Digital Age

To obtain copyright, the creation needs to be **original** work of authorship fixed in a tangible medium of **expression**. It is important to note that copyright is strictly about the expression, not the underlying ideas. The bar for the originality of the work is low. The expression needs only to be different, but it doesn't need to fulfill any criteria related to its artistic or aesthetic value or usefulness. In the digital world, tangibility of the medium is fulfilled if the work is stored in a computer hard drive. Thus, all original digital content in the form of text, numbers, sounds, images, or symbols stored on a computer is automatically protected by copyright. There is no need to register the creations with the Copyright Office.

Copyright gives the **exclusive right** to make copies of an original creation. This applies to selling, licensing, and distributing the work, as well as publicly displaying or performing it, or adapting and modifying it, but for a "limited" time. Initially in the first (1790) Copyright Act of the United States the term was 14 years, with an additional 14 years if the author was alive at the end of the first term. This act was an almost perfect copy of the British Statute of Anne from 1710. Gradually, the copyright term length kept growing over the years, first to 28 + 14 years (1831), then 28 + 28 years (1909), and, in 1976, to the life of the author + 50 years, or 75 years for corporate creations.

When digital technologies began to shift the communication landscape in the 1990s, US lawmakers started developing a new framework which was launched as the Digital Millennium Copyright Act, or DMCA, in 1998. It coincided with the Sonny Bono Copyright Extension Act that further extended the copyright term to life of the author + 70 years, or 95 years for corporate creations. This extension came in the nick of time to protect Mickey Mouse, the extremely valuable intellectual property of Disney, from lapsing into the public domain.[3] Mickey's

---

[2] Lemley, M. and Shapiro, C. (2005). Probabilistic patents. *Journal of Economic Perspectives* 19(2): 75–98. Retrieved from www.aeaweb.org/articles?id=10.1257/0895330054048650 in August 2022.

[3] Lee, T.B. (2018). Why Mickey Mouse's 1998 copyright extension probably won't happen again. ArsTechnica, January 8, 2018. Retrieved from https://arstechnica.com/tech-policy/2018/01/hollywood-says-its-not-planning-another-copyright-extension-push/ in August 2022.

character was first published in 1928 as "Steamboat Willie" and it appears the character will enter the public domain by 2024 – barring any lobbying campaign by the content industries.[4]

Copying or publishing a copyright-protected work without authorization is direct **infringement** on the copyright. For example, if I perform my favorite Adele song publicly, I will be infringing on Adele's rights to exclude others from performing her songs in the US and she could sue me. Indeed, a mother who posted a video of her baby dancing to a song by the artist at the time known as Prince on YouTube was sued by the rights holder Universal Music for direct infringement in 2007.[5] The case was so outrageous that the Electronic Frontier Foundation pursued it on the mother's behalf for 10 years until the US Supreme Court refused to hear it. After that the parties decided to settle in 2018.[6]

Indirect infringement can be *contributory*, such as in the case of a rock band manager who would know my song list and substantially participate in planning and arranging my public performance of Adele's song. *Vicarious* infringement, in contrast, might concern the performance space owner such as a bar that might financially benefit (or suffer) from my public performance of the copyrighted song. The space owner would have controlled the process of making infringing material available and realized direct financial benefit (if any).

The definition of vicarious infringement puts electronics device makers and internet service providers (ISPs) in a grey area. The DMCA of 1998 in the United States attempted to clear ISPs of the liability of their users sharing infringing material that they enabled by providing internet service to a household and by financially profiting from that. However, with rampant digital piracy in some content industries, the US Congress subsequently attempted to strengthen the legal role of ISPs in monitoring pirated content in their networks. For example, SOPA (Stop Online Piracy Act) and PIPA (Preventing Real Online Threats to Economic Creativity and Theft of Intellectual Property Act) of 2011 failed to revise the DMCA and provide protection against foreign sources of piracy. These legislative attempts would have required that website owners, search engines, ISPs and anyone with "information location tools" pointing to or enabling infringing online content would need to remove the links or shut down the infringing website upon receiving a take-down notice. Fortunately, these proposed laws did not succeed after massive protests by activists, academics, and major digital service

---

[4] Lee, T.B. (2019). Mickey Mouse will be public domain soon – here's what that means. ArsTechnica, January 1, 2019. Retrieved from https://arstechnica.com/tech-policy/2019/01/a-whole-years-worth-of-works-just-fell-into-the-public-domain/ in August 2022.

[5] McCarthy, K. (2018). Infamous 'Dancing Baby' copyright battle settled just before YouTube tot becomes a teen. The Register, June 27, 2018. Retrieved from www.theregister.co.uk/2018/06/27/dancing_baby_settlement/ retrieved in August 2022.

[6] Even earlier in 1993, the artist himself had considered the music label as excessively greedy and decided to give up his name and become a symbol. Cf. Whatley, J. (2020). Why Prince changed his name to a symbol. Far Out, November 25, 2020. Retrieved from https://faroutmagazine.co.uk/why-prince-changed-his-name-to-a-symbol/ in August 2022.

companies (e.g., the English-language Wikipedia and other major websites coordinated a blackout on January 18, 2012). These Acts would potentially have made it possible to shut down legitimate content simply with a single claim of infringement without any legal due process, prompting severe concerns about the freedom of speech online. Nevertheless, the role of such enabling technologies and services ("information location tools") remained precarious and at risk of legislative action in the future.

Digital technologies can not only rapidly disseminate lots of copyrighted material but also facilitate protecting or exposing such material. Peer-to-peer (P2P) file sharing technologies such as Napster and Gnutella emerged in the 1990s and facilitated large-scale distribution of digital content directly between "peers," that is, without a central storage location. Various Digital Rights Management (DRM) systems have attempted to technologically prevent dissemination of copyrighted content by adding code to the file that prevents its copying or opening. The DMCA in 1998 criminalized technologies intended to circumvent DRM systems, or even to communicate about or use such systems. While DRMs have probably provided some degree of protection by slowing down copying, they set up a never-ending race to upgrade protection technologies as they get hacked and the ways to circumvent DRMs disseminate online. For example, Content Scramble System (CSS) was introduced by the DVD Forum to protect DVD content in 1996, and in 1999 the deCSS software was made widely available by a Norwegian teenager.[7] Most DRM technologies have met the same fate within years, months, or sometimes just weeks, of their launch.

17.2   Evolution of the US Copyright Regime

Digital innovation and legal conflicts have co-existed from the very beginning. The emergence of electronics technologies in the mid-1970s gave rise to the first era of heated copyright debates. Sony had developed the revolutionary Betamax Video Cassette Recorder (VCR) and an associated file format and was in the process of commercializing the device. Betamax was a major contender in the first "format war" against JVC's VHS format. Both types of devices were capable of recording directly from a TV signal, which was a feature that scared movie and TV content providers out of their minds.[8] First the content industry tried to shut down VCR devices altogether in the *Sony* v. *Universal* case, and when they were (very narrowly!) unsuccessful, they attempted to kill the video rental business model without realizing that this was actually going to be a very beneficial way

---

[7] Techopedia (2011). De-content scrambling systems. Techopedia, August 18, 2011. Retrieved from www.techopedia.com/definition/24879/de-content-scrambling-system-decss in August 2022.

[8] Riley, C. (2015). Sony is finally killing its ancient Betamax format. CNN Business, November 10, 2015. Retrieved from https://money.cnn.com/2015/11/10/technology/sony-betamax/index.html in August 2022.

to version their content and build new audiences. While the numbers of viewers at movie theaters declined, households and particularly families with small children adopted habits of watching rented movies at home.

The Sony copyright case almost spelled the end of Sony as a company and VCR as a technology.[9] The *Sony* v. *Universal* case had been decided for Sony in the District Court but against the company in the Court of Appeals. Sony appealed to the Supreme Court and got its hearing in 1984. The Supreme Court decided in favor of Sony in a split 5–4 decision. The major arguments for Sony's Betamax included that it was *capable of substantial non-infringing uses*, and, therefore, the manufacturer should not be held liable for any copyright infringement of its users. Furthermore, the Court declared that "*time shifting*" programming by recording it to watch later was not a copyright violation. These were the essential features of what became to be called the Sony Standard among legal experts. Consequently, we still have a video recording industry.

The next major copyright watershed event was the rise of peer-to-peer (P2P) file sharing in the late 1990s. Pioneering companies such as Napster and later imitators such as Grokster, Kazaa, and BitTorrent enabled file sharing on a massive scale. Napster was shut down by a US court in 2001. Grokster was designed to avoid the pitfalls of Napster by not having a centralized list of files or any other type of central control. It was only a software program that was held on users' computers together with the files. Grokster, the company, simply made the software available to the users who used it in whatever ways they did. The software program certainly was "capable of non-infringing uses" – many types of files, not only infringing content, could be shared within the network. Nevertheless it got sued in another landmark copyright case that progressed to the US Supreme Court in 2005.[10]

In the *Grokster* case, MGM, the lead plaintiff, argued that 90 percent of file traffic on Grokster was infringing copyrights, and that Grokster knew and encouraged such uses. Grokster, in contrast, was supported by arguments that it was aligned with the Sony Standard and that changing the standard might slow down innovation in the software and content industries. It was also debated whether P2P downloads actually reduced album sales – the data at the time were inconclusive.

This time the Supreme Court was unanimous in their decision against Grokster:

> The tension between the competing values of supporting creativity through copyright protection and promoting technological innovation by limiting infringement liability is the subject of this case. Despite offsetting considerations, the argument for imposing indirect liability here is powerful, given the number of infringing downloads that occur daily using respondents' software. When a widely shared product is used to commit infringement, it may be impossible to enforce rights in the protected work effectively

---

[9]   Khanna, D. (2013). A look back at how the content industry almost killed Blockbuster and Netflix (and the VCR). TechCrunch, December 28, 2013. Retrieved from https://techcrunch.com/2013/12/27/how-the-content-industry-almost-killed-blockbuster-and-netflix/ in August 2022.

[10] EFF (2022). *MGM* v. *Grokster*. Electronic Frontier Foundation. Retrieved from http://w2.eff.org/IP/P2P/MGM_v_Grokster/ in August 2022.

against all direct infringers, so that the only practical alternative is to go against the device's distributor for secondary liability on a theory of contributory or vicarious infringement. One infringes contributorily by intentionally inducing or encouraging direct infringement, and infringes vicariously by profiting from direct infringement while declining to exercise the right to stop or limit it.

Thus, although the software was capable of substantial non-infringing uses, the company had *incited* infringement, which was viewed as contributory infringement. This was the new "*inducement doctrine*" within the US copyright case law. The Supreme Court judges were divided in some other interpretations about the case, but the sheer volume of infringement and the small volume of non-infringing uses convinced them all to decide against Grokster. However, the much-publicized case did not really make much difference in the music market. As articulated by Hilary Rosen, the former CEO of the Recording Industry Association of America:

> While the victory of whoever wins maybe important psychologically, it just won't really matter in the marketplace (...) Consumer is left with few legitimate services that offer some great content and lots more illegal P2P choices that offer ALL the content plus spyware, bad files and unwanted risk. (...) These are not legal decisions or trade association PR responsibilities. They are fundamentally business issues that must be addressed in the marketplace.[11]

In other words, she foresaw that until the music industry innovated legitimate streaming service business models with the right price point, piracy would go on under different names and the industry would continue to decline.

Figure 17.1 illustrates the evolution of different music formats in terms of total industry revenues. It is clear that total music industry revenue has significantly declined since 1999 and a part of the explanation is surely illegal file sharing and, later on, music streaming. However, overall music consumption has continued to grow, and consumers are much better off with access to large libraries of music from streaming services such as Pandora and Spotify. Indeed, there is no evidence that the quality of music declined with the new industry structure.[12] Moreover, the internet enabled the entry of a much more diverse set of creators through independent labels and digital-only production models. In fact, the total quantity of new albums has dramatically increased since 2000. Also, with legitimate subscription services, artists were compensated according to the consumption decisions and the overall willingness to pay by consumers. Overall, this seemed like a welfare-improving outcome from a societal perspective. Consumers got easy and reasonably priced access to a larger catalog of music, and independent musicians could enter the marketplace more easily. The main losers appeared to be major

---

[11] Rosen, H. (2011). The supreme wisdom of not relying on the court. Huffington Post, The Blog May 25, 2011. Retrieved from www.huffingtonpost.com/hilary-rosen/the-supreme-wisdom-of-not_b_3221.html in August 2022.

[12] Waldfogel, Joel (2012). Copyright protection, technological change, and the quality of new products: evidence from recorded music since Napster, *The Journal of Law and Economics* 55 (4): 715–740.

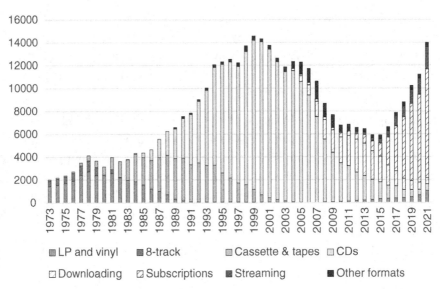

Figure 17.1 Music industry revenues by format
Note: The total revenue of the US recorded music industry dramatically decreased between 1999 and 2010, driven by the shrinking sales of music CDs. Digital music distribution started to grow initially through content downloading and subsequently through the subscription streaming services from 2012. Data source: Recording Industry Association of America (2021). Music Industry Revenues by Format. Retrieved from www.riaa.com/u-s-sales-database/ in October, 2021.

labels whose "star-making machine" was broken, with regular spats between the labels and the streaming platforms about licensing rates and content access, such as the dispute between Eminem's publisher and Spotify in 2019.[13] However, there were thorny unresolved issues in the arrangement where the major labels were essentially allowed to collude in the negotiation of licensing rates against music platforms, but on the other side, consumers and music creators were threatened by the potential monopolization of distribution into just one or two major platforms. One step forward, the 2018 Music Modernization Act provided a central database to calculate and pay the royalties to copyright holders and clarified the rate-setting process to increase transparency of the system, but the industry structure and its institutional foundation continued to evolve.

17.3   Software Patents

Software that underlies most digital innovations has undergone fundamental changes in its intellectual property right regime. Until the 1980s, copyrights or trade secrets were the primary protection of software, although there were a few patents

---

[13] Gardner, E. (2019). Eminem publisher sues Spotify claiming massive copyright breach, "unconstitutional" law. *The Hollywood Reporter*, August 21, 2019. Retrieved from www .hollywoodreporter.com/thr-esq/eminem-publisher-sues-spotify-claiming-massive-copyright-breach-unconstitutional-law-1233362 in August 2022.

for software embedded in physical devices. The creation of the more patent-friendly Court of Appeals of the Federal Circuit in 1982, and its *State Street* decision in 1998 that established that an algorithm that produces a "useful, concrete and tangible result such as a price" was patent-eligible, opened the door for software patenting. As a result, new algorithms could be patented without any novelty in terms of the associated physical device that runs them.

Patents can protect new technical ideas that are original, contain an "inventive step" that is not obvious to a person skilled in the field of technology, and are capable of industrial application. In the United States, patents are potentially valid up to 20 years, but the patent holder must continue to pay maintenance fees to the Patent and Trademark Office (PTO) after 3.5 years, 7.5 years, and again after 11.5 years to maintain their validity. Many patents are not maintained and fall into the public domain for not containing much industrial value after all. Maintenance fees increase over the life of the patent such that the patents that "survive" until 20 years are likely to be much more valuable than an average granted patent.

When an inventor submits a patent application to the PTO, a patent examiner familiar with that field of technology will carry out a search for **prior art**. Prior art are earlier inventions and scientific discoveries that are related to and provide a foundation for the new invention. The list of prior art in the patent application limits the scope of the potential patent and helps the examiner assess whether the new invention truly contains an inventive step.

A newer feature of the US patent system is the Patent Trial and Appeal Board (PTAB). Since the major revision of patent legislation in the America Invents Act (AIA) of 2012, other patent holders or third parties could challenge the validity of a new patent through Post Grant Review or Inter Partes Review. These new procedures were instituted to reduce the number of patents with dubious claims of novelty or non-obviousness. They gave the competitors of an inventor an opportunity and an incentive to show that the invention is pre-existing, obvious, or too incremental beyond the state-of-the-art in the technology field. It appeared that the new board and a few other legislative changes of the AIA had made it substantially easier to invalidate claims of new patents and reduce the volume of patent litigation (see Figure 17.2).

The patent system was set up to motivate invention activity by giving the inventor exclusive rights to the invention for a limited time – up to 20 years. However, when patenting expanded into software-based technologies, including business methods, patents were often granted to inventions that were well-known business methods simply codified in software. When such patenting was successful, firms could raise the costs of rivals by forcing them to work around the patented business activity. One highly controversial patent was Amazon's one-click patent, a "Method and System for Placing a Purchase Order via a Communication Network" (US patent 5,960,411). The inventors, Peri Hartman, Jeffrey P. Bezos, Shel Kaphan, and Joel Spiegel of Seattle, Washington, filed the patent application in 1997 and the USPTO granted the patent two years later. The patent was assigned to Amazon .com Inc. Amazon.com was an online bookstore founded in 1994 by one of the

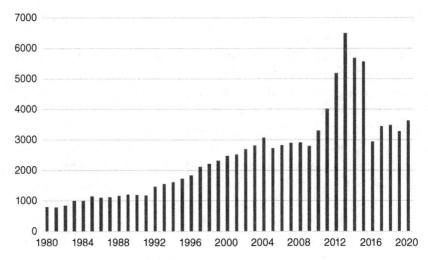

Figure 17.2 Patent litigation 1980–2020
Note: The number of patent lawsuits grew rapidly between 2009 and 2013. However, after the AIA of 2012, the number of filed lawsuits declined by nearly 40 percent between 2013 and 2017.
Source: Quinn, G. (2021). Patent litigation in the U.S., 1980 to 2020. IP Watchdog, November 4, 2021. Retrieved from https://ipwatchdog.com/2021/11/04/patent-litigation-in-the-united-states-1980-to-2020/ id=139510/# in October 2022.

inventors. This patent was the prime example for arguments that "a broad patent on a trivially obvious software concept can have a profoundly anti-competitive impact on a wide segment of the industry."[14]

The one-click patent cited 12 US patents and 7 foreign (European or World Intellectual Property Office) patents as prior art, including two earlier patents by Jeff Bezos filed in 1995. Amazon.com was thus filing software and business method patents early in its corporate history, and Bezos personally was a named inventor on at least 30 patents filed between 1995 and 2005. The one-click invention described a process to carry out a transaction in one single click (see Figure 17.3).

The process looked fairly simple: retrieve the customer's ID, set single-action ordering, return to confirming web page, and "Done." Nevertheless, the patent was deemed novel, non-obvious, and capable of industrial application by USPTO patent examiners. Amazon also used the patent to commercial advantage by suing Barnes & Noble in 2000 to prevent the rival from offering a one-click ordering process called Express Lane. A court issued a preliminary injunction, and Barnes & Noble had to add a click to its checkout process. Nevertheless, many industry commentators felt this was an obvious patent and the Electronic Frontier Foundation placed it on its shortlist of problem patents.[15]

---

[14] Paul, R. (2010). Controversial Amazon 1-click patent survives review. ArsTechnica, March 10, 2010. Retrieved from https://arstechnica.com/tech-policy/2010/03/controversial-amazon-1-click-patent-survives-review/# in August 2022.

[15] Bangeman, E. (2004). Electronic Frontier Foundation will contest problematic patents. ArsTechnica, April 20, 2004. Retrieved from https://arstechnica.com/uncategorized/2004/04/3681-2/ in August 2022.

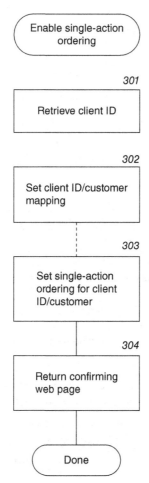

Figure 17.3 Amazon's one-click ordering patent
Note: Amazon's infamous one-click patent consisted of just six simple steps.
U.S. Patent 5960411A: Method and system for placing a purchase order via a communications network. Retrieved from https://patentimages.storage.googleapis.com/37/e6/81/3ebb1f33c41b4a/US5960411.pdf in August, 2022.

In 2006, New Zealander actor and activist Peter Calveley presented a new set of prior art and raised funding to request that USPTO re-examine the patent.[16] The PTO agreed and found that 21 of the patent's 26 novelty claims were not valid. Furthermore, the European Patent Office denied its patent application in Europe, meaning that in Europe, anyone could offer one-click transactions. Nevertheless, Apple licensed the patent for its iTunes store until it expired in 2017. Meanwhile, Jeffrey P. Bezos, that prolific software inventor, wrote in a public letter in 2000: "business method and software patents are fundamentally different from other kinds of patents" and "the lifespan of such patents should

---

[16] Anderson, N. (2006). Amazon's "one-click" patent reconsidered. ArsTechnica, May 19, 2006. Retrieved from https://arstechnica.com/uncategorized/2006/05/6872-2/ in August 2022.

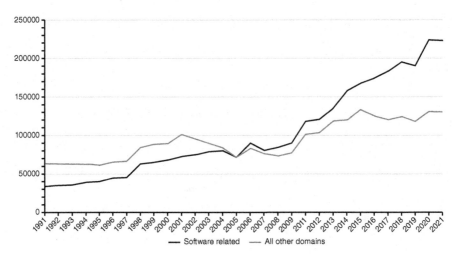

Figure 17.4 The volume of software-related patents versus other patents
Note: The growth of software patents was brisk after 1998 and the number of software patents exceeded other patents in 2006.
Source: Millien, R. (2021): Seven years after Alice, 63.2% of the U.S. patents issued in 2020 were software-related. IP Watchdog. Retrieved from https://ipwatchdog.com/2021/03/17/seven-years-after-alice-63-2-of-the-u-s-patents-issued-in-2020-were-software-related/id=130978/ in October, 2022.

be 3 to 5 years, and there should be a public comment period before the patent is issued to allow for the submission of prior art references."[17] Bezos himself observed that the economy needed fewer, higher-quality, and shorter patents for software and business methods. Meanwhile, the number of software patents kept growing and by 2005 there were as many software patents as all other types of patents (see Figure 17.4).

The America Invents Act addressed the quality issue with the PTAB process to eliminate poor-quality inventions quickly, but there were still many patents with dubious and excessively broad claims in the fast-moving software industry. The Supreme Court of the United States took on some patent cases such as *eBay* v. *MercExchange* (2006), which reduced the availability of injunction and thus lowered the cost of infringement. They also considered the *Bilski* v. *Kappos* case (2010) that limited the broad availability of business method patents as specified in the earlier *State Street* case: "processes involving transformation of abstract financial data are probably patent ineligible." Finally, in *Alice* v. *CLS Bank*, 2014, the Supreme Court decided that if the invention is an abstract idea such as a mathematical formula, it must contain an inventive concept – simply digitizing a conventional concept such as the escrow is not sufficient for patent eligibility.

Poor-quality patents may validate worthless inventions and give outsize legal power to parties who will not use it to further innovation in the economy but to

---

[17] Bezos, J. (2000). An open letter from Jeff Bezos on the subject of patents. *Tech Law Journal*, Mar 9, 2000. Retrieved from www.techlawjournal.com/intelpro/20000309bez.htm in August 2022.

extort money from other parties. One such company was Shipping and Transit, previously known as ArrivalStar. Shipping & Transit held a small portfolio of e-commerce patents primarily invented by its founder, a former professional tennis player who had no engineering experience. The patents were related to common business activities such as sending a shipping confirmation by email or using GPS to find where vehicles are located. Through a series of unfortunate mistakes, the USPTO had granted these patents, and the company took full advantage to collect licensing fees from over 800 small companies. It subsequently turned to public transit systems that used GPS devices to manage the transit.

After the *Alice* decision of the US Supreme Court that determined that just automating a well-known idea using a computer is not patentable, therefore anyone who was threatened with these Shipping & Transit patents could have sought to invalidate them for example through the Inter Partes Review process. However, this process could cost $200,000 in legal fees, and it involved some risk taking – one can never be sure what the court will decide. Before the AIA, going through the lawsuit might have cost over $1 million in legal fees, with even more uncertainty about the decision. Therefore, Shipping & Transit continued to threaten small businesses with lawsuits and asked them to pay anything between $15,000 and $100,000. This would be much less than the legal fees to challenge the patent validity, so the target companies simply paid up and settled. If anyone decided to fight back, the company would dismiss the lawsuit and find other, more vulnerable and ignorant parties to threaten. In this way, the company managed to collect over $15 million over a decade. However, by 2017, victims of this strategy finally started to push back and use courts to invalidate the patents and the infringement claims.[18] Soon after, Shipping & Transit filed for bankruptcy in 2018, with a portfolio of 34 patents valued at $34.

KEY IDEAS

- Digital distribution made it difficult to sell digital content because of the ease of imitation.
- Governments attempted to gain control of rampant online piracy by creating ways to punish copying through regulatory, legislative, and judicial changes.
- Rights holders also attempted to legally prevent copying of their information goods, but sometimes such schemes inflicted great PR damage to the rights holders themselves.
- Software patents, particularly software-based business methods, have been a problematic area of patenting, with intense litigation and questionable inventions.

---

[18] Nazer, D. (2017). Court orders prolific patent troll Shipping & Transit LLC to pay defendant's legal bill. Electronic Frontier Foundation, July 7, 2017. Retrieved from www.eff.org/deeplinks/2017/07/court-orders-prolific-patent-troll-shipping-transit-llc-pay-defendants-legal-bill in August 2022.

Ranieri, V. (2017). Death knell is tolling for Shipping & Transit LLC. Electronic Frontier Foundation, July 11, 2017. Retrieved from www.eff.org/deeplinks/2017/07/death-knell-tolling-shipping-transit-llc in August 2022.

- The America Invents Act (2012) facilitated invalidation of bad patents and reduced litigation, making it difficult to pursue the most egregious forms of patent trolling.
- Wisely used, software patents can strengthen the value of software innovation and lower the risk of being legally targeted by rivals, because a strong patent portfolio can be a desirable asset in cross-licensing negotiations.
- Generally, legal methods of protecting intangible assets are incomplete and evolving, making it best to not build business models that primarily rely on intellectual property rights for strategic control of the market.

DEFINITIONS

Intellectual property rights give **exclusive rights** to use or make copies of the creation for a limited period of time. They do not give permanent ownership rights in the same way property rights to physical assets do.

Infringement of intellectual property rights happens when others make copies, use, or commercially benefit from the creative asset without a license.

Original expression refers to sequences of symbols that are not copyrighted by another party. Even a short amount of text or visual expression may qualify for protection.

Prior art includes all the pre-existing inventions either patented or in the public domain that the current invention builds on. A new invention must cite the prior art that is relevant to defining the novel aspects of the invention

DISCUSSION QUESTIONS

1. How could a game developer apply software patenting and copyright enforcement to reduce the imitability of games?
2. Do the changes of the US copyright regime over time facilitate or complicate these efforts?
3. What aspects of the intellectual property (IP) regime are conducive to innovation and which ones make innovation more challenging?
4. How could a digital innovator strategically address the challenges of the IP regime?

FURTHER READING

Cockburn Iain M. and MacGarvie, Megan J. 2011. Entry and patenting in the software industry. *Management Science* 57(5): 915–933.

Giorcelli, Michela and Moser, Petra. 2020. Copyrights and creativity: evidence from Italian opera in the Napoleonic Age. *Journal of Political Economy* 128(11): 4163–4210.

Waldfogel, Joel. 2017. How digitization has created a golden age of music, movies, books, and television. *Journal of Economic Perspectives*, 31 (3): 195–214.

Webb, Michael, Short, Nick, Bloom, Nicholas, and Lerner, Josh. 2018. *Some Facts of High-Tech Patenting*. National Bureau of Economic Research Working Paper 24793. Retrieved from www.nber.org/system/files/working_papers/w24793/w24793.pdf in October 2021.

CASE 5: SPOTIFY: "LISTENING IS EVERYTHING"

Daniel Ek and Martin Lorentzon founded Spotify in 2006 in Stockholm, Sweden. The platform grew as a response to rampant online piracy afflicting the music industry. After Napster, LimeWire, and other file-sharing services "disrupted" the traditional music model, Spotify entered in Pandora's footsteps by offering a free service funded through advertising. However, Spotify's goal was to funnel users towards an ad-free subscription service. "I realised that you can never legislate away from piracy," Daniel Ek reportedly told *The Telegraph* in 2010. "The only way to solve the problem was to create a service that was better than piracy and at the same time compensates the music industry."[19]

Although Pandora remained the US market leader,[20] globally Spotify's main rival was Apple Music. Apple cornered a market by securing exclusive deals with popular artists such as Drake, Frank Ocean, and Taylor Swift. Whereas Apple's iTunes operated under a "sales" model of music, Apple Music launched with a subscription model for unlimited access to a library of music. Similarly, SoundCloud launched the SoundCloud Go subscription service in 2016. Originally SoundCloud created a platform for new and unsigned musicians and DJs, but later diversified toward major label content.

Music streaming services operated by licensing content from record labels and independent artists and then paying the artists, songwriters, and labels royalties depending on how often the music was streamed. Some superstars objected to this model, however. In 2014, Taylor Swift was very vocal about rejecting the revenue share arrangement between platforms like Spotify and artists.[21] "I'm not willing to contribute my life's work to an experiment that I don't feel fairly compensates the writers, producers, artists, and creators of this music," Swift said.[22] In 2015, Jay Z and Beyoncé acquired a rival music service, the Norwegian platform Tidal, and created a superstar-owned model with Rihanna, Kanye West, Alicia Keys, and others.[23] Eventually, Swift ended the feud with Spotify and put all her music back on the platform in 2017.

[19] BBC (2018). How Spotify came to be worth billions. BBC Newsbeat, March 1, 2018. Retrieved from www.bbc.com/news/newsbeat-43240886 in August 2022.

[20] Sun, L. (2019). A foolish take: the Top 4 music-streaming services in the US. The Motley Fool, Yahoo Movies, April 1, 2019. Retrieved from https://ca.movies.yahoo.com/foolish-top-4-music-streaming-160000141.html in August 2022.

[21] Butterly, A. (2014). Taylor Swift's entire back catalogue removed from Spotify. BBC Newsbeat, November 3, 2014. Retrieved from www.bbc.com/news/newsbeat-29885973 in August 2022.

[22] Willman, C. (2014). Taylor Swift on being pop's instantly platinum wonder ... and why she is paddling against the streams. Yahoo! Entertainment, November 6, 2014. Retrieved from www.yahoo.com/entertainment/blogs/music-news/exclusive--taylor-swift-on-being-pop-s-instantly-platinum-wonder-and-why-she-s-paddling-against-the-streams-085041907.html in August 2022.

[23] See www.ibtimes.co.uk/tidal-launch-livestream-watch-jay-z-relaunching-high-fidelity-music-streaming-service-1494210 retrieved in August 2022.

Case 5.1 Background

Spotify had been growing rapidly since 2011. It took the company five years to reach 10 million users, and just two more years to reach 20 million users. In 2018, Spotify completed a direct listing of ordinary shares on the New York Stock Exchange. With subsequent acquisitions of Anchor FM, Gimlet Media, and Cutler Media, Spotify sought to diversify into the emerging market for podcasts and other non-music audio content. By the end of 2019, Spotify had 271 million Monthly Active Users (MAUs) and 124 million premium subscribers, making it the largest global audio streaming platform, with a presence in 79 countries and territories. Its mission was to "unlock the potential of human creativity by giving a million creative artists the opportunity to live off their art and billions of fans the opportunity to enjoy and be inspired by these creators."[24]

In 2019, the rapid growth continued at about 30 percent annual rate in terms of both total active users, subscribers, and advertising revenue. The global recorded music industry revenues grew at 10 percent rate, primarily driven by streaming revenues. Spotify's payments to artists, music labels, and publishers also grew at 30 percent annual rate, and by end of 2019 the company had paid more than €15 billion in royalties to rights holders since launch.

The streaming industry transformed the way people access and enjoy music. Users switched from a transaction-based experience of buying and holding music to an access-based model which allowed users to stream music on demand. The traditional radio relied on a linear distribution model with little freedom of choice. Spotify was also attempting to expand into podcasts and other forms of alternative and spoken-word content to complement the music offerings. The company believed that offering a wider variety of content would generate more user engagement.

Whereas Pandora excelled in music discovery through its Music Genome Project, Spotify offered a more traditional recommendation engine based on listening patterns. Recommendations accounted for how long users listened to songs, and whether they skipped songs or added them to playlists, to guide users to new types of music and entertainment. The recommendation engine utilized collaborative filtering to recommend items that users with similar preference profiles enjoyed, and natural language processing to identify similarities in written content, including song lyrics and playlist titles. Additionally, in a computerized nod to Pandora's Music Genome Project, automated audio models analyzed the audio pattern of entirely new songs and then Spotify was able to recommend new songs to people who were likely to enjoy them because they had previously enjoyed songs with similar audio patterns. Spotify believed that

---

[24] Annual report, 2019. Retrieved from https://s29.q4cdn.com/175625835/files/doc_financials/2019/AR/2019-AR.pdf in August 2022.

discovery drove delight, and delight drove engagement. The company stated that it "reflects culture but also occasionally creates it by turning listening data into recommendations that remind people of the role music plays in their lives."[25]

Case 5.2 Business Model

Spotify was based on two service and revenue models. The Ad-Supported Service was a viable stand-alone product but it also served as a funnel driving new Premium Subscribers. The Premium Subscribers provided a steadier stream of revenue and were slightly "stickier" in terms of their commitment and engagement with the platform.

Spotify expected continued development of new features and functionality for users and creators, particularly personalization of the user experience, to unlock higher user engagement and enjoyment. The company's usage data indicated that the hours of streamed content increased by 34 percent, faster than the numbers of users. Spotify saw this as an indication that users were spending more time on the platform.

The Premium Service provided subscribers with unlimited online and offline streaming access to a catalog of music and podcasts without commercial breaks. Premium Services were sold directly to end users and through partners such as telecommunications companies that bundled the subscription with their own services or collected payment for the stand-alone subscriptions from end customers. There were a variety of subscription pricing plans ranging from the standard individual plan ($9.99/month), to a family plan ($14.99/month for up to six accounts), and student plan ($4.99/month) to appeal to users with different lifestyles and across various demographics and age groups. The plans also offered varying features, for example, the student plan was bundled with Hulu and Showtime video streaming services and the family plan blocked music with explicit lyrics.

Most new subscribers originated from the conversion of ad-supported users to subscribers. Conversion strategies included product links, campaigns targeting existing users, and marketing across social media platforms. New subscribers also originated from free or discounted trial programs (see Figure C5.1).

Spotify relied on a monthly revenue measure Premium ARPU (Average Revenue Per User) defined as Premium Service revenue recognized in the quarter divided by the average daily Premium Subscribers in the quarter, divided by three months. Premium ARPU had decreased from €5.32 in 2017 to €4.81 in 2018 and €4.72 in 2019. Spotify stated that the reasons behind the decline included switching to the family plan from individual plans and the increase in subscribers on free trials

---

[25] Annual report 2019. Retrieved from https://s29.q4cdn.com/175625835/files/doc_financials/2019/AR/2019-AR.pdf in August 2022.

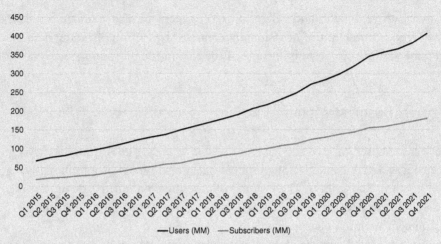

Figure C5.1 Worldwide Spotify users and premium users (subscribers), millions
Note: The numbers of users and subscribers of Spotify have grown steadily and even accelerated after 2018.
Data source: Business of Apps. Retrieved from www.businessofapps.com/data/spotify-statistics/ in
August 2022.

which were included in the Premium Service numbers but didn't yet generate
any revenue. Premium Services were also bundled with third-party services and
products, priced on a per-subscriber rate in a negotiated agreement.

Spotify's ad-supported service provided users with limited on-demand online
access to the song catalog and unlimited access to the catalog of podcasts.
The company monetized these users through the sale of display, audio, and
video advertising delivered through ad impressions across the music and podcast
content. Ad agencies would purchase ads on Spotify's platform on behalf of their
clients specifying the type of ad, pricing, insertion dates, and the number of
impressions. Ad revenue depended on the number of users, total content hours
per user, and ad product innovations relevant to these users. Ad revenues were
also enhanced by ad sale innovations and analytics that helped evaluate and
improve the effectiveness of ad campaigns on behalf of ad clients. Increasingly,
Spotify allowed advertisers to self-serve on the ad platform, improving its
efficiency and scalability.

Case 5.3 Licensing Agreements

In order to stream content to its users, Spotify needed to secure licenses
from and pay royalties to the rights holders. These included the largest music
companies such as Universal Music Group, Sony Music Entertainment, and
Warner Music Group, as well as Merlin, which represented many independent
record labels. Worldwide license agreements typically lasted one to two years
and gave the record labels the right to audit Spotify for compliance with
agreement terms.

Spotify usually licensed both mechanical rights and public performance rights. In the United States, the governmental agency Copyright Royalty Board set royalty rates for compositions, and a third-party company, the Harry Fox Agency, administered all licenses. Together with Google, Amazon, and Pandora, Spotify appealed the rates set by the Copyright Royalty Board to obtain lower content acquisition costs, but there were no guarantees for rates becoming more advantageous for the streaming platforms. In other parts of the world, including Europe, Asia Pacific, and Latin America, Spotify obtained musical licenses through local collecting societies representing publishers or from publishers directly. Such agreements lasted for one to three years and included reporting obligations for Spotify and auditing rights for the licensors.

Spotify obtained rights to non-music content directly from rights holders. These multiyear commitments involved revenue sharing and other payments based on the performance of the content.

Case 5.4 Operations and Financials

Spotify's principal offices were located in Stockholm and New York, with sales and marketing subsidiaries in the US, UK, India, Japan, Brazil, Australia, Canada, and several EU countries.

Revenue

Subscription revenue comprised 90 percent of Spotify's total revenue, and advertising just 10 percent. In 2019, subscription revenue grew by 29 percent, while advertising revenue grew about 25 percent. Advertising grew primarily in terms of the number of impressions sold through programmatic ad sales. Podcasts generated a smaller revenue of €19 million (see Table C5.1).

Cost of Revenue

Royalty and distribution costs were the major sources of variable cost. Premium Service royalties were calculated based on revenue generated and the number

Table C5.1 Spotify revenue, 2017–2021 (millions of euros)

	2021	2020	2019	2018	2017
Premium	8,460	7,135	6,086	4,717	3,674
Ad-supported	1,208	745	678	542	416
Total	9,668	7,880	6,764	5,259	4,090

Note: Spotify's revenue primarily originated from subscription customers, although advertising revenue had grown as rapidly as subscription revenue.
Source: Spotify Annual Reports. Retrieved from https://investors.spotify.com/financials/default.aspx in August 2022.

Table C5.2 Spotify cost of revenue, 2017–2021 (millions of euros)					
	2021	2020	2019	2018	2017
Premium	5,986	5,126	4,465	3,461	2,868
Ad-supported	1,091	739	577	445	373
Total	7,077	5,865	5,042	3,906	3,241

Note: Cost of revenue was relatively higher for ad-supported services, in part because licensing rates were higher for these services.
Source: Spotify Annual Reports. Retrieved from https://investors.spotify.com/financials/default.aspx in August 2022.

of users. Ad-supported service royalties were usually a percentage of revenue, although sometimes streaming frequencies were accounted too. Lower-priced subscription plans (family and student plans) had lower royalty commitments, but some agreements required that Spotify pay royalties in advance or minimum guaranteed amounts independent of revenue generated. Usually un-recouped advances or minimum guarantees were not a substantial issue. Royalty rates varied significantly by country. Costs of revenue also included costs arising from payment processing, customer service, cloud computing, streaming, facility, equipment, and podcast and other content production. Costs of revenue tended to be a relatively stable share of revenue. Premium Services' cost of revenue was about 73 percent of revenue, whereas ad-supported services were less profitable, with costs amounting to about 85 percent of revenue (see Table C5.2).

Case 5.5 Other Activities and Associated Costs

Research and Development
Spotify viewed technological innovation as central to its long-term success. Investments in research and development (R&D) focused on improving user engagement and satisfaction. The company assumed that better user experience translated to user growth, in turn driving subscriber growth through their adoption funnel, and advertising opportunities for ad-supported users. R&D investments were a rather high share of revenue: 9 percent annually. R&D projects centered on improvements of the platform, service products, advertising products, mobile and desktop applications, and streaming. These involved significant engineering resources and large investments of time and money. New technologies were risky to develop and launch.

Sales and Marketing
Sales and marketing were a critical part of Spotify's operations. Sales involved managing customer relationships, public relations, and branding and advertising. As for any growth platform, customer acquisition was a big challenge, driving

Table C5.3 Spotify operations data, 2017–2021 (millions of euros)

	2021	2020	2019	2018	2017	2016	2015
Revenue	9,668	7,880	6,764	5,259	4,090	2,952	1,940
Cost of revenue	7,077	5,865	5,042	3,906	3,241	2,551	1,714
Gross profit	2,591	2,015	1,722	1,353	849	401	226
Research and development	912	837	615	493	396	207	136
Sales and marketing	1,135	1,029	826	620	567	368	219
General and administrative	450	442	354	283	264	175	106
Operating profit (loss)	94	(293)	(73)	(43)	(387)	(349)	(235)

Note: Although cost of revenue remained high, it had declined as a share of revenue, allowing Spotify to show a positive operating profit by 2021.
Source: Spotify Annual Reports. Retrieved from https://investors.spotify.com/financials/default.aspx in August 2022.

the growth and profitability of the business model. This entailed advertising of the services, live events and trade shows, promotion of new content on the platform, and offering free trials of premium services. Much of the cost of sales and marketing, like R&D, was due to highly-skilled employees, but it also included expenditures related to advertising channels and promotion events.

Managing the Platform

Another major cost category was general and administrative functions. These included business functions such as finance and accounting, analytics, legal, and human resource management. Additional expenses came from consulting, facility, and equipment (see Table C5.3).

Case 5.6 Competition in the Ecosystem

Spotify's competitors in the US market included music services such as Pandora, Apple, Amazon, and Google. Among these rivals, Pandora was not a major player in the global marketplace. Globally, Spotify had managed to retain and even grow its lead over Apple Music (see Figure C5.2).

Competition against the major digital platforms Apple, Amazon, and Google was extremely challenging, because Spotify was a specialized music streaming service, whereas the rivals had gigantic and well-resourced platforms that they were able to leverage in the music streaming market. Apple had a hugely profitable position in the handheld device market and it could subsidize music services with the profits from devices. Similarly, Google controlled almost 90 percent of the global market for mobile device operating systems with its Android system, which allowed it to push its own music service through subsidies to its three billion users. Either platform could reduce the accessibility of Spotify's application in their systems and thereby reduce Spotify's appeal with

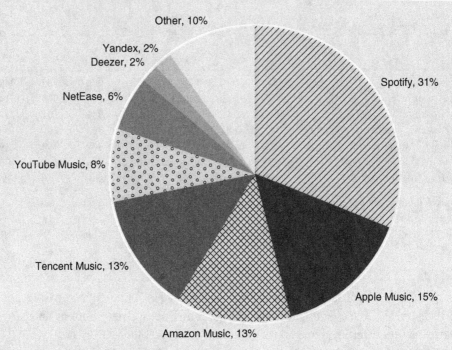

Figure C5.2 Spotify's global market share in 2021
Note: By 2021, Spotify had become the dominant music subscription platform in the global market.
Source: MIDiA Research. Retrieved from www.midiaresearch.com/blog/music-subscriber-market-shares-q2-2021 in August 2022.

consumers in subtle ways. They also controlled the application stores on their popular platforms and charged in-app purchase fees to app makers including Spotify. Their own applications did not have to pay such fees, which created an additional competitive disadvantage. Meanwhile, Amazon was the dominant e-commerce platform for thousands of products, including streaming content such as e-books and video – and now music. Within the preceding five years, competition in the streaming media marketplace had certainly heated up (see Figure C5.3).

Digital platforms were not the only source of competitive pressure for Spotify. The media market was complex and rapidly evolving, with innovative business models and services continuously entering and exiting. Some internet radio and satellite radio providers were able to offer more extensive content libraries or leverage their infrastructure, content libraries, brand recognition, and user bases to augment their services with on-demand music. On the other hand, many terrestrial radio providers were now broadcasting high-quality digital audio for free to users, and funded their services through advertising or other sources of support.

Spotify was concerned that entrants with a combination of technical expertise, brand recognition, financial resources, and digital media experience could pose a significant threat in on-demand audio distribution. If a company

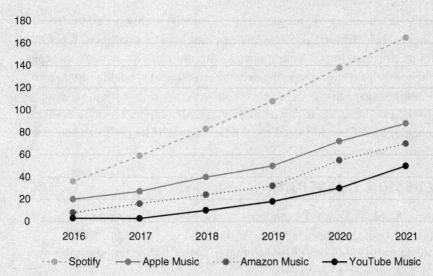

Figure C5.3 Growth of the main music platforms, millions of users 2016–2021
Note: Spotify had been the fastest-growing music subscription platform for an extended period.
Data source: Business of Apps. Retrieved from www.businessofapps.com/data/spotify-statistics/ in
March, 2022.

like Facebook chose to enter, they would have greater resources, a huge
existing user base, and proprietary technologies to provide services that
users and advertisers might prefer. It appeared that the keys to competitive
advantage in this market included brand recognition, operational knowhow,
a large user base, relationships with content holders and mobile device
manufacturers, and sophisticated technologies. Deep pockets of funding didn't
hurt, because they allowed acquiring any missing resources. Some rivals with
some of these assets might form greater threats by merging, as Sirius XM and
Pandora had done, to combine and leverage their resources and audiences.
And, at any time, rivals might innovate new features, technologies, or business
models that would be difficult to imitate and improve upon, leading Spotify to
lose ground.

    On the other side of the platform, Spotify competed for a share of advertisers'
marketing budgets with other content providers. Here, key factors included the
return on investment, effectiveness and relevance of the advertising products,
the pricing structure, and an ability to deliver large volumes or precise types of
advertisements to targeted user demographics. The advertising market included
not only Google and Amazon but also social media companies Facebook
and Twitter and traditional advertising channels such as terrestrial radio and
television.

    It was perhaps fortunate that Spotify did not rely primarily on advertising
revenue, as the large internet platforms had greater brand recognition, sales
personnel, advertising inventory, proprietary advertising technologies, and user
traffic that impacted ad pricing.

Spotify depended on the music industry that was highly concentrated. Just four major labels (Universal, Sony, Warner, and Merlin) accounted for over 80 percent of streamed music. Relationships with music rights holders was thus extremely important and made for delicate negotiations. Locally dominant rights holders in specific local markets were also often in a position to demand high royalties. Therefore, if any of these powerful suppliers were to sever the relationship, Spotify would need to take the music off its platform and lose significant numbers of users.

DISCUSSION QUESTIONS

1. How imitable is Spotify? Compare the degree of differentiation of Spotify and its main rivals and discuss how Spotify could reduce its imitability.
2. How does the evolution of intellectual property rights regimes influence Spotify's prospects for profitability?
3. Describe Spotify's ecosystem and highlight the critical complements to its music streaming service. Who controls external complements and what can Spotify do about it?
4. What architectural strategies might Spotify deploy to influence the ecosystem structure to its advantage?
5. Can you propose any strategic investments that might alleviate the ecosystem bottlenecks that are controlled by external parties?

EPILOGUE: RECOGNIZING OPPORTUNITIES FOR INNOVATION WITH NEXT-GENERATION COMMUNICATION NETWORKS

Communication technologies change relentlessly and "co-evolve" with the social and economic systems within which they are embedded, particularly with the dynamics of the marketplace. Many high-technology industries evolve through a cyclical pattern that helps predict how the next-generation networks and services may take shape and grow. We will study this pattern of evolution to understand what to expect in information and communication technology markets and how to make decisions about adopting and innovating new information and communication services. We then discuss the implications of this pattern for future communication networks and products.

E.1 Cycles of Innovation in Communication Systems

A technology cycle[1] often begins with a radical innovation that offers to improve performance by an order of magnitude. For example, compared to 4G, 5G is expected to improve download speeds and latency by a factor of 10. Moreover, the technological basis of the radical innovation is often novel, requiring firms to develop new capabilities. Such technological discontinuities thus bring about "competence destruction" for incumbents,[2] creating an opening for new entrants. Entirely new types of applications that were not feasible before can be developed. Such a radical innovation tends to facilitate a flurry of other innovations. Usually this industry-wide process of follow-on innovation takes several years to play out (see Figure E.1).

Over time, performance improvements in the system will begin to slow down. Innovation opportunities become incremental as the technology matures. Eventually, a new cycle begins with another radical innovation, introducing a new discontinuity in the pattern of evolution.

Firms' innovation strategies need to change over the technology cycle. There is a great deal of product innovation in the early years when companies are exploring new technological options and product designs. Markets and services are quite turbulent because new firms enter and old firms exit – there is a lot of uncertainty

---

[1] Anderson, P. and Tushman, M.L. (1990). Technological discontinuities and dominant designs: a cyclical model of technological change. *Administrative Science Quarterly* 35(4): 604–633.

[2] Tushman, M.L. and Anderson, P. (1986). Technological discontinuities and organizational environments. *Administrative Science Quarterly* 31(3): 439–465.

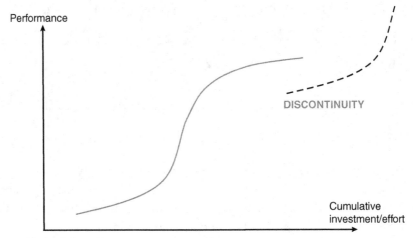

Figure E.1 Technology cycle
Note: The technology cycle describes product performance as a function of cumulative investment in R&D. The rate of improvement slows after the growth phase as it becomes more difficult to find innovation opportunities. A discontinuous innovation may set off the growth phase again, but it may initially offer an inferior performance.

about both consumer preferences and new technologies. Some of these market experiments succeed, but most fail. Particularly in communication technology markets, consumer preferences and social dynamics play a decisive role. Communication networks and applications are adopted and used in social groups such as business organizations, families, or educational communities. Therefore, the success of the innovation depends on the group dynamics. Does the social group find that the application or technology enhances the way they communicate and work together? If not, the innovation will be discarded and never take-off on a large scale.

Those innovations that succeed are likely to attract large numbers of users quickly once they reach a critical mass of users. They may become the dominant designs either through intentional standardization of technical interfaces or just through organic adoption and market growth. Once a set of dominant designs are defined and selected through product development and standardization, product and service innovations begin to slow down. The opportunities to improve product performance eventually become scarce, and firms begin to generate more profits from operational efficiency improvements rather than product improvements. Their focus, therefore, shifts toward process innovation and scaling up operations (Figure E.2).

The Three Stages of the Innovation Cycle

In a classic conceptual framework, Abernathy and Utterback (1975)[3] characterized the three stages of the innovation cycle as fluid, transitional, and specific.

---

[3] Utterback, J.M. and Abernathy, W.J. (1975). A dynamic model of process and product innovation. *Omega* 3(6), 639–656.

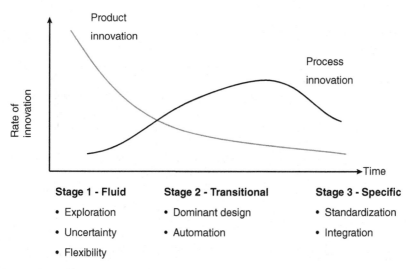

Figure E.2 Industry life cycle
Note: While product innovation dominates in the early stages of the innovation cycle, process innovation becomes more prominent over time as product innovation opportunities are depleted and consumer preferences identified.
Adapted from Abernathy, W.J. and Utterback, J.M. (1978). Patterns of industrial innovation. *Technology Review* 80(7): 40–47.

Fluid Stage

In this stage, when the product designs are emergent and variable, firm scale tends to be small and production processes generic. Firms compete on product performance that is improving rapidly. Because of the rapid market and technological change, organizations are informal and flexible, and often entrepreneurial.

Transitional Stage

During the transitional stage, stability, specificity, and standardization begin to emerge in terms of both product designs and production processes. As consumer preferences are becoming clearer, some product designs are starting to attract greater demand and their production volumes are picking up. This calls for more attention to efficiency.

Specific Stage

In the specific stage, product designs are stable and fewer in number, and competition is increasingly based on price – products are becoming commoditized. Consequently, firms begin to emphasize cost reduction through process innovation. Production processes and organizational structures are formalized and more specific to the products produced (see Table E.1).

Table E.1 Stages of the innovation cycle

	Stage 1. Fluid	Stage 2. Transitional	Stage 3. Specific
Innovation	Frequent major product changes	Major process changes required by rising demand	Incremental product and cumulative improvements
Products	Diverse designs, often customized	A product design emerges that is popular and stable enough to scale	Mostly undifferentiated, standard products
R&D	Focus unspecified because of uncertainty	Focused on specific product features	Focus on incremental product technologies and process efficiency
Production process	Small scale, located near user	General purpose with specialized sections	Large scale, highly specific to product
Costs of process change	Low	Medium	High
Basis of competition	Product performance	Product variation	Price
Vulnerabilities of industry leaders	To imitators and to successful breakthroughs	To more efficient and higher-quality producers	To technological innovations that present superior product substitutes
Organizational control	Informal and entrepreneurial	Through project and task groups	Structure, rules and goals

Note: The evolution of technology influences innovation strategies of the industry participants. In addition to the transition from product to process innovation, firms need to adjust their organization, investments, and competitive strategies.
Sources: Adapted from Abernathy and Utterback (1978) and Klepper (1996)
Ibid., and Klepper, S. (1996). Entry, exit, growth, and innovation over the product life cycle. *American Economic Review* 86(3): 562–583.

E.2   From Wireless Telecommunication to Data Networks to the Internet of Everything: What Comes Next?

In emerging communication networks, one can expect many creative ideas for harnessing the anticipated performance improvements. Higher data transfer speeds, greater reliability, lower latency, and greater data transfer capacity promised by 5G might be utilized in a myriad of ways such as high-precision remote medical procedures, virtual reality communications, or large-scale digital events. Discovering the ones that are the most valuable for users will take time and countless experimental services and products. Specifically, 5G offered three main new capabilities:

1. **Instrumentation and device proliferation:** 5G enabled a myriad of wireless devices: mobile phones and other personal devices; computers large and small; automobiles; robots, sensors and RFID tags. Basically, every product or appliance, even people and animals, could contain sensors that were connected to mobile communication networks. This meant that there would be many devices per square mile of network coverage, posing challenges to the base stations that were in charge of the signal being transmitted over the air.

2. **Low latency and high reliability:** 5G was developed for highly time-sensitive applications such as autonomous transportation. This required the network to be always available and respond to devices quickly and reliably. For example, when two autonomous cranes operated in a port carrying loads worth thousands or millions of dollars, they needed to be able to rely on the communication network to quickly and correctly allow the machines to coordinate their actions.

3. **Speed and volume:** As with each of the earlier network generations, 5G was designed to accommodate faster data transfer and larger volumes of data in terms of throughput per device and per area. Applications such as ultra-high-definition streaming and virtual or augmented reality required such speed and volume, particularly considering that the number of devices per area and the overall data traffic volume were growing rapidly. The worldwide monthly data traffic in smartphones was estimated to be 50 petabytes in 2021, which was about 12 times the traffic in the year 2016.[4]

The increased traffic and speed of 5G necessitated a lot of additional radio spectrum as well as more "spectrally-efficient" technologies. Higher-frequency spectrum bands were deployed for this purpose, but they were limited to a shorter distance from a base station: Higher frequencies meant that cell sizes were going to be smaller.[5] Although high-frequency bands increased the data transfer capacity of the network, they were suited for indoor hotspots and outdoor small-cell scenarios. Additional base stations needed to be installed to provide adequate coverage and make sure that each user would compete with fewer peers to get access to the network. New techniques such as "multiplexing" also facilitated efficient allocation of the spectrum resource. These new frequencies were also used by other radiocommunication services, notably satellite communications, weather forecasting, and Earth and climate change monitoring, raising questions about interference.

Maintaining an agile and flexible organization and developing multiple strategic options through R&D investments during this period of experimentation was going to be critical. Next we explore some industrial use cases to illustrate how 5G generated digital innovation opportunities and how those opportunities could be evaluated.

---

[4] Ericsson AB, "Traffic exploration tool," Online tool. Retrieved from www.ericsson.com/en/reports-and-papers/mobility-report/mobility-visualizer?f=1&ft=2&tr=2,3,4,5,6,7,8,9&t=1,2,3,4,5,6,7&s=4&u=1&ty=2021,2027&c=3 in August 2022

[5] Morgado, A., Huq, K.M.S, and Mumtaz, S. (2018). A survey of 5G technologies: regulatory, standardization and industrial perspectives. *Digital Communications and Networks* 4: 87–97.

E.3   Assessment of Opportunities for Innovation

New communication systems such as the internet or 5G can turn into huge global innovation projects. As had happened with the internet, a plethora of new activities and applications were going to connect to the 5G system, and almost 700 companies participated just in the global 5G standard-development process. The initial use cases varied in terms of the technologies utilized and the capabilities offered. A transportation system would be designed and managed quite differently from an entertainment application or an industrial Internet of Things system. To narrow down the network requirements for such diverse scenarios of use, the 5G standard was developed around three key scenarios: enhanced mobile broadband, ultra-reliable low-latency communications, and massive machine-type communication.

Enhanced mobile broadband concerned the consumer-facing 5G wireless telecommunication networks. These systems would deliver a faster speed of transmission and a greater capacity to handle large volumes of data per area. As a result of the network innovations, the cost per gigabit of data transferred over the network was decreasing, and it became possible to handle large amounts of data within a smaller location such as an event with thousands of participants. One innovation opportunity here was *multiplayer gaming events*.

Ultra-reliable low-latency communications required extremely fast response times, usually under 1 microsecond, and a dense network coverage. These were services involving mobility such as autonomous vehicles or drones, but also services such as remote surgery. These types of applications were mission-critical and needed 100 percent reliability, otherwise participants might be seriously harmed. Transportation, including *autonomous trucking* was an important innovation opportunity in this use case.

Massive machine-type communication required fewer new capabilities from the network and more effort and innovation on the part of the industrial users to instrument and digitize their activities. It was defined as fully automatic data generation, transfer, analysis, and actuation among intelligent machines.[6] Humans thus interfered very little with these network operations, or not at all. As billions of new devices connected to mobile networks, communication among machines constituted the majority of traffic in communication networks. Each device could generate small amounts of data at some intervals (e.g., temperature reading every hour), or collect and transfer a constant, real-time stream of data about the performance of an industrial machine. For example, the sensor-enhanced ball bearings of the Swedish company SKF constantly collected data about the number

---

[6] Bockelman, C., Pratas, N., Nikopour, H., et al. (2016). Massive machine-type communications in 5G: physical and MAC-layer solutions. *IEEE Communications Magazine* 54(9): 1–13. Retrieved from www.researchgate.net/publication/305881263_Massive_Machine-type_Communications_in_5G_Physical_and_MAC-layer_solutions in August 2022.

of revolutions, speed, direction of rotation, relative position, acceleration, and deceleration of ball bearings in mission-critical machinery.[7] Instrumentation of any smart space, such as a *smart seaport*, would require deployment of massive machine-type communication networks.

With all the new technologies becoming available, how could a digital innovator begin to make sense of the emerging innovation opportunities? Next we will consider a few actual opportunities that arose with the launch of 5G networks and evaluate their potential for building viable business models. We do so by carrying out an opportunity assessment based on information that was available in 2020, at the time of the launch of the standard. A useful starting point for assessing an innovation opportunity is an analysis of potential and existing user needs. Understanding how a problem or an activity is currently done and what the greatest bottlenecks are that constrain productivity or the user experience is essential for any innovation project. Next, mapping out the new technologies becoming available and their potential trajectories of improvement will help assess whether the innovation opportunity might create substantial value with respect to the user needs by providing significant improvements compared with the existing product or service set-up. Finally, an innovator would want to examine whether, and in what time frame, there is reasonable profit potential to cover the cost of development and build a sustainable business. The following aspects of the innovation will thus critically influence early design choices:

CLIENT: Who are the users, individual consumers or industrial companies, and what are their needs and existing patterns of technology use? This determines whether the innovation involves a consumer or a business communication network, and how the service is launched in the marketplace. Who would pay for the system, individual users or affiliated companies?

SERVICE FEATURES: What is the innovative application idea? Is the new service primarily about data collection and real-time transfer, about downloading and streaming, or about interaction among the users/participants? Do the services entail mobility or just depend on quality of service in a given location? Is the service time-sensitive or can it tolerate delays? Analysis of service features will reveal how the innovation idea connects with and benefits from the rapidly evolving communication network.

STATE-OF-THE-ART: How is the need currently addressed through existing services and what are the performance issues? In other words, what is the "pain point"? Can the emerging technological improvements alleviate some of the performance issues?

INVESTMENT: What is the anticipated cost of developing and launching the service? Compared to the currently exhibited willingness to pay of users and customers, how

---

[7] SKF (2020). New wireless sensors enable automated machine monitoring for reliable rotation in heavy industries. SKF News and events, March 27, 2020. Retrieved from www.skf.com/us/news-and-events/news/2020/2020-03-27-new-wireless-sensors-enable-automated-machine-monitoring-for-reliable-rotation-in-heavy-industries in August 2022.

long would it take to cover the fixed cost of development from anticipated revenues? This is a very rough analysis that illuminates whether the innovation is too early at this time, or if it is feasible to launch in the near future. If the development cost far exceeds potential revenue within a few years, it is likely that the technology development required is excessive and the technologies are too early stage for this application at this time.

Next, we evaluate three innovation opportunities that potentially take advantage of the new capabilities offered by 5G communication networks.

Case 1: Multiplayer-Augmented Reality Game with Geolocation

Multiplayer AR games such as Pokemon GO and Ingress work by digitally augmenting what users see or experience in the physical environment. Both were created by Niantic Studios and enjoyed millions of downloads. They collected revenue from in-app purchases of digital items that allowed players to improve their performance. In Pokemon GO, players collected pokemons that appeared and disappeared in their environment. Users needed to be in the exact physical location in order to "catch" the creature. In Ingress, players battled for world dominance by discovering and capturing energy sources digitally hidden in the physical environment. Like Pokemon Go, this game was global in reach and by walking around a city one could follow the evolving game plot and look for the energy sources. In 2018, about 50 live events were organized around the world where players gathered for a more intense gaming experience simultaneously.

Looking at the game Ingress as a starting point to explore whether 5G could enhance the multiplayer AR gaming experience, we first summarize the dimensions of the innovation opportunity (see Table E.2).

Table E.2 Multiplayer AR gaming opportunity assessment

Opportunity dimension	Assessment
CLIENT	Clients are individual players who would download the game (for a fee or free) and potentially purchase in-app items. It is thus a consumer application, monetized either directly (game fees) or indirectly via location-based advertising.
SERVICE FEATURES	Both downloading content from game servers and uploading game actions to be visible by other players would be relevant. Depending on the speed of the game, this application might require a low-latency wireless network. Lower latencies would enable more rapid interactive game features (e.g., "shooting" a moving AR target). AR gaming may also involve mobility but usually players are moving around on foot. Such games are ideally offered globally and the diverse quality of networks available across global markets might influence user experience.

Table E.2 (cont.)	
Opportunity dimension	Assessment
STATE-OF-THE-ART	As of 2020, multiplayer AR games existed and were very popular. Ingress had recently been significantly updated. According to game reviews on Google's Play Store app market, the main issues related to the user experience included:
	– Slow performance due to the special effects on the interface
	– Big images consumed bandwidth
	– Too many bugs and crashes
	– AR images were distorted
	– Visuals and images were not clear
	– Visuals were prioritized over playability (speed)
	– 30-second delays
	– High CPU usage
	– Large amount of data transferred wirelessly while playing
	– Compatibility issues with devices
	– Battery drain
	– High latency
	– App freezes when data is uploaded
INVESTMENT	This application would primarily rely on public 5G networks built and provided by consumer wireless telecom service providers (telecom operators). It would simply be an application in mobile app stores that provides a software-based service that allows players to access the visual content and interact with each other in physical and digital shared locations. It would not be a cheap investment – as a point of reference, Niantic raised $200 million to develop Pokémon Go and Ingress.

Note: The opportunity assessment framework applied to the multiplayer AR gaming innovation suggests that, as 5G networks become more widespread, AR gaming becomes a lucrative innovation opportunity because the faster networks offer to significantly enhance the user experience.

It appears that many of the performance issues in AR gaming involved speed (both uploading and downloading) and latency. There were also apparent bandwidth issues, and data volume could be a problem considering the advanced graphics and the number of players attempting to access the game data at the same time from the same location. It also seemed that many players had inadequate handsets for the game features, so device upgrades would potentially make a significant difference. This application thus seemed like a great candidate for innovation when 5G networks were becoming widely available.

In conclusion, multiplayer AR gaming offered a promising innovation opportunity with improved wireless networks, as it would take advantage of many of the new capabilities of 5G and potentially significantly improve user experience.

However, this required both large R&D investment in game development and user adoption of advanced devices. Coordinated timing of R&D and network adoption would be critical.

Case 2: Autonomous Trucking

Trucking was a 700 billion-dollar industry in the United States, transporting over 70 percent of the nation's freight by weight, with 700,000 private carriers (trucking companies) and over 33 million trucks registered for business purposes.[8] However, the industry was chronically short of drivers, and the gap was estimated to be 80, 000 drivers in the US in 2022.[9] A total of 3.5 million truck drivers were employed. An average driver earned $73,000 per year, amounting to about a third of the total industry sales revenue ($250 billion). The industry could thus save enormous amounts of money if trucks could operate autonomously without drivers. An autonomous trucking service could provide a competitive service for a lower price, once the fixed costs of R&D and equipment investment had been covered, see Table E.3.

In conclusion, the industry could save enormous amounts of money if trucks could operate autonomously without drivers. An autonomous trucking service could provide a competitive service for a lower price, once the fixed costs of R&D and equipment investment into autonomous driving and fleet management would be covered. It would require both robust ultra-reliable and low-latency 5G covering the road network and device-to-device (such as Vehicle-to-X, or V2X) communication technologies to enable safe transportation without drivers. If these became available and approved by transportation safety regulators (which may take several years), shipping and transportation systems could be automated to some degree because of the high labor cost and significant driver shortage. However, as of 2020, the development of autonomous trucking systems was unfeasible because too many of the essential system components were either missing or under development. Overall, a hybrid system of both autonomous and human driving where the driver could rest while the autonomous system drove e.g. along an interstate highway segment of a long haul seemed more viable, at least in the medium term.

Case 3: Smart Seaports

Internet of Things technologies apply to many industrial or logistical situations, and one context that could significantly benefit is seaports. Large ports are busy with hundreds of ships, trucks, and taxicabs coming and going any given day, with thousands of individuals and dozens of lifting and carrying machinery (forklifts,

---

[8] American Trucking Associations (2022). Economics and industry data. Retrieved from www .trucking.org/economics-and-industry-data in August 2022.

[9] Goodman, P.S. (2022). The real reason America doesn't have enough truck drivers. *The New York Times*, February 9, 2022. Retrieved from www.nytimes.com/2022/02/09/business/truck-driver-shortage.html in August 2022.

Table E.3 Autonomous trucking opportunity assessment

Opportunity dimension	Assessment
CLIENT	Autonomous trucking service would be offered for businesses or individuals needing long-distance heavy transportation.
SERVICE FEATURES	Autonomous trucking requires a wireless network supporting and managing autonomous vehicles involving both uploading and downloading large amounts of data with low latency so instrumentation and network speed would be critical. This service depends on long-distance mobility and the entire road network would probably need to be covered. Interactions would be extremely time-sensitive and require very low latency in order to provide a safe and reliable transportation service. Trucks and the network "edge" devices would also need high computational capacity.
STATE-OF-THE-ART	As of 2020, truck driving was challenging work and not enough drivers were available.
INVESTMENT	The autonomous transportation network would likely rely on a public 5G network because it would need to be available in public spaces along major roads and highways. Software- and sensor-based systems in the vehicles that sense the environment (location, obstacles, traffic rules and regulations) and drive the vehicle would be the critical complements. Autonomous vehicle systems were under development but were enormously complex and likely to require billions of R&D to become acceptable on public roads. At the same time, laws and traffic regulations needed to change to accommodate autonomous vehicles in public spaces. Also, an ultra-reliable and low-latency communication network might need to cover the whole road system unless there were significant advances in radar and LIDAR (Light Detection and Ranging) technologies.

Note: The innovation opportunity assessment framework highlights concerns about the early stage of the autonomous driving systems and the incomplete regulatory and legal frameworks that will govern autonomous driving activities in society.

cranes, etc.) mixed in. For everyone involved, quick processing and short waiting times save money. However, that is usually not the case.

For example, on any given day there were about 1,000 vessels in the Port of Singapore, one of the largest ports in the world in terms of tonnage and shipping containers. Every 2–3 minutes a ship arrived or left the port.[10] Even though the

---

[10] SeaNews (2018). The Busiest Ports in the World and How they Handle Operations. January 11, 2018. Retrieved from https://seanews.co.uk/features/the-busiest-ports-in-the-world-and-how-they-handle-operations-part-ii-singapore/ in September, 2022.

port was able to move 66 containers per ship per hour, it took 1.38 days on average to handle the ship from arrival to departure.[11] The sheer volume of tonnage transported was a challenge, but on top of that, orchestrating the ship loading and unloading with land transport to move the goods to shore and to their final destinations was a complex logistical problem. While ports may seem huge, they typically are constrained in space, meaning that they can only allow a land vehicle to enter the loading area when it's their turn to load or unload. This means that the truck has to be ready to move in, but ideally not need to wait outside of the loading area for hours. Nevertheless, as of 2020, in most ports, land and sea shipping companies did not directly share data about arrivals, departures, or cargo characteristics, leading to complicated offline interactions. Even in major ports, some of these messages were delivered to transportation service providers offline and printed on paper. It is thus easy to imagine how digitization of the information flow and coordination of operations could improve productivity, in particular, turnaround times of ships and trucks. However, few ports had such digital "port operating systems" in use.

Digitization of port operations from ship and cargo characteristics to the physical operations of the vehicles in the port area could dramatically reduce the turnaround times. For example, IBM helped the Port of Rotterdam to collect data about tides, currents, temperatures, wind, humidity, turbidity, and salinity of water with sensors installed in quay walls and buoys. Combined with weather data and information about vessel, and land transport arrival and departure times, such data could be analyzed and operations optimized with the help of artificial intelligence to predict optimal docking times and coordinate the berth and land operations. According to IBM, shrinking the turnaround time for a ship by just one hour could reduce costs by $80,000.[12]

However, this amount of data was not easy to collect, organize, and analyze for intelligent and actionable insights. Furthermore, high-end ports such as Rotterdam aimed to operate with autonomous vessels by 2025. It was thus imperative that ports become able to optimize and connect their operations via faster communication systems within a few years. The advantages seemed substantial, but so were the challenges of adoption and implementation. Table E.4 summarises the innovation opportunity.

To conclude, digitization of seaports offered an attractive innovation opportunity that could evolve as autonomous shipping and trucking applications emerged. Digitization of port operations from ship and cargo data to the operation

[11] Tan, M. (2015). Singapore's container port faces a productivity question. The Business Times, July 21, 2015. Retrieved from www.businesstimes.com.sg/companies-markets/singapores-container-port-faces-a-productivity-question in September 2022.

[12] IBM Mediacenter: Port of Rotterdam: transforming Europe's largest port through digitalization. Retrieved from https://mediacenter.ibm.com/media/Port+of+RotterdamA+Transforming+Europe's+largest+port+through+digitalization/1_0jcv9na8 in September 2022.

Table E.4 Smart seaport opportunity assessment

Opportunity dimension	Assessment
CLIENT	The communication system could be adopted and provided by the port operating company as a private industrial 5G communication system. The port company would need to facilitate adoption by all the transport companies visiting the port.
SERVICE FEATURES	The smart seaport would involve both uploading and downloading information and the data volume and analytical demands were likely to be challenging. This innovation idea is to some degree about mobility and the system needs to seamlessly cover the whole port area, but these areas are not huge compared to, for example, road networks. There would also be other coordination and communication applications that do not depend on managing mobility. There would be both extremely time-sensitive activities requiring very low latency in order to provide safe cargo handling, and coordination activities where greater time delays could be tolerated.
STATE-OF-THE-ART	Many of the hundreds of companies and thousands of individual vehicles visiting a major port on a daily basis were not digitally connected, leading to long wait times both in the berths and on land.
INVESTMENT	The port operating system enabling autonomous vehicles and equipment to operate would rely on private 5G network investment by the port authority. As with transportation systems, it would be complemented by software- and sensor-based systems in the machinery that would sense the environment (location, obstacles, rules) and operate the machinery. The challenge was to ensure adoption by the land and sea shipping companies. Global adoption would likely require global cooperative arrangements such as the SITA alliance in airport communications.

Note: For smart seaports, the innovation opportunity assessment framework suggests an incremental path of digitization that can over time lead to interoperability between communication systems of various port operators and shipping companies across the globe.

of the vehicles in the port area could dramatically reduce turnaround times, and adding intelligence into systems as autonomous equipment became widely available would offer an incremental development trajectory. However, coordinated adoption across international shipping companies was a critical concern, although cooperative organizations and systems in other industries provided templates for steps forward.

As communication networks evolve beyond 5G, these use case illustrations and many other types of service innovations will be developed, launched, and most of them will fail, at least initially. Successful innovations will likely implement the design principles and the business model framework that allow the innovations to grow with the technological system and the demand patterns. They will then launch new networks, build momentum and scale, and perhaps evolve into large platform ecosystems. Once standardization and regulation take place, these platforms will become more rigid and even static, with many formal structures, rules, and organizational features, and sometimes popular backlash against their market power.

However, the transition to scale, consolidation, and commoditization in the innovation cycle can be quick and take some firms by surprise, especially if industry leaders pre-empt organic growth via mergers and acquisitions. During the transitional phase, innovators need to keep track of rivals' ability to increase market momentum for some of their products and thereby solidify their control of the market. They may also proactively work with select rivals and partners to create ecosystems and standards that support their complementary products and services and slow down competing ecosystems. Most information and communication services involve some network effects as well as supply-side economies of scale. Therefore, after standardization of the desirable "form factors" during the transition, scaling, consolidation, and formalization of processes and organization structures during the specific stage can take place rapidly. However, through network effects and other sources of switching costs, platforms that succeed in growing large tend to persist for long periods of time. At least until the next disruptive innovation.

E.4   Playing the Tape Forward: How Will the Digital Economy Evolve?

The market response to digital innovations will, in part, depend on their power to disrupt existing patterns and networks of information consumption. The framework of disruptive innovation in Chapter 2 suggests that if an innovation introduces entirely new features or performance trajectories, especially if it launches new and open or public sources of previously proprietary information, it might have the capacity to disrupt existing markets. Such disruptive products might initially address new or underserved parts of the market and be simpler and cheaper.

Regarding the three 5G innovations discussed above, AR gaming could initially evolve in a sustaining fashion. It could be adopted as a mobile app by individuals with smartphones without having to invest in new hardware or learn new skills. There is already a large market for such gaming apps. However, if, for example, AR gaming evolved into more of a blended offline–online event such that gamers get together in a location to interact with each other, the innovation might become disruptive by introducing an entirely new set of features. Such new features might eventually be adopted by many other existing games, making AR communities a new and disruptive gaming phenomenon.

Similarly, autonomous trucking would highly likely be disruptive. Autonomous driving is a very new and distinct feature, and it would dramatically change the interactions among the industry participants and organizations. Meanwhile it seems that smart ports might be more sustaining rather than disruptive in their market impact. Established ports are likely to gradually invest in advanced communication systems. They might not offer dramatically new features or services, but will likely significantly improve the efficiency and quality of existing services. This analysis thus suggests that in some contexts, new communication networks such as the 5G can be expected to disrupt existing markets, but in others they might be adopted in a more incremental and sustaining fashion.

As the rapid pace of technological change continues and new innovation opportunities are revealed, the design principles for innovating the digital society in Chapter 3 are likely to be as relevant as ever. Design for the future means creating systems and products that can adapt as the network capabilities evolve. For example, by 2022, some autonomous driving could already be implemented in closed environments such as ports, but not nationally in the interstate highway network. Thus, innovating products that facilitate autonomous mobility could initially focus on closed industrial environments and later be adapted for public transportation needs. Smart companies build that flexibility into their product development strategy. Similarly, design for change addresses the unpredictable aspects of this rapid technological evolution. While technology roadmaps help planning for future product development trajectories, there may be unexpected discoveries or failures that disrupt such plans with surprise opportunities or challenges. Products, systems, and organizations that support them need to be able to adapt in the face of unexpected events. This means scanning the environment for sources of disruption and quickly adjusting the approach as new challenges or opportunities emerge. Finally, designing the products and systems for generativity allows both the innovator and their partners to rapidly extend the innovation in directions that users care about. Open standards and interfaces are important drivers of generativity that contribute to dynamic, rather than static, efficiency: constantly innovating the best possible products rather than optimizing the efficiency of a fixed set of products.

How will these emerging digital innovators compete? Most likely, especially in the early stages of the innovation cycle, competition focuses on differentiation as discussed in Chapter 4. Although innovators may successfully launch new products or services, they may quickly need to be upgraded, improved, or even replaced by newer versions. Costs of R&D will be very substantial in all three use cases as innovators attempt to integrate rapidly changing technologies while discovering user preferences and latent needs.

What are the revenue mechanisms for 5G innovations? Chapter 5 gives us some insights. AR gaming might rely on well-known freemium models with in-app purchases. There may however be new revenue streams to discover from AR events where a physical venue could pay to implement custom content for a specific event. Snapchat has been a pioneer in developing these types of affiliate opportunities. In autonomous trucking, the revenue models of trucking per se will probably not change, but the revenue sharing in the communication system that enables autonomous driving will likely be a complicated arrangement. Trucking companies will pay for licenses and access to the autonomous driving system and technologies, and those fees will be divided among the contributors to the system based on their market power. While such licensing arrangements have already been used in wireless telecommunications for years, they have been extremely contentious and litigious. With autonomous driving, the automobile industry and a variety of new component technology providers will participate in the licensing scheme, and it might be even more complicated, with regulators also playing a role. Meanwhile, in systems such as smart cities and seaports, revenues will be collected through various access fees, but it will be challenging to get the participants to adopt the system when there is an entrance fee.

Indeed, the key strategic challenges in such system innovations are around network launch. Each of the 5G examples involves setting up a network where participants cooperate and coordinate their actions in some way. The benefits from the system arise from large numbers of users agreeing to participate. Thus, per Chapter 9, there are strong network effects and, because the systems are expensive, the critical mass issue will be central. Switching costs originate from the need to purchase hardware and restructure activities and practices. Getting gamers to adopt a freemium AR game will be an order of magnitude simpler than getting large numbers of drivers or trucking companies to adopt autonomous driving systems, and that assumes that regulation and legislation are supportive. The most challenging case might be the coordinated adoption of port communication systems by ports around the world. Nevertheless, coordination will be necessary so that shipping companies will not have to adopt a different system for each port that their vessels visit. Network strategies will thus play a central role in the launch and growth of these innovations. Considering the scale of the adoption problem, perhaps with the exception of gaming, strategies that emphasize open standards and open platforms are likely to win in the marketplace. Ports might consider arrangements such as the airport consortium SITA that has done exactly that for airport communication systems.

What kinds of organizations might successfully commercialize these innovations? Although digitization makes the inverted firm often more efficient at orchestrating economic activities, at least in the early stages, 5G innovations require very large investments in R&D. Interestingly, even the most successful inverted digital firms conduct much of their R&D internally. As we saw in Chapter 12, this is because of the overriding need for the integration of expertise that is difficult to accomplish in a dispersed fashion. The results of R&D are also extremely valuable and strategic, and intellectual property rights and contracts may not sufficiently protect them if they are revealed to outsiders. Secrecy may be essential for early-stage R&D activities. As a result, while inverted firms might implement some of these innovations in their activities, they are less likely to innovate new 5G products and systems.

The value configurations created by these use cases will probably largely rely on value networks. The value created by a new communication product is inherently dependent on the interactions of the participants in gaming, production, or transportation settings. Value networks create efficiency through scale and liquidity. Indeed, any successful product design has to accommodate efficient scaling, as argued in Chapter 8. Furthermore, revenue mechanisms for value networks are tricky because users' willingness to pay depends on the size of the network. Therefore, innovators should attempt to create systems where users reveal their valuations. That might involve versioning, such as the freemium model, or dynamic pricing such as auctions or surge pricing for network access, or market segmentation based on predicted WTP. In other words, business models for digital innovations need to be compatible with user behavior, such that it's not easy for users to breach the terms and conditions.

Once such innovations are developed into business models, Chapter 15 suggests experimental strategies that help refine the product and business model design and successfully launch the innovation within a supportive ecosystem. Successful innovators will closely observe users and their social behavior, collect and analyze detailed usage data, and quickly evolve the product and the business model accordingly. The next set of strategic questions revolves around how innovators can protect their profit streams. Online games tend to be difficult to protect, despite network effects, and require constant improvement and upgrading. However, some of the AR features could potentially be protected by patents, although enforcement of software patents can be costly and risky. Autonomous transportation systems will involve a large number of hardware and software components. If some of these components become dominant and standardized, the owners of associated intellectual property may be in a lucrative position to collect royalties from a very large potential market. On the adoption side, in contrast, it is not clear if any trucking or transportation company will profit from these systems in the long term, and licensing fees may be high. Nevertheless, the systems may become essential for survival in the industry, and larger companies will likely be in positions to adopt early and drive down marginal cost. Similarly, in smart cities and other smart places, the system innovators will likely benefit, whereas the adopters may be able to offer improved services but pay a high price for them due to the small number of technology innovators licensing their hardware and software. In short, there are large profits to be generated in the Internet of Everything, but those will likely primarily accrue to a smaller number of parties that control the enabling technologies and systems. This is not unlike earlier generations of the wireless and wired internet: the most profitable companies in the digital realm have been hardware and software platform providers. Everyone else will simply have to adopt these technologies, because they provide such significant benefits to users that companies not providing digitized services will not survive.

KEY IDEAS

- Innovations tend to emerge in a cyclical pattern
- Early stages of the innovation cycle tend to be chaotic and creative, with many ideas for possible products and services.

- Once innovators discover consumer preferences, the innovation cycle transitions to more formalized and large-scale networks.
- It is best for digital innovators to enter in the early stages when no market player yet has dominant scale.
- While it is usually not necessary to be the first-to-market, being the first-to-scale is often advantageous.

DISCUSSION QUESTIONS

1. Using the innovation cycle framework to predict market dynamics of the autonomous trucking industry, what strategies should an innovator follow in the next stage?
2. How is standardization of products related to scaling? How might standardization occur in the market for AR or VR gaming?
3. Why is "first-to-scale" usually more important than "first-to-market"? What would that mean for a company building IoT networks for airports or seaports?

FURTHER READING

Anderson, P. and Tushman, M.L. (1990). Technological discontinuities and dominant designs: a cyclical model of technological change. *Administrative Science Quarterly* 35(4): 604–633.

Klepper, S. (1996). Entry, exit, growth, and innovation over the product life cycle. *American Economic Review* 86(3): 562–583.

Tushman, M.L. and Anderson, P. (1986). Technological discontinuities and organizational environments. *Administrative Science Quarterly* 31(3): 439–465.

Utterback, J.M. and Abernathy, W.J. (1975) A dynamic model of process and product innovation. *Omega* 3, 639–656.

Index

Printed in the United States
by Baker & Taylor Publisher Services